AT LARGE

By the same Author

American in Italy
Easter in Sicily
Varieties of Love
Italy (LIFE WORLD LIBRARY)
The Whistling Zone
Switzerland (LIFE WORLD LIBRARY)

HERBERT
KUBLY

AT LARGE

with a foreword
by KAY BOYLE

DOUBLEDAY & COMPANY, INC.
GARDEN CITY, NEW YORK
1964

ACKNOWLEDGMENTS

From Bayreuth to Salzburg, Copyright © 1956 by The Atlantic
Monthly Company. *Native's Return,* Copyright © 1957 by The
Conde Nast Publications, Inc. *The Isle of Exile—Elba,* Copyright ©
1959 by The Curtis Publishing Company. *The Passions of Sardinia,*
Copyright © 1957 by The Curtis Publishing Company. *Ambivalent
Adria,* which appeared in *Holiday* as *Italy's Adriatic Coast,* Copy-
right © 1959 by The Curtis Publishing Company. *Rome's Liveliest
Quarter,* which appeared in *Holiday* as *Trastevere,* Copyright ©
1960 by The Curtis Publishing Company. *Renaissance in a Company
Town,* which appeared in *Holiday* as *Pittsburgh,* Copyright © 1959
by The Curtis Publishing Company. *Where Are You, Hazel Hop-
kins?,* which appeared in *Holiday* as *Wisconsin North* and *Life is
Good in Madison,* Copyright © 1960 by The Curtis Publishing Company. *A Village of Wilhelm Tells,* Copyright © 1958 by The Curtis
Publishing Company. *The Town of Many Faces,* Copyright © 1956
by Esquire, Inc. *Siegfried's Wine Journey* first appeared in *Cornhill.*
The Marquise's Holy Mountain was first published in *Vogue,* as was
Masks of the Mountain People, which appears in this book under the
title *The Valley of the Masks.*

LIBRARY OF CONGRESS CATALOG CARD NUMBER 64–18496
COPYRIGHT © 1960, 1961, 1963, 1964 BY HERBERT KUBLY

to the memory of two friends
Curtis Bok *and* Irving Fine

All photographs by the author with the exception of numbers 2 and 8.

CONTENTS

A MOUNTAIN MAN

Foreword by Kay Boyle

Men who love mountains have a quality that is alien to valley men. They have a restlessness, an uneasiness, that nothing quiets. They have a loneliness that is present like a shadow even in the rain. It is there in their eyes when you meet them crossing a glacier, packs on their backs, mounting or descending staircases of eternal ice, on an endless journey not only to the limits of the land but to the limits of themselves. They are on their dogged way to another place, following paths that lash high above timber line and edge precipices of shale or granite, bound for a destination they will never reach, for mountains unfold forever, and the highest point is always farther, beyond the blue of the crevasses, higher than either land or man can go. In this collection and in other of Herbert Kubly's books, the restlessness, the loneliness, the uneasiness, of the mountain man is there like another dimension, and the gayest yodeling of voices in his pages is as nostalgic as the winding of the hunter's horn at dusk. For beneath the deceptive insouciance of his writing, there is hard, unembellished, and disconcerting fact. As we dance the polka or as we waltz, we learn, for instance, that Switzerland—with the Scandinavian countries—leads Europe in both suicides and mental disturbances, and that "part of the trouble is the sense of inadequacy which mountains give to people living intimately with them." Thus, whatever the country, or city, or state of mind, of which Kubly writes, there are two identities present: the gay dancer with his dark shadow pursuing him, and the mountain man of tenacious courage who is at the same time desperately concerned with fear.

Each of us, whether consciously or not, I believe makes a choice between the mountains and the sea. Go down to the sea, if that is what you have chosen; lie on its shore and be lulled and rocked into sleep, or drift will-less on its current, giving acquiescence to the embittered statements of the gulls. The mountains are something else; they ask man where he is going, and many are afraid to hear this question asked. In Kubly's best essays, and in his introduction to them, he is setting down the words of his own answer, writing them with gravity and conscience at the same time that he gives ear to the dancing and the music. For on every page, or in every other paragraph, or in every other sentence, the music of zithers, or chamber instruments, or opera arias, or tremendous orchestras, accompany the words of the answer he is seeking to give.

The opening pieces in this collection, in which Kubly establishes the blood relationship between his home town and home state, New Glarus, Wisconsin, and Glarus, Switzerland, are among the most eloquent in the book. If they are romanticized, they are as well, clear-eyed and factual as his judgment on the Reformation Zurichers, whom he describes as substituting "a lust for money" and banking in place of the renounced pleasures of the flesh. "During all the monetary crises that have shaken Europe during the first half of the twentieth century," Kubly writes, "the banks of Switzerland stood solid. When the last war ended, Zürich's Bahnhofstrasse was the banking center of Continental Europe and world-wide deposit vault. The Swiss love other people's money almost as much as their own and they've never had any scruples about whose money they husband. Fascist fortunes were secure behind the red geranium window-boxes, and Latin American dictators stashed away their piles there." But even for this libretto there is music that will not be stilled, and dancers who move to the sound of it across the glaciers; and while percentages are tabulated and dividends paid, the mountain torrents roar their implacable questions out. Although Kubly is deeply aware of his commitments to his forebears, still he can write with ruthless honesty that the *malaise Suisse* had been diagnosed as "an internal emptiness." He quotes a Swiss psychiatrist who attributes that inner emptiness to the fact that "we have no national crisis upon which to externalize our emotions. Business is good. We don't fight wars. There is nothing to unite us to each other in a common effort. We're unhappy, but we don't know why."

The fiction writer can resort to any number of disguises, but in the essay or poem the reflection of the man himself is unequivocally there. In these pieces of Kubly's, the man revealed loves movement and change, and the color of twilight, and music at any altitude, and mountain and church silences and sounds. It is the fear of his own loneliness that has sent him shrewdly probing into the meaning of countries and their people, a scrutiny akin—although lighter in tone —to D. H. Lawrence's anxious challenging of the psyche of the lands through which he moved. Even in Kubly's airiest phrases there is the solid ground of truth, and national character is revealed in oblique ways. Read, for instance, his description of the Bayreuth Wagner festival on an evening when, during an intermission in *Götterdämmerung*, a storm rolls out of the "Czechoslovakian mountains on the eastern horizon." One hears as one reads the violent music competing with the violence of the storm, "and then, at the moment of the closing of the cycle, the storm ceases and the theme of tranquil nature purged of evil" is heard in the softly falling rain outside, and rises as well "sweetly and gently from the orchestra" as the curtain falls. The tears of the audience that night, the shouts, the twenty-one curtain calls, send the author walking the wet streets all night, asking himself if the men and women in the opera house wept "for the immolation in a bunker under the chancellory" and for "their own death as gods."

There is, besides the sound of music, the endless beauty of the scenes, the quickly changing décor, to please the senses, and there is as well in this book a respect for fact and myth that satisfies the mind. In one of the pieces on Italy there is the legend of the Holy House in which a more tender, but no less accurately rendered, world is evoked than the world of Switzerland, or Germany, or New Glarus, Wisconsin, or Pittsburgh, Pa. The Holy House, in which the Virgin Mary is said to have been born, and in which her son, Jesus, is believed to have lived until his thirtieth year, was transported by angels' hands from Palestine to Dalmatia during the thirteenth century Moslem invasions. And then the Holy House and its black cedar Madonna—still borne by angels—were moved across the Adriatic into a forest near Revanti, and, finally, to the laurel grove in Loreto, where it now stands. At this famed shrine, hundreds of pilgrims press during the hot hours of the afternoon around a truck of watermelons, and quench "their thirst on its scarlet fruit," and kneel in prayer as night falls. In the warm dark, skyrockets soar across the sky, "bursting in graceful tendrils of pink and purple stars, to float down toward the shrine and flicker away," and the pilgrims watch as, at the climax, the heavens light up with the words *Ave Maria* in clearest gold.

There are such pictures as these, and there are other, quite different things. In his introduction, Kubly tells us that he created in these pieces an image of himself that is "true only in part, being the most amiable of the many persons that I am." From the evidence presented in this book, he appears to have sought through country after country, city after city, festival after festival, ritual after ritual, for the affirmation of what he himself is. And because he is still seeking the limits of that self, he believes he has "been no place, belonged nowhere." If this is true, then "no place" is a remarkably diverse terrain, and "belonging nowhere" should be acknowledged as the unique heritage of all mountain men.

K. B.

introduction

It may not be essential for a writer to have been a liar as a child, but I suspect it helps. For the genesis of fiction is really organized prevaricating—an escape from reality by creating and living in a world of the imagination.

I remember an incident when I was six. I had been deeply stirred by the death of the sister of a playmate and on the day of the funeral, in June, I saw, quite clearly, her soul being carried on the arms of angels up through a clear blue sky toward heaven. I spread the joyful tidings and the people of the town, while committed to the *theory* of my observation by their fundamentalist religion, concluded nevertheless that I was an odd child. In New Glarus, Wisconsin, I certainly was.

The maturing of a writer begins with a critical sense, the ability to separate his worlds of fantasy and of fact. The alternative to being a writer, if the critical faculty did not develop, would be madness. In my own case, the sense of separation and organization was stimulated early by my parents repeating to me in *Schwyzerdütsch* the Ninth Commandment and by a kindergarten teacher who spanked me whenever she caught me in a lie. Her influence I believe to have been somewhat premature and it is she I blame for all those self-conscious blocks which torment me when I am working and for a persisting sense of guilt that I am a writer at all.

Being a lonely child in the country, I became at the age of four a determined student, walking two miles to and from school each day. Though I was just learning to speak English, I would leaf absorbedly through books, feeling the mysterious inviolability of printed words. It was another two years before I became a reader, a curious species in a community where reading was frowned upon. My father read a newspaper and some farm journals in a rocking chair by the fire on winter evenings. Of the books in our house I remember some German Bibles and hymnals, a moralistic volume called *The Last Days of Pompeii,* and biographies of William McKinley and Theodore Roosevelt bought from itinerant book salesmen who had appealed to my parents' patriotism. At my grandmother's house there was an illustrated German-language Dante with which I was fascinated but could look into only surreptitiously because of the nudity in the Doré illustrations. A budding Calvinist, I was far more fascinated by the naked bodies writhing in Hell than by the robed choirs marching glumly into Paradise.

Having read through the school library, I began a library of my own, sending to Sears Roebuck for the collected works of Horatio Alger whose rags-to-riches fantasies enlarged the horizons of my own daydreams. "You'll give yourself a headache, filling it so full," my father said, and for him I was a cross to bear, sneaking into the woods or haymow with books while other men's sons plunged with healthy exuberance into the long days of planting, cultivating, and milking cows. "We never had anything like him in the family before," said my grandfather, an activist who considered any position other than one of vertical motion a condition of laziness.

All this reading, much of it in bed by bad light, crossed my eyes and I was fitted for spectacles, an ignominy which further marked me as an outsider. Not having learned at that age the wisdom of conforming, I became a sort of pariah in my school; at the age of eight my pattern of an individual against the mob was irrevocably established. My escape was to read more books, which only compounded my isolation and loneliness.

I was also writing poems. We had a trout stream on the farm, to which I escaped whenever I could, bringing home each afternoon two or three poems and a bucket of fish. I did not care about eating the fish that I caught and this refuge came to an end with my father's ultimatum that I either eat the fish or stop catching them. Success came at the age of twelve when I won first prize—three dollars—in a "stewardship" essay contest sponsored by our Swiss Reformed Church. My nominee for a Christian steward was *The Ladies' Home Journal* editor, Edward Bok, whose autobiography, *The Americanization of Edward Bok*, I had just read. Some thirty years later, during the writing of these lines, I sat at Edward Bok's desk in Philadelphia, revisiting the pages of the book which was such an influence in my life, and for the first time I understood why my identification with it had been so complete. The story of the immigrant Dutch boy's rise to fame and riches and his marriage to the boss's daughter was a palpable recapitulation of Horatio Alger.

Here, for example, is the story of eight-year-old Edward's first employment:

> The owner of the bakery, who had just placed in the window a series of trays filled with buns, tarts, and pies, came outside to look at the display. He found the hungry boy wistfully regarding the tempting-looking wares.
>
> "Look pretty good, don't they?" asked the baker.
>
> "They would," answered the Dutch boy with his national passion for cleanliness, "if your window were clean."
>
> "That's so, too," mused the baker. "Perhaps you'll clean it."
>
> "I will," was the laconic reply. And Edward Bok, there

and then, got his first job. The salary was to be fifty cents per week!

At the age of thirteen, the young hero became a Western Union office boy:

> And, as such things will fall out in this curiously strange world, it happened that as Edward Bok drew up his chair for the first time to his desk on that Monday morning, there had been born in Boston, exactly twelve hours before, a girl baby who was destined to become his wife. Thus, at the earliest possible moment after her birth, Edward Bok started to work for her!

Three years later, having discovered that "This is America, where one can do anything if it is honest," Edward Bok decided to call on the President of the United States.

> He had no sooner handed his card to the butler than the dignitary, looking at it, announced: "The President and Mrs. Hayes are waiting for you! . . ." And he a boy of sixteen!

As I read, it seemed that *Tattered Tom* or *Ragged Dick* were before me. I understood why Horatio Alger was the best-selling American author of the nineteenth century and why Edward Bok was a best-seller of the 1920s. Except for the Western frontiersmen, the poor boy rising from rags to riches was the most powerful myth in our American culture.

Following the example set by Bok I decided to be a journalist and began my fulfillment of the American dream by editing our high school paper. I should say I wrote it, since my staff was not as fired as I was by a passion for perfection. On the side I wrote tragic short stories of unrequited love, usually ending in suicide. Self-inflicted death was as casual an occurrence among us Swiss in Wisconsin as it still is in Switzerland, but a more common cause than love, both in New Glarus and Switzerland, is financial reverses. During the depression years when bankruptcy foreclosures on farms were common, three of our neighbors took their own lives.

The favored method was hanging in the silo, and my father was usually called to cut down the corpses of his friends. When my father, himself, became depressed over some losses my mother would send me out to look for him, and in the vividness of my imagination, I half expected to find him hanging from a rope.

My father was an overpowering, sometimes violent man, who kept his small family in more or less constant turmoil. My sister insists that he and I were much alike, with the same mercurial vacillation from gaiety to melancholy, the same flashing temper and the same mildly paranoic anger at injustices, both toward ourselves and others. Yet the worlds we lived in kept us apart, and in our frequent wars the weapon we used toward one another was silence. It wasn't until years later when I took his name—Nick—for my own, that I realized how much I was his son.

Reconciled to my unfitness for farming, my father agreed I should go to the state university. I enrolled in journalism and was guided by an adviser into history, literature, and social science courses. Looking back on it now it seems to have been an admirable liberal arts program. My parents felt some apprehension when they read in the newspapers that an entire printing of the student literary magazine, *The Rocking Horse*, had been confiscated because a story by an anonymous student was considered by the dean to be obscene. My father and mother had the uneasy feeling that a university where such stories were written might not be a proper place for me. They did not know that the story, described in the press as "the account of the way of a man with a maid," was mine. The incident was my first brush with censorship.

In my junior year I joined the creative writing workshop of Helen White, a teacher whose warm encouragement and sharp criticism steered me away from self-conscious imitations of Joyce, James, or whomever I might be reading, toward a straightforward style which, while hardly distinguished, was at least my own. I was also writing farm articles for agricultural journals, feature stories for the Milwaukee *Journal*, a column for the university newspaper, *The Daily Cardinal*, and lurid confessions of imagined erotic adventures ("She was my fraternity brother's sweetheart") which I sold to *True Story*. My aim in this indiscriminate output was to make money; I had become a fraternity member, a man-about-sororities, and life was expensive.

It never occurred to me in those days that my double-purposed aspirations—to become a popular journalist and a good writer—might, like Troilus' wild steeds dragging him to his destruction, betray me. My reputation as a campus journalist won me an offer to become a "Hearstling," a twenty-five-dollar-a-week apprentice on a Hearst newspaper. I longed to get to New York, so when I was promised assignment to the New York *American*, I accepted. The week of my graduation the *American* folded, and two days later I received telegraphed orders to report for work on the Pittsburgh *Sun-Telegraph*. I considered not going, but Father persuaded me to give Pittsburgh a chance. A tenacious peasant quality of seeing things through was strong in both of us and we decided I should try it for six months, until Christmas. Then if I found Pittsburgh not to my liking I would come home.

In order to break the long train ride my family arranged for me to stop off in Ohio for an overnight visit with a cousin who was superintendent of an insane asylum. In the morning he took me on a tour of his hospital, showing me bedlam cages of men and women in advanced stages of lunacy; the implied warning to a country boy was that such were the wages of urban sin. I continued apprehensively on my journey. My anxieties were not much eased when my train creaked slowly on trestles through Stygian black canyons into Pittsburgh's hot steaming station. Like a forlorn Horatio Alger hero I barricaded myself in the YMCA—which I discovered soon enough was right around the corner from a street of cabarets and women, and a burlesque house.

Of the assortment of characters I met the next morning at the *Sun-Telegraph*, many are now dead. The most memorable one was William "Fuzzy" Pfarr, an assistant city editor, who loathed above all things academic eruditeness. "A collitch man," was his epithet for me, "he has intellectual orgasms." My opportunity to deal with him came on my third day when he assigned me to cover a rape hearing in a police station in the slums. The alleged crime had taken place in a cemetery, and the defendant was a thin, pale boy of fifteen and the plaintiff a frayed virago in her thirties. I suspected that her charge had some sort of revenge motive, and back in the office I told Pfarr I didn't think the rape story stood up.

"Why not?" he asked.

"Well, he didn't have a weapon. She was certainly no virgin and she didn't seem exactly reluctant to me."

"What's your intellectual view of the case?" asked Pfarr.

I handed him a piece of paper on which I'd typed. "Woman molests minor."

"O.K., Professor," said Pfarr, spiking the story.

In November I was sent to cover one of Mrs. Eleanor Roosevelt's famous descents into the coal mines of West Virginia. On a Saturday night in a mining town schoolhouse I square danced with the First Lady, with the result that I was the only reporter on the assignment to whom she gave an interview. I had a "scoop"; there was no doubt of it. I phoned my story to Pittsburgh in high excitement, expecting my first front-page by-line. The next day the story which covered the right side of the page under a headline was mine, but the name at the head of the column was that of the rewrite man, William Pfarr.

Still, perhaps partly because he had usurped my glory, Fuzzy Pfarr's attitude toward me underwent a change. There was a mellowing in the antagonism between us, and after a time a kind of respect and perverse affection replaced it. On

Christmas, the day set by my father and myself when I should decide whether to leave Pittsburgh or stay, I was at a Croatian party in the home of the Yugoslav consul whose daughter was a reporter on the paper. There was no longer any question of leaving. The town with a reputation for ugliness had won me completely. It was dramatic, exciting and, sometimes at night when the furnaces lit up the heavens like Biblical pillars of fire, even beautiful.

After two years on the city desk, I received an unexpected promotion. It was in October of 1940, the afternoon before the formal opening of the Carnegie International Art Show. The *Sun-Telegraph's* critic, a lady, disagreeing with Fuzzy Pfarr over how the story should be handled, quit her job and walked out of the office. Someone had to review the show. A quick roll-call revealed that I was the only man on the staff who had a full-dress suit (left over from university proms), so I was sent to the exhibition. My review was a success and the next day I was the official art critic.

I knew very little about art, but I was filled with curiosity and I was happy to be on my own. I found an apartment in the tree-shaded Schenley Park area near Carnegie Museum, and there I did most of my writing, going into the office no more than was necessary. Art was not a full-time assignment, so I was given what Fuzzy Pfarr called "the culture beat," which included the University of Pittsburgh, the Carnegie Institute of Technology, and the Pittsburgh Symphony Orchestra. Fritz Reiner was conductor of the Symphony and I enjoyed the musical part of my work even more than the art. As interviewer of "cultural" visitors, an important journalistic assignment in a provincial town, I met Sergei Rachmaninoff, Béla Bartók, Serge Koussevitsky and all the opera singers, movie stars, and even the burlesque queens who came to town. In the Casino Theatre's dressing room one day I found one of the strippers—I believe it was Ann Corio—reading Proust. My story about the lady's refined literary tastes was put on the Associated Press wire and thereafter every stripper arrived in Pittsburgh prepared for an interview with the boxed edition of *Remembrance of Things Past*.

One gray winter day I went to an art gallery to cover the show of a native artist named Mary Shaw Marohnic. She arrived late for our appointment, offering the excuse that she'd torn her girdle and had to stop at a gas station to get it vulcanized. The logic of the explanation enchanted me and Mary Shaw and I became close friends. She was a large woman, a Junoesque earth mother with golden hair and the enveloping warmth and tenderness of the eternal female. Through our friendship I acquired some of the indefatigable joy she seemed to find in every moment of her life. Mary Shaw showed me her vision of the apocalyptic beauty of her city; Pittsburgh became the place of my growing-up, and my commitment to it was complete. She introduced me to "The Stable," a band of artists and little-theatre actors who made their headquarters in a renovated horse barn in Squirrel Hill. "The Stable" was actually the home of Dr. John Bowman, a research chemist who was the son of the Chancellor of the University of Pittsburgh, and his wife at the time, Melita Fils. In those days if you got off a train in Pittsburgh and ordered a taxi driver to "The Stable," he would know where to go.

Several of the girls in the group were painters, and another journalist and I would accompany them for painting weekends in the mountains of Pennsylvania and West Virginia. Our favorite place was the village of Somerfield, seventy miles south of Pittsburgh on the Youghiogheny River. Because of such unconventional behavior, Presbyterian Pittsburgh considered The Stable set rather racy. Its ebullience was a combination of energy and innocence, compounded by anxieties, for we knew our time was running out. The war had begun in Europe, and though I had been deferred in the first call for defective vision, one after another of the men in our group was being drafted. The Stable's last big party was on my birthday in the spring of 1941. Someone brought two psychology professors who were in town for a convention; they stayed, like the rest of us, for two days, as if they were afraid to have it end.

Later that summer in Wisconsin I was in an automobile accident which hospitalized me for four months and eventually left my right leg an inch shorter. When my draft number came up for reclassification, I was deferred as an invalid. Not to be in the war was a different torment from the torment of combat. For a writer to miss the most cataclysmic human experience of his epoch could hardly be considered good fortune.

Early in 1942, I returned to the *Sun-Telegraph*. My activities in the affairs of the Newspaper Guild displeased the editors and I was taken from my art and "culture" beats and assigned to the coventry of the radio desk, where my duties were tabulating program listings. After a week of focusing on eight-point type, my vision became a blur and I resigned from the *Sun-Telegraph* and went to New York where I found a job on the *Herald Tribune*.

The day before I left Pittsburgh I drove to Somerfield with Mary Shaw. A flood-control dam had been built by U. S. Army engineers ten miles down the Youghiogheny, and the valley was slowly turning into a lake. Our summer village had disappeared. Trees were cut, houses were razed, and even the bones of the dead in the cemetery had been moved to higher ground. Standing on the old stones of the Washington's Crossing Bridge, I looked over the naked hills and the ravaged village, feeling in my heart that the rising waters would be the grave of my youth, knowing that the sustaining warmth of the friend beside me must now pass out of my life.

Reading over these lines I have written I am aware of the shadowy presence in them of the Horatio Alger-Edward Bok "American Dream" syndrome. There is a curiously familiar tone to this record, with myself a vaguely smug hero, almost pretentiously reminiscent of "Tattered Tom" and "Ready

Eddy." The tone seems fitting to my story to this point. Now, admitting to a certain maturity both as person and as writer, the humor begins to change. For five years in Pittsburgh I had done little writing except for the newspaper. In New York I found an apartment in Greenwich Village and began to write—short stories, and magazine pieces about the Swiss in New Glarus. One day I was sent by the *Herald Tribune* city editor to Brooklyn to investigate the story of an anxious young sailor who had gone AWOL to be with his wife during the birth of their baby, only to find that she had disappeared. She was discovered hiding because the baby which she said she was expecting nine months after her husband's last visit home had been fathered by another sailor and was not due for another two months. The story of young love caught in the confusion of war haunted me. I wrote it, first as a short story and then as a play.

Another *Herald Tribune* reporter, Margaret Parton, read the play and suggested I submit it to Producer Eddie Dowling. On my way to work one Friday noon late in April, I took a script to Dowling's office and left it with a secretary who assured me it would be read. I was not convinced, for I had heard stories of scripts languishing in producers' offices, so I took another copy to the office of an agent whose name someone had given me. On the next Monday, so early that I was still asleep, I was called to the phone, a pay box in the hall of my rooming house.

"Hello, Herbert," said a strange voice. "This is Eddie. I want to buy your play."

Believing the voice to be a prankster's from the *Tribune*, I responded with an obscene epithet and hung up. In a few minutes the phone rang again. This time the same voice, somewhat more formal, said, "Is this Mr. Kubly? This is Mr. Dowling. . . ."

I was not convinced, but I agreed, nevertheless, to call at Mr. Dowling's office on my way to work. When I arrived Mr. Dowling was waiting, and a contract was on his desk.

"Who's your agent?" he asked, and I replied: "What do I need an agent for if the play is sold?"

"You'll need an agent to handle the movie rights," said Mr. Dowling. I gave him the name of Audrey Wood at whose office I had left a script, and in a moment he had her on the telephone. "Audrey, I'm buying one of your plays," he said. "*Men to the Sea*, by Herbert Kubly." "Who is Kubly?" said Miss Wood.

For a while I thought about writing a book about the madnesses of that summer, but others who have survived a similar experience have told about it and the story is familiar. Still being a somewhat credulous farm boy, I believed everything that was happening to me. Probably to get me out of his hair, Dowling made me major-domo of the casting couch. So absorbing was the responsibility of interviewing actresses that I resigned my job on the *Herald Tribune*. Few of my choices ended up in the cast; one of the parts was eventually given to the girl friend of an investor, another to the wife of an investor, and both were unsuited to their roles. In the newspapers I read Dowling's statement that my play was a religious drama, a profound Christian parable. It was not quite what I had had in mind, but I believed even that. By the time we opened in New Haven, the protagonist of the play was a pious Roman Catholic girl who prayed to a madonna on her fireplace mantel. Some nuns rustled out of a matinee in a high dudgeon at the end of the first act to complain to the police, and a magistrate who hadn't seen the play ("I don't go to dirty shows") ordered the madonna on the mantel replaced by a crucifix. This done, we finished the run and went to Boston.

Alerted by the hullaballoo in New Haven, the censor, a Mayor Curley appointee named Spencer, had sent for a script. When we arrived in Boston it was returned to us with eighty-three lines marked for excision. Boston had no objection to the madonna—which was duly returned to the mantel—but objected to the singing of *Silent Night* during a second act Christmas scene.

The result of all the publicity was that we were a roaring hit, and our two-weeks' booking was extended to three. Things were just calming down when an actor[1] in the play took a late-hour nightclub job singing patter songs, including one called *Spencer the Censor*, each verse of which ended with the refrain, "They won't let you do it in Boston." This brought a new attack from the censor's office. Newspapers carried my photograph, blinking through shell-rimmed spectacles like a pained Aldous Huxley. Out in Wisconsin, my parents saw it and prayed for my salvation; the caption over the picture said "Blasphemer!" (This confused me; one night I had visited the Old Howard burlesque house, where my Wisconsin puritanism was shocked by references to fornication, *pederasty*, and excretion.)

The Boston run of *Men to the Sea* was finally closed by a hurricane which cut off the power; my pious producer uneasily suspected that this was a divine manifestation of God's judgment. Understandably, therefore, the play's New York opening was a nervous affair. The critic on the *Herald Tribune* called it "a leaking boat." The *World-Telegram* said it was a "conspicuous and distinguished achievement of depth, power, compassion and intelligence," and the *Daily News* called it, "a superior work of vigor, humor and tenderness." While the controversy went on in the press, a sermon was preached against the play in St. Patrick's Cathedral and word came from Washington that the Secretary of the Navy (who had neither seen nor read it) reported that it undermined the morale of our men at war. The Reverend Edward N. West, Canon of the Episcopal Cathedral of St. John the Di-

---

[1] The most incredible character in the whole enterprise, this actor went on to a career as rodeo rider and circus clown, and is said to have finally committed suicide in a Havana hotel. He left a note signed "Jean Genet" and, if his myth is to be believed, was buried in Cuba under the French writer's name.

vine, had read the script and he said in a letter, "The play is distinctly a moral one." In spite of his judgment, the nervous Mr. Dowling and his associates closed the play after three weeks.

Still, I was a playwright—or so I was led to believe by the press, by producers, agents, and Hollywood flacks. For one of the latter I worked two months on a comedy about a woman psychiatrist in an Army mental hospital, but the plot was so grotesque that it was inevitable I foul it up.

Unemployed and filled with guilt for my idleness in war, I decided to take a factory defense job, in February 1945. Dressing for the role in dungarees I went to the offices of the United States Employment Service. The interviewer considered my experience and said I had no qualifications for a factory job; instead, he suggested that I apply at *Time* magazine. "They're a defense industry," he said. "They need writers." I protested—a writing job was the last thing I desired. I wanted to work with my hands. The interviewer said that though a factory foreman would have little interest in me *Time* probably would, and so I took the subway to Rockefeller Center. There a personnel clerk who had heard of my play sent me to the managing editor, Dana Tasker, who said he needed a music critic.

I told him I was not qualified, that I did not know enough. Art, books, or theatre perhaps, but not music. "We don't need a musicologist, we need a writer," he said. "Think it over." After an Automat lunch I went to the public library and read through six months of *Time's* music sections. My confidence soared; my years of Pittsburgh concert-going could be made to pay off. I returned in the afternoon to *Time's* offices and took the job.

It began well. For a farm boy, music in New York was a magic world, and I had the energy and enthusiasm to make the most of it. I glutted myself on a smorgasbord of symphonies, ballet, and opera—I went to the Metropolitan two or three times a week. Opera singers, composers, and conductors became my friends; I conducted an orchestra on the radio and appeared on panels and juries as critic and musicologist. I was neither of course; I was never anything but an intuitively perspicacious amateur with a bounding love for music and musicians.

Because of a mild sense of vertigo when I was alone in my thirtieth-floor office, I often worked with the door open. One day a shadow fell across my typewriter; when I looked up James Agee was standing there. His office was several doors down the hall, but we had never spoken. I was awed by him, his preponderant presence, his solemnity, his achievement. Now he was filling my door with his large frame, watching me, his eyes penetrating as an X ray. "I trust you're writing great words," he said.

He did not enter, but stood there asking perceptive questions, finding out all he wanted to know, and then he left. A few days later he returned, for a sort of sympathy had been struck between us, an awareness of certain parallels. We were small-town boys from rural America; we were individualists involved in a sophisticated, sometimes cynical group enterprise, a kind of totalitarianism of talent in which the individual was lost in a mass. I told him that I had begun to sense that my life on *Time* was an escape hatch from myself and that if I continued there, the writer which I believed in my heart that I was would end up without having a thing to say. Agee was giving up *Time's* movie reviews in order to do special features which he hoped would be a more satisfying way of expressing himself. We spoke of what we wanted to do, and of what we believed were the differences in the circumstances of writers in America and in Europe where I had never been and he had been once in his youth. In America, Agee said, the writer was outside the human family, set apart by a distrust of the intellectual; in Europe he was a prophet in his own house. Jim Agee's conversational flights were more engaging than anything he ever wrote. He could carry you along in his excitement, making you feel that he passionately cared. Aside from his sympathetic voice and ear, he represented for me my own imprisonment and my yearnings for freedom, but for him his plight became the plight of Everyman. He was older than I, more mature and more accomplished; still, like myself he needed the immediacy of involvement, the sense of being within, rather than outside, the human effort. The battle we shared was between our need for a daily social consummation which journalism filled, and a deeper, more elusive yearning toward literature. I suppose it was really a battle between the extrovert and introvert that was in us both.

In my own case the problem of involvement with *Time* was moving toward a resolution and a result of my friendship with Jim Agee was that my discontent kept growing. As I became more knowledgeable about music, and began to have confidence in my judgments, my difficulties in the office increased. The surer I grew of my opinions, the more the processes of anonymous group journalism became a burden. I found it increasingly intolerable to have my evaluations of music or musicians modified by a senior editor who had not heard a performance, and after a series of arguments I was called into the editor's office and told I was not "working out."

That afternoon I went back to my desk and emptied the contents of the drawers out of my office window. As I watched the papers fluttering down to Forty-eighth Street, like an accolade for a hero, I felt both the joy of liberation and despair at my failure. It was the second time I had felt this despair, the second time I had failed. I seemed to be mourning for a death, for the death of Horatio Alger, for the death of my faith in my omniscience.

Jim Agee was away from the office on the day I was fired. A few days later a note, thickly scrawled with a copy pencil, came to me at home. It said, "Am thinking a favor's been done you. This time try going it alone, make it a beginning."

I returned to writing plays, living on unemployment insurance checks, by part-time office work, by typing for others, by all the denigrating ways by which an artist, compulsive about his work, somehow keeps alive. I was elected secretary of the Dramatists Guild of America for a two-year term, and in 1948 my play, *Inherit the Wind*, a title I found in the Book of Proverbs, was produced at the St. James's Theatre in London. Though twice optioned in America, it was never produced. By a curious coincidence the successful 1955 American play, *Inherit the Wind*, was handled by the same agent who was holding my own.

I wrote three more plays, none of which was produced. It was a long and bitter period before I realized that I was operating in a quicksand of false premises, one of which was my dogged clinging to a chimeric dream of Broadway fame and affluence which had once seemed just within grasp and then was lost. The final and most disheartening episode of my involvements with Broadway came in 1959 when my agent "sold" a script and involved me once more in the frantic cycle of rewriting and casting. The only money that my fraudulent producers seem to have raised came from some trusting New Hampshire souls who were my friends, and the one palpable result of those eight months of hysteria was that they were bilked of their investments. By this time I had won recognition with some books, and the degrading waste of authorship in the commercial theatre had cured me, I would like to think, for good. It is on observation made, of course, from the cold bleak climate of failure.

A second, more basic, false premise that goaded me at this time was my mania for having to solve the material framework of my life in order to earn my right to live it. What this had turned into was a denial of life which a friend who is a psychiatrist told me was really an evasion, a fear of responsibility and of maturity. He could not have known the stern Swiss peasant axiom bred into my bones, flowing in my blood like another Commandment: "Thou shalt provide a home and a secure life before thou takest unto thyself a wife and children." In my strange life two hungers were struggling, canceling one another out—the passion to write, to *be a writer*, and the hunger to enter the family of man, to take up the natural cycle of life, to marry, to have children. The gregariousness of my youth had been an urge to fill the vacuum in my life, to give love to anyone who would receive it and to many who would not. There had also been rejection, great rejection, in an indifference to my work, in my failure of recognition, and the two channels of frustration flowed together into a dammed-up Niagara of love which I released sometimes in my work but more often held back until it lashed out in floods of bitterness, hostility, and anger.

In the Greenwich Village ambience in which I was living in the late 1940s, companionship was easy enough. But the carnival of gregariousness offered less and less, and finally the heart itself cried out in protest, and it was the voices of my patriarchal ancestors which I seemed to hear within me. The five proud brothers of my father's family had begotten more daughters than sons, and in the generation after me there was only one male to bear the Kubly name. In my guilt I began to think of returning to the farm where I was born, of marrying and siring sons.

So I married, as much in despair as in love, someone as security-minded as myself. The apprehensions which had kept me from marriage proliferated in the new relationship, for I felt deeply the unexpressed anxieties of my wife and her family over what seemed to them my lack of responsibility. I took free-lance jobs, providing an erratic sustenance. Writing became frantic and joyless, and no matter how hard I worked I had the feeling of being—in the New Glarus, in the American sense—a gold-bricking bum. In the end I merely succeeded in proving the validity of my apprehensions about marriage.

In 1949 I had to get a job. That autumn I received an offer from the University of Illinois to become an associate professor, teaching playwriting. At that moment the opportunity seemed providential. It was necessary that I fly out at once, and my wife agreed to follow me within the month. But when I had started teaching, she decided she could not give up her life and job in New York to live in a small town in the Midwest. There was more to it, of course, than that; when two persons, believing themselves maligned, are reduced to maligning one another it is no longer a matter of right or wrong—the tragedy of a divorce is the end of a hope, the debasement of a trust.

The despair and the loneliness in a strange and alien world during those autumn months were the most devastating I had yet known. My escape was my teaching. I looked forward to each class meeting with an eager excitement; the closing bell was a signal for sadness. As they developed the classes became more and more a workshop in human experience, not only in theatre but in all literature and the arts. The students responded with enthusiasm—at the end of my first semester we produced in the university theatre three plays written in the class. There was considerably less approval of what I was doing from some of my colleagues. My concepts of teaching were certainly less formal than their own. When students came to me with their personal problems, I answered their questions. By encouraging students' efforts and talents, by sharing with them my broader non-academic experience, I believed I was doing for them what others had not the perception to do. Without quite realizing that it was happening, I found myself aligned with students in a hostile academic situation. One day a student called to my attention Thomas Wolfe's sensitive delineation of academics in words spoken by the editor, Foxhall Edwards, to his daughter, in *You Can't Go Home Again.*

". . . the people that you find in school are academic people"—he says—"and these other people—the poets—are not academic people . . . they are people—who discover things for themselves, who burst through and make another world —and the academic people cannot understand them—so that's why what academic people say about them is not much good. It's a pity!"

I imagined at the time that these words applied to me. But I was not as right as I believed. In aligning myself with the young I was also escaping from my own solitude, I was falling into the danger of every lonely bachelor and spinster teacher on every lonely campus. To such a teacher young students may respond with love, but older professors see it as a betrayal of their ranks. In my failure to accept the mature role of teacher I was aligning myself on the wrong side of the schism between the two generations.

So I learned more that year than any of my students. In the spring the U. S. State Department offered me a Fulbright grant as research scholar and lecturer in Italian universities. The fifteen months in Italy turned out to be the happiest and most decisive of my life. The moment I stepped from the *Vulcania* on an October morning and walked through the labyrinthian tumult of Naples, I had the feeling that I had lived before among these people and that my arrival now was a reconciliation. The devastated beauty around me every-where aroused all my senses. After two months of studying Italian in Rome, I began my travels up and down the land, speaking to students. I was in a golden season of my life, like some pilgrim in a paradise regained, a sightseer wandering in and out of centuries, moving through time as well as geo-graphic space, and the landscape that interested me was the human one. My joy must have been obvious, for wherever I went I found a reciprocation of warmth and friendship. I like to listen, and Italians dearly love a listener. I made notes in shorthand and bought a little typewriter; soon my tran-scribed pages filled boxes.

In summer I went to Switzerland and was welcomed as a prodigal son in the alpine village of Elm from which my ancestors had emigrated more than a century before. It was delightful to discover an Italian origin for the Kublis in the cantonal archives of Glarus for it seemed to explain the mysterious blood response I had felt. It was as if I had been suddenly liberated into a sunlight of freedom from the stifling cocoon of Swiss Calvinism and American Puritanism.

I did not want to return to the campus in the American Midwest, yet I never considered that I would not. Not to go back would have been an admission of weakness I was unable to make. It was a kind of obligation, a Calvinist equating of the dark with the light which made it necessary for me to pay my debt for my happy life in Italy, to earn my right to it. An American living abroad is confronted with the question of his own identity as many expatriates have found. The confusion comes from his new European view of his country. After viewing America through the eyes of my Italian friends and through my own Italianized eyes, I needed to return to see how it would appear to me at home.

In December there was a farewell party in Naples, in Father Borelli's home for homeless children, the Casa dello Scugnizzo, and the next day a band of the *scugnizzi* escorted me to the pier. Because it was feared the boys might stow away, my convoy was not allowed on the ship. I said goodbye at the gate, and when the ship slid out of the harbor my eyes were blinded by tears. I was parting from a land and a people which that moment I loved more deeply than my own.

A new group of students were waiting for me at the university. But faculty amiability had not improved, a situation for which my own inability to join with my colleagues was partly responsible. One professor advised students against taking my course because I was a "commercial hack who writes for *Esquire*," and when I developed a friendship with one of my graduate students, a lady professor warned her against the "compromise" of associating with me outside of class. The dilemma of students caught up in such a quagmire troubled me. I did not want disciples—discipleship was a danger both to teacher and to student. Yet just such a relationship was being forced upon me. The students had a right to expect not to be abandoned by a teacher, they had a right to hear a voice speak above the babble of evasion and out of the silence which surrounded them. But they demanded too much, and my insoluble problem was how to give them the confirmation they sought without giving too much of myself.

I should have left the university that spring, but the year was 1952 and I had another reason for wishing to remain in Illinois. I had become acquainted with the governor of the state, Adlai Stevenson. In Chicago I met a group of professors and lawyers who planned to "draft" Stevenson for the Democratic nomination. At the convention in July, I worked with the Volunteers for Stevenson, and after the convention I plunged into Democratic politicking in the Republican center of the state. By the time school opened in the fall a group of us had formed a University Volunteers for Stevenson organization. I was informed by a dean that as a state employee I had not the right to engage in politics; my reply was that as a teacher I did not think I had the right not to take up my citizen's responsibility in the political life of my country. I continued in the campaign, never doubting that "the Governor" would win. My disillusionment came the night before the election in the Springfield headquarters, when it suddenly became apparent that Stevenson himself no longer believed in a victory.

After the election, life on campus grew even more difficult than before. Illinois had a Republican Governor; the following July the university's President, Dr. George D. Stoddard, under whose administration I had been employed, was asked to resign. As a tenured professor I could not be fired; the method in such a case was to make one's situation so unendurable one resigned. In the spring I became ill, with dizzy fainting spells accompanied by painful chest spasms, and my symptoms were described as psychosomatic.

That summer, in Wisconsin, I alternated between periods of melancholy and spurts of work, trying to shape my boxes of Italian notes into a book, and in September I returned to the Illinois campus. After one week I collapsed and my illness was diagnosed as anxiety neurosis and depression. By now my breakdown was complete. I was cut off from human contact, and my despair was a physical pain churning in my gut. One of my students drove me back to Madison, and this time my journey was flight from terror.

In Madison a doctor, Annette Washburne, who had just retired from the University of Wisconsin's health service, understood my illness for what it was, a capitulation to defeat and failure. I had failed as a playwright, I had failed as music critic, I had failed as a husband. Now, having failed also as a professor, I was at the end of my endurance; my failure was complete. Dr. Washburne began by showing me how my failures were not failures of accomplishment, but failures in measuring up to the high standard of achievement I had always set for myself. In the Illinois discord, Dr. Washburne convinced me I had been morally right and that the forces—real and imagined—which I had opposed were wrong. My culpability had been an immaturity, a childishly naïve attitude fixed in me since my own undergraduate days, of the infallible wisdom and goodness of professors. As a child is incapable of believing in the evil of adults, so I had been unable to conceive of the hostilities of insecure men when they feel themselves threatened. Challenging the whole academic structure, I had placed myself unequivocally in the path of destruction.

Dr. Washburne urged me to write—prodding, jogging, shaming me to work on the Italy book—for she understood above all things that the artist's redemption is in his work, in creating. In the spring the book was finished, and almost immediately a publisher offered me a contract. It was 1954, the season when Senator McCarthy, that unbridled anti-intellectual from my own state, was spreading his lunatic terror over the land. I had become obsessed with the idea that insecurity, distrust, and hostility were the lot of the intellectual in America. For this reason Dr. Washburne advised me to take the money I had received for my book and return to Europe. When I stopped feeling it necessary to apologize for myself, she felt, I would re-establish my identity as a man.

I went to London and Paris, and then to Zürich to meet a British music critic with an automobile who had invited me to accompany him on a summer reconnaissance of music festivals. For two months we whizzed around Europe, listening to operas and concerts, at Verona, Aix-en-Provence, Lucerne, Bregenz, and Munich, persevering through a ceremonial Ring at Bayreuth and then going on to Salzburg to be restored by Mozart. Late one August Saturday, driving from Salzburg to Bolzano, we entered a village at the foot of the Grossglockner Pass and were met by a chorus of singing children who threw flowers in our path. It did not matter that they had just greeted a visiting bishop and were offering us leftover blossoms and songs. My eyes filled with tears of joy, as if I had suddenly emerged from a deep dark cave and stepped into sunlight. That evening I danced *Ländlers* and *Schuhplattlers* in the local *Wirtshaus* and at midnight I ran with dirndled girls and lederhosened youths after a local flutist up to an alpine meadow and danced in the moonlight on autumn crocuses. It was a season of larkish self-indulgence, a second youth-time of my life, and it made no difference at the moment that it had come fifteen years too late.

When I entered Italy, finally, to live, in October, it was through a back door from Nice to Sardinia. After two weeks on that tempestuous, primitively beautiful island I went to Rome, to the American Academy on the Gianicolo Hill where I began work on a new book about Sicily. In March when *American in Italy* was published in New York, I was in Sicily. Late one day I was having a martini in a Taormina bar. Through the window I could see my friend, Carmelo Intelisano, the "Roy Rogers Postman" in *American in Italy*, come running down the Via Umberto from the post office, waving a large envelope. "*Sono arrivate le recensioni!*" he shouted out so that everyone in the bar could hear. I opened the envelope and read the reviews, translating them as well as I could for my friends. "A breathtaking loveletter to Italy," the New York *Times* said of *American in Italy*. "A wonderfully flexible writer," said *The New Yorker*. There was also a dissenter, a lady in Baltimore who said I had found no common ground with Italians "save in the matters of sex and wine." I ordered a round of drinks for my Sicilian friends and we drank to the Baltimore lady's health.

In the days that followed I received publishers' letters about a contract for my new book, and cables from agents urging me to return to America. Though I was not ready to face a decision, I was increasingly aware that I did not want to go home. In May I heard of the death in New York of James Agee and in some illogical way this increased my determination to remain in Europe. I returned to Sardinia in the spring, and in summer, on an invitation from my English publisher, Victor Gollancz, I went to London. In the autumn I lived for two months in a borrowed house on Lago Maggiore, in the Italian-Swiss village of Ascona, and in the winter of 1955 I was back in Rome.

While I was there a politically rightist magazine, *Il Borghese*, published a condemning article about me which bore the title *"Un Calvinista in Italia."* The writer, an ex-Mussolini apologist living in New York, described me as "the little Parsival from Wisconsin" and complained that my friends in Italy were from the lower working classes, including "the son of the Communist writer, Elio Vittorini,"[2] and that I had no interest in persons of "a superior caliber." The immediate result of this was that Italian newspapers began publishing favorable notices of my book. At the same time some Italian friends told me they had been unable to get my book in the United States Information Service library on the Via Veneto. I went to the library and asked for it, and the Amer-

[2] My friend, Giusto Vittorini, a journalist, had died of cancer two months before the article appeared.

ican lady at the desk replied stiffly, "I'm sorry, we don't keep that sort of book."

"What sort of book?" I asked.

"Subversive," she said.

I identified myself and the lady ran off in an agitated state. Finally, an older woman came back to say that decisions about "controversial books" were not up to library officials, but—she cast her eyes to the Embassy across the street—to "the policy makers." I wrote letters to friends in London, Paris, and Munich and found that the book was absent also from American libraries in those cities. The U. S. State Department, which had made my book possible by sending me on a Fulbright grant to Italy, was now banning it.

My expatriatism seemed complete. In my mind America was a hazard, a threat to which I had no wish to return. In my resolution I was supported, curiously, by my publishers, who had found themselves faced with three libel suits and possibly thought (*I have no evidence for it*) that their attorneys could get the actions dismissed on the ground that I was an indispensable party and could not be summoned into court. I began to think of changing my citizenship. Italian citizenship was difficult to come by, but I learned that the residual Swiss citizenship inherited from my Swiss ancestors would easily be activated. I began negotiations. Not even anxious letters from relatives hinting at the declining health of my father persuaded me; nothing, I resolved, would bring me back.

That is how matters stood one morning in the New Year, 1956, when I found the blue envelope of a cablegram in my mailbox at the American Academy. Since cables from America had come to mean catastrophe, I did not open this one at once. Instead I went in to breakfast. It was not a happy meal; my mind was speculating what new disaster might have befallen me.

My father's illness, a rejection on the new book, an unfavorable judgment in a libel suit—all these and much more went through my mind. Finally, I mustered courage to open the envelope, and I read:

ITALY WON NATIONAL BOOK AWARD CONFIDENTIAL CON-
GRATULATIONS MLS AND RAE.

The initials and name were M. L. Schuster's of Simon and Schuster, and his wife's, both of whom I had met once in London. I decided the cable was someone's practical joke and did not reply to it. The next day a second cable, this time from my editor, asked me to return to America at once. The idea filled me with panic. For several hours that morning I wandered along the edge of the Gianicolo Hill, looking down upon the gold, shimmering city which had become my home. By noon I was physically ill. I stumbled into the Salvator Mundi Hospital, seeking out my friend, Dr. Nick Musacchio. "I can't do it," I said to him. "I can't go back." That great good man, a Manhattan-born expatriate who had become an Italian citizen, burst into tears and said, "You must! If you don't, you'll regret it the rest of your life." He gave me a sedative to prepare me for the flight home. Before I left I took the precaution of buying a round-trip ticket to make sure I would be back as soon as possible, before the summer.

Under the circumstances, it was an incredible homecoming. I was welcomed with all that razzle-dazzle with which America greets its heroes, no matter how small. The book award address was by Senator John F. Kennedy whom I had met four years before in Chicago, while working on the Stevenson campaign. There was a month of parties and interviews and speech-making, through all of which I moved in a sort of dream, never quite free of the sense that it was a comedy happening to someone else. When it was over I went to Wisconsin, carrying the gold award medallion to my father, and there, too, the welcome was festive and warm. In spite of my feelings of unreality, I was experiencing a kind of therapy. Like the wayfaring prodigal of the Bible I was discovering that I belonged, that America and not Europe was my reality and that I—or at least the image of me which was projected by my book—was esteemed and loved.

From a doctor I learned how critically ill my father was, and I decided not to return to Rome at once. I accepted an invitation to spend the summer at MacDowell Colony, in New Hampshire, and this too was like a homecoming, for I had been there three times in the late 1940s. In a forest studio, with the thrushes singing as sweetly as the nightingales in the marshes of the Po, I finished *Easter in Sicily*. In September I returned to New Glarus for *Wilhelm Tell*, the Schiller play performed each autumn by the people of New Glarus in the forest amphitheatre on our farm. My father seemed better and I made my plans to go to Rome for the winter. Then, early in October, he died suddenly and I went back to Wisconsin. He had been reading a review copy of my new book, *Easter in Sicily*, and my National Book Award gold medallion was hanging in his room. In the last year of his life he had become reconciled to my being a writer; he even had been proud of me. Several weeks later a reviewer for *Commonweal Magazine*, writing favorably of *Easter in Sicily*, said he found in it evidences that pointed toward my conversion to Catholicism. It is just as well that my father didn't live to read that. His stern Calvinism could hardly have endured the shock of such a suggestion.

The next May, using the return ticket I had cherished through fifteen months, I returned to Europe. But this time my journey was neither flight nor escape, but professional; I had three assignments from *Holiday* magazine. I rented a house in Ascona, on the Swiss shores of Maggiore, with a garden of bananas and figs, drenched with the scents of jasmine, honeysuckle, and lime. It was a summer of mountain climbing, of limpid voyages on Maggiore and Lugano, of sudden Alpine tempests. I was serene and at peace, feeling the same joyful harmony with a place that I had discovered in Italy six years before. Using the town (which I called *Celesto*) and the misty silvery lake (named *Priori*) as settings, I wrote four stories which were published a year later in *Varieties of Love*. In August I went to Elba for *Holiday*, and in September I toured the Adriatic coast of Italy, from Ravenna to Loreto. I returned to Ascona for the autumn and in December I went to Rome.

That winter I received word from *Holiday's* editors that they wanted a "profile" of the city of Pittsburgh which that year was celebrating its two-hundredth birthday. My first impulse was to say "no"; I was in no hurry to return and Rome is loveliest in the spring. But the idea that someone else might take the assignment rankled. No one else would write so sympathetically of the city I had loved in my youth and which I had not seen for almost ten years. Something like homesickness set in, and in March I was on a ship, aware at last how completely the expatriate in me was dead.

I passed the springtime in Pittsburgh, seeking out familiar places, familiar faces, like an aroused Rip Van Winkle, and it came to me as never before that my mood was the mood of the wanderer, the uprooted, who, not remaining long enough in one place, coming back only now and then, sees nothing but the change. The skies were fresh and clear of smog and old slums had been replaced by civic centers and green parks. Much was different and some of it was marvelous. To orient myself I sought out that which was un-changed—the Frick forests, the north-side slums, the Croatian church at Millvale—and on my birthday Mary Shaw mustered what old hands she could find to her Victorian house for a party. But time could not be redeemed, and before I left Pittsburgh in May a kind of melancholia had set in. I had heard too many statistics, too many accountings of costs, too much talk of "the image." The bicentennial cele-bration languished and finally perished for lack of public sup-port. The only spontaneity I had found was at a folk festival of Pittsburgh's nationality groups where workers played the music and danced the dances of their European ancestors. The new city rising was an astonishing monument, but if it had a soul it was there in the workers' festival and in the Croatian church across the Allegheny, and the master builders had no knowledge of it. When I left it was with a feeling that an old chapter in my life had finally closed.

That summer of 1958 I went to MacDowell Colony to begin the novel which I had been waiting to write for five years. In the dark days of my illness back in Madison, Dr. Washburne had said, "Some day you will write a book and it will be your most painful, perhaps your most important work. But it will take a long time—perhaps five or ten years —until you will be able to do it." She was right. The writing did not come easily. I had written two books in the first person, creating an image of myself as a carefree *bon vivant*, and they had come easily because the personality I was creating, while not false, was true only in part, being the most amiable of the many persons that I am. The image was corroborated by a profile in *Esquire* which portrayed me as an *enfant terrible*, a rampaging soldier of fortune who had once joined up with a band of Sardinian bandits. It made good copy, but it was not me. Now, writing in the third person, I seemed to be portraying myself for the first time and it was an agony. It become clear to me that the greatest enemy to my creativity was my Calvinist reticence, my inherited Swiss passion for anonymity. My mother's admonishments, repeated over and over in my childhood, rang in my mind's ear; "What will people think, what will people say?" They seemed to have influenced every act of my life and now to me, the writer, they were forged fetters, iron chains of restraint. I have vast admiration for two astonishing writers of my generation, James Baldwin and Norman Mailer, because they can unburden so uninhibitedly all their hostilities and frustrations. For me such self-revelation was laborious and painful, with every instinct blocking my way.

Still, with a dogged kind of masochism, I plunged deep,

deep into the sealed-off labyrinths of myself, and in the descent I relived all the agonies from the dark seasons of my life. I wrote two versions of the novel in two years and then I showed the manuscript to editors and to friends. The responses were catastrophic: the advice—that I abandon the book at once. When one editor said, "I don't believe a bit of it," I realized how completely I had failed, for it was the truest book I had ever tried to write.

How had I failed? With self-conscious deliberation I had set out to return the vanished hero to the novel, to create a teacher who was a really good man. What I succeeded in producing was a Calvinist protagonist frozen by conscience to inaction: a sterile portrait of a passive prig. There is, said Dostoevski, after finishing *The Idiot*, nothing in the world more difficult to do than to portray a "positively good man." Writers are doomed to fail "because the good is an ideal, and the ideal is still too far in our civilization from having been worked out."

From one friend there was encouragement. "There is life on every page," said Kay Boyle. "I believe in the things that you are saying, that there can be no salvation for man until he can accept and give love." Spurred on, I began again, trying to relate my hero, Christian Mawther, to human life, trying to balance his Calvinist conscience with a toleration for people and an identification with them.

I wrote two more versions; it had taken four years to free myself of my commitment. Then, on the day I should have finished, I was in Massachusetts at the funeral of a friend, one exactly my own age, who had turned me toward teaching in 1949 and who had suggested the Fulbright in Italy. Among all the persons I knew he had come closest to the image of a teacher that I had tried to create in the book. I sat in stunned unreality, listening to a Beethoven quartet, and then a university president eulogizing my friend, saying, "His whole ethos was transmitted to his students . . . he gave himself completely . . . he was a man born without gall and without

bile. . . ." Later, standing in the hot August sun at the grave
with my friend's wife and his children, I wondered why the
devotion of a family had never been mine, why love had been
something I mistrusted and feared, and why, when I had
loved, it had been only those who could not give love entirely
and who did not threaten my liberty. I wondered why I had
cherished the image of myself as a lonely outcast when in
reality my solitude was no greater than the solitude of other
men. When I heard the rabbi murmur, out of his own sense
of helplessness, "There is nothing else to say," it seemed to
me that I was at the grave of Christian Mawther, at the
funeral of myself in the flesh of another man, and that everything that had happened before that day had happened a hundred years ago.

During the long self-analysis of the writing of *The Whistling Zone*, the realization had returned to me that I had another vocation, that I was a teacher. I began, exploring my
way, with writing classes at New York's New School for
Social Research and at Columbia University.

Writing courses are an absurdity, I often hear it said, and
sometimes it seems so. Nelson Algren says one writer cannot
help another and William Styron says that writing cannot be
taught. Both are right, and yet I disagree, for most of us
have had the good fortune, along the way, of a sensitive
perceptive teacher who offered criticism and direction. Styron's was William Blackburn at Duke University; mine was
Helen White at Wisconsin. If one student responds then a
teacher's effort is worthwhile. From my five semesters of
students at Illinois, two have become professional writers and
perhaps three more have drifted into such peripheral areas
as journalism and television. I cannot believe that for the
scores of others, their time and my energies have been wasted.

If education is going to fulfill its role in the new epoch of
shortened work hours, it will need to shift its emphasis from
training for a profession to the Aristotelian concept of teach-

ing a more rewarding use of leisure. In our future culture of automation, citizens will need to be weaned away from the stern puritan tradition that man's sole salvation is labor. When a teacher brings to his students a comprehension of the anguish of Kafka or Camus and an appreciation of the technical skill of Proust, he is giving them a respect for literature and making them better readers. The good teacher spurs young imaginations beyond self-pity and the simoleon pursuits to an acceptance of the human experience, toward a more complete giving to life. Striking at his student's feelings, like a blow to the heart, he is teaching more than writing and literature, he is making human beings.

"I hate to travel!" I said grimly one day in New Hampshire while loading boxes into a station wagon for the autumnal return to New York.

My companion looked at me in amazement. "What did you just say?" she asked.

"I hate to travel. I'd like to be an old tree or a stone, rooted in one place forever." I was thinking how, through a curious chain of circumstances, I had become known as a "travel writer." In one respect, at least, I was like D. H. Lawrence who seemed to find the logistics of movement almost unendurable, yet was always on the move. Why did he continue to punish himself? Why do I?

Carlo Levi, writing in *The Linden Trees* of a journey to Germany, speaks of travel as "a flight, an unconscious quest, an abandonment, a longing to escape to adolescence, a desire to leave the real war of life to those who stay behind." "We know where we are going," Levi writes. "But do we know why we leave what remains behind and does not follow us?"

What Levi is saying is that travel is another elaborate escape hatch, and he is right. Wandering in foreign countries I seek and find a sort of freedom, or at least an illusion of freedom. In Italy I found a human warmth for which I seem in my whole life to have yearned, a *dolce far niente* permissive-

ness which freed me from the guilt of indolence, freed me
for enjoyment, for fulfillment instead of denial. In Switzerland I found roots, tradition, a sense of belonging to history;
perhaps my own American past had been too spurious, the
presence of my people too brief. In both Switzerland and
Italy I found what I'd been searching for my entire life: an
awareness, a recognition of myself as a person. I was accepted, not as an American with an American's troublesome
milieu of foreign aid dollars, of Hollywood's luxury fantasies,
of—during my first two visits—McCarthy politics, but as a
human being.

The experience of discovering one's Americanism by leaving America must be a common one and to an American
writer I would think almost necessary. After fighting a dozen
years to gain admission into the American writing community, I was welcomed for a book I wrote *after* my prodigal
alienation and reconciliation. *American in Italy* was as much
about America as it was about Italy. In writing it I had re-
entered into my Americanism. Europe and Europeans had
showed me the way, and the end of my alienation from
America was the real beginning of my reconciliation with
myself.

I fled my land to find my identity and what I found was
my American identity; in my separation I discovered those
bonds and loyalties which marked me inviolably American.
Looking at America through European eyes I saw its greatness, greatness not in a political or doctrinal sense, but greatness as a fulfillment in history, in the destiny of humanity.
Because I returned loving it, as I had once hated it in my
anger, I cherished zealously my privilege, my commitment,
my *duty* to criticize it.

It is only when we realize we will never meet the image of
ourselves which we have cherished, that the outlines of it
commence to take shape. Sometimes when I equate accomplishment with boyhood aspiration, my life seems to me to

have been a dismal chronicle of failure. Of all my enemies of fulfillment, the most corrosive has been poverty, or fear of poverty rather than poverty itself. In order to write I have worked at menial half-jobs, lived on unemployment insurance, borrowed from friends, but I have never known hunger or poverty as I have seen it in the Mediterranean or in the slums of our cities. Still I remain a bourgeois, descended through my ancestors from one bourgeois nation and born into another. Though I have escaped now and then into Bohemia, I could never escape into Bohemianism because I will always long for those bourgeois corporealities—family, home, financial security—which give substance to life not only in Switzerland and America but in every enduring country of the western world. But because I have chosen to be a writer, these things have been denied me, and I have not been able to make my peace with my disenfranchisement. To have to accept poverty with meekness within the affluence of our land seems to me to be a debilitating stagnation, a degradation of life. For it is not true that suffering, physical and spiritual, without an apportionate amount of fulfillment, ennobles a man. Instead it debases him, makes him bitter, envious, querulous. Another writer from Wisconsin, Glenway Wescott, has said that it is inadvisable for a writer to undertake the writing of novels unless he is sure of being able to produce a great quantity in a popular vein. If this is true, one's heart must mourn for all the fine books that are not to be written. Despite the classic example of Mozart (who could tell what he might have composed had the circumstances of his life been otherwise?) I believe the greatest poem is the one still unwritten, the greatest song the one that may be prevented from being sung.

Against things such as these I have vented my bitterness, my anger, and the most vicious part of it all has been that one is not allowed anger, is not permitted to complain, but is expected to make his humble peace with the intolerations of his life, to accept his allotment of bile.

But self-pity is a ruining force; anger is destructive and destroys the one who is angry. And so the greatest enemy to my fulfillment has been myself, believing as I have that I could rise to the potential of my talent at the same time that I would be a success in a very materialistic sense. The Horatio Alger-Edward Bok myth failed me precisely because it was a myth. Perhaps I failed it first. Having propelled myself out of the world into which I was born and never achieving the world toward which I aspired, I have been no place, belonged nowhere. Vulnerable to the stresses of life, I have been afraid to forgo the small opportunities and seek the large ones. Too many times I have stood at a fork, choosing a road I might better not have traveled, because I had not the courage to resist, because I did not clearly understand my commitment. In my scramble for security, for success, the one I was betraying was myself.

It is no accident that the anti-heroes of American novels— Saul Bellow's Augie March, Philip Roth's Gabe Wallach, Hemingway's rootless floaters and Wolfe's rebellious poets, even O'Hara's status-climbing tycoons—are outside society trying to batter their way into the human family. For that is precisely the plight of the American writer. In Europe it is work and work alone that is expected of the author and he is honored accordingly. In America, with America's deification of personality and icon of success, it is the writer's intimate life that is demanded, his body, his privacy, his curtained seclusion. By contrast, in the socially oriented novels of Balzac, Proust, Thomas Mann, and the great Russians, the protagonists are concerned with finding meaning inside the frameworks of their fixed societies because the authors are writing of *their* situations. Sociologists keep showing us how American life is an exhaustive, anxiety-ridden and effortful ascension, branch by branch, up the materialistic beanstalk toward the cornucopia of fulfillment, the frustrating rewards of luxury, status, power, and by indirection, love and sex, which awaits them at the top. Whether from choice or incapacity a vast group of American writers does not come to grips with this vertically impelled order, and so we have in American letters an inordinate preoccupation with children and adolescents, an escape from the responsibilities of adulthood into the memories, the nostalgic fantasies of childhood, or early innocence. A result is the peculiar phenomenon of the young writer, exploding like a rocket his early brilliance, and never growing to a maturity of his powers.

The price of maturing can be dear. For artists, feeding longer on their early years than ordinary men, do not move easily with resigned unawareness toward maturity. Sometimes an artist, suddenly catapulted into a realization of his middle years, loses his sense of direction and is shattered by crises which may crush him for months or even years. It is possible that a writer, taking psychic risks, needs this trial by rebirth, this cataclysmic upheaval in which the irresponsibilities of youth are discarded, and from which a shaken maturity rises from the wreckage like a soul in resurrection.

The past is unalterable and must be reconciled. I know that to make my peace with it I must understand its part in the present; I must see it as a necessary growth toward the man I now am and the man I will become. If I did not understand the past as such, the memory of mistakes made, of pain inflicted on others—deliberately or by neglect—become a last judgment inferno of demons. The only redemption from this heritage of guilt is to turn the face forward, to raise the eyes upward and accept with as much courage as possible one's human responsibility. It seems to me that this is the real meaning of Jesus, of the Christian commitment.

No doubt every writer feels that society is a conspiracy against him—it is this tendency toward paranoia that made him a writer in the first place. One of the tenets upon which all society is based, by which it survives, is its support of the conventionality of the mass against the originality of the individual. The enemies of talent—neglect, hostility, rejection, poverty—do exist and the writer must understand that the moment when he chose to be a writer he took them upon himself and that forever after they may be the terms and conditions of his life.

The fact is that the same things which bring a writer pain also spur him on, for everything that happens to him is included in the perimeter of his experience. The only real source of one's work is one's own life, where the self-destructive forces of death are eternally at war with the proliferations of life. Emily Brontë was Heathcliffe, and Dostoevski Raskolnikov; Stavrogin, Prince Myshkin and Ivan and Alyosha Karamazov are all emanations of their creator's many-faceted and tortured soul. For writing is a confession, a search for absolution from anguish, the road by which the writer, accepting life without capitulating to its injustices, survives. If he is very fortunate he may gain a measure of that which he is forever seeking—attention and sometimes a little understanding.

A soul in crisis is one without hope. The hope that remains when all others are gone is that I shall continue to write. Chekhov has said that the writer is "bound under contract by conscience and by duty." His duty is to articulate the voices that speak to him, and in the end he must be known by the quality of their truth.

one

A VILLAGE OF WILHELM TELLS

Though it is twenty years since I parted from New Glarus, the Wisconsin village of my birth, I cannot, even now, return without apprehension and guilt. To an extent this must be true of every man who has turned his back on his roots and who, as a result, never again is quite certain who he is.

In my own case the problem of identity was confused long before I was born. My people were Americans who believed themselves Swiss. The Government of Switzerland claims as a subject anyone of Swiss pedigree, no matter where he may be born. When I, a fourth-generation American, was born in Wisconsin, the news was sent to Switzerland where I was registered under a coat of arms as Herbert Oswald Kubli von Elm, thereby establishing me as a burgher of a mountain hamlet which my great-grandparents had left seventy years before.

My people were farmers with a European peasant's mystic feeling for land and cattle. "Who walks on his own land walks with God," was one of my father's favorite Swiss maxims, and on stormy winter nights he never failed in the cozy warmth of his barn to thank God for his cows. While I could understand in some measure his feeling for land, I never thought of enslavement to cattle as anything but a nuisance, and very early I determined to have none of it. One October Saturday many years ago, when I was helping my father pick the wild grapes for the wine he made every autumn, he confided to me his plan to paint across the full sweep of our barn the sign, "Nic H. Kubly & Son." The compliment of such a sign to an eight-year-old boy was tremendous, but I did not so consider it. "In that case," I said with what must have been intolerable smugness, "you shall have to have another son."

He did not have another son and my betrayal of the land was, I think, the biggest sorrow of his life. It was a matter of great pride to him that no one but a Kubly had ever lived on the farm pioneered by my great-grandfather and owned subsequently by my grandfather and then himself. In recent years the farm had gained a sort of fame as the setting of Schiller's patriotic drama, *Wilhelm Tell*, performed by the people of New Glarus every Labor Day weekend. This brought my father much pleasure. Nothing could induce him to sell and he hoped to the end that I would see the error of my ways and return. Though in the seventy-four years of his life he never left the farm, he considered himself a Swiss and spoke his *schwyzerdütsche Muttersprache* to the day he died. My relationship with him, while never hostile, was the complex father-son relationship which ordinarily exists between first- and second-generation Americans. I had determined to be not a Swiss but an American.

A psychiatrist once told me that everything I have done in my life has been an effort to prove myself to the people of New Glarus. If this is true, I have not succeeded, for I am remembered primarily for my failure at milking cows. My preference of books to Holsteins was apparent at an early age, and even my father had to admit to his friends that I was a *"Wunderlicher,"* an "odd one." His permission for me to attend the University of Wisconsin was granted only when it was apparent I would be a failure as a farmer.

The people of New Glarus don't read books, much less write them, and literature is not considered a serious vocation. So it was a curious coincidence when two books by local sons were published in New York on the same day in 1955. One—the best-selling *How to Live 365 Days a Year*—was read with interest in New Glarus because its author, the late Dr. John Schindler, a Swiss-speaking physician, drew from his experiences to write on mental health; the other was my own *American in Italy*, which an English teacher in the high school I attended wanted the public library to ban as unfit for young people. My father did not go that far, but he did write me a firm letter about the book's "strong language."

My last visit while my father lived was early one September, just before the *Wilhelm Tell* drama. I told no one I was coming. My plane crossed Lake Michigan and was winging over the checkerboard Wisconsin landscape toward Madison when I felt the palms of my hands turning moist. The symptom was familiar. As usual, I was going home like a prodigal, worrying how I would be received.

Riding the bus south and west into rolling Green County, I was moved, as always, by the beauty of the landscape. Herds of fawn-colored Swiss cows and larger black-and-white Holsteins grazed knee-deep in clover and alfalfa, filling the late afternoon with the music of their Swiss bells. The town's familiar profile—a slender church spire rising from the hills—came into view. A large billboard painted with Wilhelm Tell and his son against a background of mountains and blue skies read, "Don't miss the Swiss! Visit New Glarus. Schiller's *Wilhelm Tell* annually."

The sleepy village I remembered had no need for street names, but now brand-new streets signs—as befitted the richest farm community in the state—were mounted under brightly colored shields of the twenty-two Swiss cantons.

Similar medallions were mounted on the façade of the local movie and on a new "Alpine Restaurant." A hand-carved bulletin board in the churchyard looked like an Alpine prayer station. It was Saturday afternoon and the streets were crowded and bustling as a fair.

Leaving my bag in the bus depot, I left the village and climbed the steep east hill, one mile up, to the highest point in the township. It was a hill I had climbed, up and down, for fourteen years on my way to school. I remembered a time when I believed it to be a mountain and dreamed of a tunnel I would one day build to shorten the arduous trip to town. From the summit I could look north to the hazy outline of the village of Blue Mounds; twenty-five miles away, it used to seem like the edge of the world.

I descended into a valley of green meadows where I saw the familiar buildings of Wilhelm Tell farm, the brick house built by my father, the red barn newly painted, and the grove of oak which hid the old white cottage in which both my father and I were born. It was milking time and I found my father, despite his ill health, with my mother, milking cows in the barn, stubbornly dramatizing his devotion to the land. He embraced me and asked how I had come. The years had not made conversation between us easier; to him I was still the recalcitrant "*Wunderlicher.*" Shortly, embarrassed as always by his own emotion, he turned from me and went back to his cows.

I have many images of my father; I remember him as a handsome, supple man who, with my mother, won the waltzing contests at dances; a man with curly black hair and eyes that flashed with merriment one minute and filled with tears the next. The eyes were the barometer of his temperament, his lusty humors, his violent tempers and his deep sorrows. Even now, gray-haired, ponderous in his movements, he was a striking man.

Later, with my sister and brother-in-law—who had come from Racine for the festival with their three daughters and son—I went into the village. A street had been roped off for dancing, and parents and grandparents stood on the sidewalks watching their young people dance Swiss folk dances. The musicians, local youths, were mounted on the back of a truck. My sister and I danced the schottisches and polkas we had learned as children. They were dances I had not been able to find on my visits to Switzerland, where young people danced American jive and tangoes. On the pavements I met an old friend, Colonel Raymond Kundert. "*Hol-di-rol-yeeee*," he shouted, "*noch einmal as Chaeferfest.*" The yodel phrase and Swiss idiom—meaning "still another bug feast"—were our traditional greeting on such occasions. The colonel, a large and fun-loving extrovert, is the most indefatigable celebrant at New Glarus' festivals. The next morning he played his accordion in the lively Four Corners Tavern—a concert I did not hear, for it occurred when I was in church.

The minister, a third-generation Swiss-American named Lynn Tschudy, had announced that he would preach on the vainglory of New Glarners. Since I had not succeeded in throwing off my own New Glarus consciousness during two decades of absence, the subject interested me. In an editorial entitled "Glarners Forever" in the New Glarus *Post*, I read, "A Glarner is always a Glarner, no matter where he lives, and no matter how far away he moves. . . . Being a Glarner is a lifetime proposition."

The congregation sang *Faith of Our Fathers*, and then an anthem, *My God and I*, was sung by the Edelweiss Stars, the most famous of New Glarus' numerous yodel groups. The Reverend Tschudy began his sermon by comparing the immigration of New Glarus' pioneers to the journey of Abraham, who "left his father's home in Haran and came down to a land called Canaan to fulfill a covenant with God," a covenant leading to the ultimate birth of Christ and the founding of Christianity. "Like Abraham," the minister said, "the Glarners hadn't the slightest idea how it would all turn

out. Now look around you, at the privileges of life, at the
things God and the faith of our fathers has made possible for
us."

Reminding the New Glarners of their own lapse of faith,
he concluded, "The way of salvation is not that of nation-
alistic custom. We cannot be saved for life everlasting because
we are Glarners any more than a Jew can be saved for
life everlasting because he is a son of Abraham."

The sermon seemed to me admirable and courageous. But
the parishioners, beginning two days of patriotic activities,
had no time for self-examination. We hurried home to a meal
of *Chalberwurst* (sausages of veal and cream) and *Pfaffechlötz*
(potatoes with parsley and onion grass). My mother was
dressed in the skirt and shawls of a Swiss peasant woman;
my nieces, in embroideries and feathered caps, were a trio
of little Heidis. Before the rest of us had finished our meal
they were off with my father to the "upper forty," a half
mile from the house, for the German-language performance
of *Wilhelm Tell*.

Deciding to pass up the play in favor of an English performance the next day, I went for a walk in the village.
It glowed with summer flowers: zinnias, asters, salvias,
dahlias, and red geraniums in window boxes. In the *"Schoene
Grund"* part of town I came to the Chalet of the Golden
Fleece, the most elegant house in New Glarus. In years past,
I had frequently been a guest at the Chalet. Against its dark-
stained walls the red geraniums in the window boxes shone
with extraordinary brightness. It is built in the Bernese Oberland style, with finely leaded stained-glass windows, a second-
story veranda and stones on the roof. Fragments of German-language poetry are burned into the outside walls. Under
the high gable are the lines:

> *This house is mine and yet not mine,*
> *I leave and you enter,*
> *Who knows who shall be the last.*

The lines struck me as particularly sad. Two years before his death, the chalet's builder, a lifelong wanderer and collector of art named Edwin Barlow, reversed the usual migratory direction by retiring to Ascona in Switzerland. Before leaving, he presented the chalet and its contents to New Glarus as a museum. Inside, the rooms, which I remembered as settings for lighthearted revelries, were melancholy and funereal. Ropes and glass protected the furniture, paintings, books, and china with which I once had intimately lived. The chalet, it struck me sadly, was a mausoleum of my youth.

The evening, the most festive of the year, began with a two-hour yodeling concert in the village commons across the street from the church. Yodeling is a mountain art; it is supposed to have developed from the rise and fall of echoes of the human voice caused by the jagged skyline of mountain peaks. The technique of yodeling consists largely of a quick shift from head to chest tones. To the uninitiated the sliding arpeggios between a natural and falsetto voice may seem absurd and even unpleasant. To a New Glarner there is no lovelier music. It is best performed out of doors. The dampish night was acoustically perfect and the moonlit meadow was filled with people. The yodel songs of New Glarus are sentimental and sad, filled with a longing for Switzerland. Since many of the yodelers have never seen the land for which they seem so homesick, they are probably expressing an abstract longing for a sweetness of life, a return to the simplicity of childhood.

I listened to *Little Church* ("*high in the mountains, lonely in solitude*") and *Bells* ("*In the arms of my mother I heard church bells ring*"). Young voices are best for yodeling and the stars of the concert were two youths named Hans Neuenschwander and Robert Schneider, recently arrived from Switzerland. They sang like bewitched flutes and the people cheered them.

After the concert the crowd dispersed to the taverns. New Glarners have the same puritan compulsion about play as they do about work, and their alcoholic consumption is laudatory. There are eleven flourishing taverns, one for every 110 citizens.

The popular Four Corners was booming like a mining-camp saloon. We moved on to Puempel's where the festivities were more controlled. Otto Puempel attended high school with me; his wife, Hazel, is my cousin. Both were busy drawing beer. Their clientele seemed to be the younger middle-aged set. Colonel Kundert was there and other schoolmates, as well as two of my high school teachers. We danced schottisches and polkas while an old man in the orchestra imitated birds by pinching his nose. When the taverns closed, Colonel Kundert played for some impromptu street dancing outside the Alpine Restaurant. It was four o'clock when we finally drove over the hill to Wilhelm Tell farm. My rest was brief; before seven o'clock I was awakened by my nieces and nephew yodeling outside my window.

After lunch that day I headed for the meadow, where *Wilhelm Tell* was to be performed. The play was first produced in 1938 and is another gift to New Glarus from Edwin Barlow. Barlow modeled his production after *Tells* he saw at Interlaken and Altdorf in Switzerland. Schiller made *Tell* an autumnal play and the New Glarners selected Labor Day weekend for its presentation for two reasons: the rehearsal period falls conveniently between the hay and grain harvests of July and August and the corn harvest in September, and the weather is usually dry and sunny.

The day was perfect and the crowd was the largest in twenty years. The meadow where the play is performed is enclosed on three sides by forested hills; on the south it opens on a rolling vista of green fields in which cows grazed. I remembered the valley as a thicket of blackberry brambles through which as a child I crawled, gathering fruit. Now it was neat as a park with the forest cropped and shaped to provide settings for the play and screens for the actors and animals. The wind whipped American and Swiss flags over the field. There were pretty usherettes in lacy costumes with butterfly and cartwheel hats bright and fresh as Alpine flowers.

Checking the cast of characters, I found that at least one-third of the 150 actors were my relatives. The German-speaking Tell, a carpenter named Oswald Schneider, was a cousin on my father's side; the English Tell, a building-supplies dealer named Gilbert Ott, was a cousin on my mother's side.

Promptly at one-thirty a sonorous rumble filled the valley. It came from a ten-foot hollowed fir log called an *alphorn*, and its effect was like that of a conch shell with which a chief calls a tribal council. The crowd quieted into a reverential silence, and a falsetto melody, the familiar *Wengernalp* yodel, filled the valley like bird song. From the south came a procession of singing men, cows, and goats garlanded with flowers and tinkling bells and a placidly wagging St. Bernard dog.

The scene of Schiller's *Wilhelm Tell* is Lake Lucerne in the thirteenth century, when Switzerland was under Austrian rule. It is the end of summer and men and animals are returning from Alpine meadows to winter in the valley villages. From the north came a second procession of women and children, greeting husbands and fathers. In the running mob I saw my mother, carrying a bundle of hay on her back, and my three nieces. The mood of rustic joy ended quickly with the rise of a storm, suggested by electrically produced wind and thunder. A young patriot fleeing from Austrian soldiers is rescued in a boat by Wilhelm Tell, and the summer exiles are caught up in a revolution which fomented while they were grazing their cattle on mountain meadows.

Each time Tell made his appearance a hush fell over the forest. In part this was due to Schiller's characterization of the hero as more god than man, a *deus ex machina* who

enters the drama at each crisis to set things right and then
disappears into the forest until his superhuman powers are
needed again. But the veneration of the audience was height-
ened by the acting of Gilbert Ott, who made Schiller's creation a living character.[1] He was a strongly built, romantic
figure who might have stepped out of a nineteeth-century
engraving of Tell. He moved with calm deliberation and,
with a powerfully resonant voice, spoke the epic lines so
eloquently from the heart that he seemed to become Tell.
Though the apple-shooting is faked (when the arrow is shot
the child flicks the apple from his head and produces an
arrow-pierced apple hidden in his clothing), Ott rehearsed
the scene by shooting an arrow through an apple at a distance of fifty yards. "How could I be Tell," Ott said, "if
I could not shoot an arrow through an apple?"

The climax of the play comes when Tell arches his bow
for the last time, aiming for his enemy, the Austrian governor. He says:

> *This day I'll make*
> *My master shot and win the highest prize*
> *Within the highest circumference of the mountains.*

The prize is freedom and with the fatal shot Tell becomes
the symbol of Swiss liberty. The audience rose to its feet
as a costumed chorus waved the bright flags of the Swiss
cantons and the young yodeler, Robert Schneider, hurled a
large Swiss flag fifty feet into the air. The red silk crackled
as it cut the wind and returned to Schneider, who sent it
back again and again like a flaming rocket. To proclaim
the birth of the Swiss Republic, church bells pealed in the
village and bonfires burned in the hills. This is a moment
which has never failed to move me to tears.

As the crowd trailed off, storm clouds appeared and in
the evening a real storm broke as wildly as the imaginary

---

[1] Ott died, a victim of cancer, seven weeks after giving his final performance in 1961.

one with which Schiller opens his play. The actors seemed to welcome it; their concern for the harvest left no time for the depression that usually descends on them when the play is finished.

I went to a party at the home of Wilhelm Tell. Most of the guests were actors in the play and they wore their black velvet yodel jackets embroidered with red and silver edelweiss. Our host sat in a corner, sullen and brooding, deep in the melancholy which always seemed to come over him when the play was finished. His wife, Dora, who was wardrobe mistress of the play, served wine and beer and a supper of sausages and cheeses.

The men in the room offered toasts and sang sentimental songs about mountains and snowy villages, Alpine flowers and girls with flowery names. Ott said, "Schiller didn't create Tell. He was created by the Swiss people. Tell is a lone wolf of great strength, of deep pride and no fear. He is a warrior who is a pacifist, a peasant who is also a philosopher."

I was beginning to understand Tell and the Swiss need for him. The neat materialism of life in Switzerland and in New Glarus, no matter how prosperous, will never be quite enough. It has brought on a neglect of the spirit, resulting in *mal de Suisse* (a phrase invented by Zürich psychiatrists) with its easy despair and casual suicide. That is why during their restless centuries of tight conformism the Swiss have comforted themselves with a nonconforming folk hero who rebels. "Tell is the kind of man every Swiss would like to be and knows he can't," said Gilbert Ott.

Someone remembered that sleeping in the house next door was the oldest resident of the town, ninety-two-year-old Mrs. Elsbeth Jenny, who came from Canton Glarus sixty-nine years before and never returned. The old lady's daughter went to awaken her and the men formed an arc under her window and sang a song called *Homesickness*. The voices of the two youths from Switzerland wove in and out of the chorus like silver whistles.

All my hope is gone,
That I will see my home again,
I live in a strange land without happiness,
I have only one wish before my death,
I would like to see the Alpine roses blooming . . .

The old lady listened in her bed and tears flowed from the eyes of the men. "We're all so damned lonely," Colonel Kundert muttered. Whatever we were, whether it was Swiss trying to be American or Americans trying to be Swiss, what we have all been seeking for a century is an identity.

In the morning Tell returned to his lumberyard and other Swiss patriots made cheese and cut corn. The amphitheatre was boarded up and my father and I removed the electric fence so that the cows could graze again in the meadow. The storm had washed everything green as spring. We climbed to a forested hill where he showed me the vines of wild grapes which were ripening for wine. We looked to the south over the hills which my father owned, and to the east over the hills which he coveted. "Man must have roots like a tree," he said. "To live without land is like living without God."

My father died a month later while working near his cows in the barn, speaking his last words in *Schwyzerdütsch*. He had just finished mashing the grapes, preparing to make the season's wine.

When I arrived from New York for the funeral, Wisconsin was on fire with autumn, glowing with the warmth of dissolution. Standing in sunlight in the cemetery looking out over the flaming hills, the day seemed like a benediction. The next day my sister and I went into the village to read the will. Wilhelm Tell Farm had been left in trust to her and to me. We returned over the east hill, my sister driving the car. At the summit she stopped and we looked down into the valley. Wilhelm Tell Farm had never looked so beautiful to me. The maples were scarlet, the birch and poplars golden, the oaks the color of wine. Breaking down finally after a long, sad week, my sister said, "We can't do it! We can't sell!"

When we arrived home I boiled vats of water for the wine, the first wine I had ever made.

two

The village in Switzerland, at which my citizenship was registered when I was born in New Glarus, Wisconsin, was the hamlet of Elm, Canton Glarus. Since my eight great-grandparents had left Elm in the 1840s and 1850s, no one in the family had been back there. But Switzerland never disclaims her own, no matter how far removed, and one of the first things I was taught to remember was that I was a Swiss.

Though I was a fourth-generation American, my childhood could not have been more Swiss if my peasant ancestors had never left Switzerland. In New Glarus we observed Swiss holidays, ate Swiss food, played Swiss games, yodeled and spoke only *Muttersprache*, the *schwyzerdütsch* patois of Elm.

One hundred and two years after my ancestors' departure from Switzerland I was the first of their descendants to return for a visit. Though it had rained almost constantly since I had entered Switzerland, the July morning was bright. The snowy Alps toward which I was headed were visible beyond Zürich Lake. It was Saturday and the train was jammed with ruddy youths on their way to Canton Glarus, a favorite weekend bivouac for Zürichers. We followed the shore of Zürich Lake, alive with swimmers and sailing boats looking like coveys of white butterflies. Soon after leaving the lake we arrived at Ziegelbruecke, the gateway to Canton Glarus. The entire canton, under twenty-five miles long and in the shape of "Y," is only a brisk Sunday hike for a sturdy mountaineer. As the train traveled up the valley, the mountain walls grew higher and closer, with each village huddling in claustrophobic peril.

Glarus town is near the head of the main valley, just below the fork in the "Y." Here the railroad station was surprisingly cosmopolitan, with kiosks of American magazines and French and English books. I had expected an old town with narrow streets cluttered by goats and peasants. What I saw was a graciously open city with wide streets, neoclassic palaces, public gardens, and fountains. Destroyed by fire in 1861, the town was wisely redesigned. Despite the oppressive mountains, it has a feeling of space where no space exists. The planners succeeded in creating an atmosphere of light and air, like a miniature Paris. The town's 5000 citizens are 40 per cent Catholic and 60 per cent Swiss Reformed. The municipally owned cathedral, where Ulrich Zwingli was a parish priest before he became a reformer, is used by both faiths, the Catholics occupying it the first half of each Sunday morning, and the Protestants the second half.

My purpose in stopping in Glarus was to trace my family tree. For this I went to the courthouse, a large stone building in the heart of the town, not far from the twin-spired cathedral. A box of geraniums made a scarlet cornice over the door. I was directed to the second floor, down a long corridor to a door which said "Landesarchiv." A thin, large-framed man came out of a corridor and peered at me over his glasses. He was Herr Doktor Jacob Winteler-Marti, custodian of what must be one of the world's most astounding genealogical records. The volumes which filled the room are the works of a genealogist named John Jacob Kubli-Mueller, a distant relative, who devoted his life to tracing the histories of every cantonal family back to the sixteenth century—and, in some cases, further. When he died in 1933 Herr Kubli-Mueller left his records to the government, which moved them to the courthouse, and employed Dr. Winteler-Marti to keep them up to date. Today every citizen of the canton—and very nearly every citizen of New Glarus, Wisconsin, if he so desires—can go to the archives and trace his ancestry back more than three hundred years.

The first thing I learned is that the Kublis (the name was anglicized with a "y" in America) of Glarus are not an old family at all, but upstart *Auslanders*. Their arrival in the fourteenth century is considered somewhat mysterious. According to Dr. Winteler-Marti, the founders of the family were probably Italian peasant immigrants named Capelli, an Italian word which means hair. The first Kublis mentioned in the archives are identified either as *"Kubli genannt Zopfi"* (Kubli named Zopfi), or *"Zopfi genannt Kubli."* *Zopfi*, in *Schwyzerdütsch*, means a braid of hair and the appellation, stemming from the Italian *"Capelli,"* seems to have referred to the custom of Kubli men to wear their hair long. The first member of the clan to appear in the records is Hans Kubli, born in 1446. His fiercely patriotic sons and grandsons distinguished themselves as soldiers against the dukes of their ancestral Italy. In 1513 Felix was killed in a foolhardy Swiss campaign to wrest Milan from the Viscontis, and twelve years later Thomas joined another Italian campaign to capture Pavia. Of the Kublis who stayed home, some became governors and judges. But not all were so respectable. In 1549, Paulus Kubli was ordered by a judge to stop drinking and in the next generation Peter and Fridli Kubli were on trial for a crime which the records discreetly fail to name. In 1589, Jost Kubli won first prize in an annual arms inventory. He possessed one suit of armor, three guns, three large spears, eight small spears, one large sword and one *"Tachsengablen,"* which is a sort of pronged devil's pitchfork.

In 1597, Yodel Kubli was married to Margaret Luchsinger

(historian Kubli-Mueller designates marriages with the abbreviation *"cop'd"* for the archaic *"copuliert"*) and this union is the beginning of an unbroken line down to the present. Yodel and Margaret had eight children, of which the sixth, Jacob, was born in 1615. He *"cop'd"* with Anna Maria Stauffacher and had seven children. One of them, Rudolf, also had seven children and was killed in a landslide in 1701. On August 6, 1723, Rudolf's youngest son, Hans Peter, married Magdalena Wild, and on December 1 of that year, the first of their seven children, Hans Rudolf, was born. I note the dates to show Hans Peter's observance of a Kubli tradition of shotgun marriages which has continued, unbroken in my family, almost to the present day. Because marriage and birth records are sketchy before Hans Peter, it is impossible to say just when this custom began. It has always pleased me to think of it as evidence of hot Kubli blood, but the real explanation is less romantic. To an Alpine landowner a barren wife is a catastrophe and it was the custom of mountain peasants to demand irrefutable evidence of fertility as a prerequisite to matrimony.

Hans Peter filled the family quota of seven children, but his son, Hans Rudolf, fell one short with six. Hans Rudolf's sons, Hans Ulrich, born in 1762, is my favorite ancestor. At the age of twenty he *"cop'd"* with a widow, Verena Rhyner, who was eleven years his senior and five months with child. They had four children. In 1814 Verena died and two years later Hans Ulrich, aged fifty-four, *"cop'd"* with Susanna Schneider, younger than his children and seven months pregnant. He fathered nine more children before he died in 1831. An infant son, Oswald, died in 1818, and a year later there was a second Oswald, who in 1842 married Barbara Schrapfar, according to the records a girl from a "charity family." In 1853, Oswald and Barbara emigrated to America with their four children, and cleared the land in Wisconsin upon which the family has lived since. The next year, on August 3, two of the children died of cholera, leaving two sons, Hans Ulrich, who ten years later was to lose a leg in the Civil War, and Oswald, who became my grandfather. In New Glarus the young Oswald married Anna Marie Elmer-Elmer von Elm, a proud patrician woman who, though she left Switzerland at the age of two and did not return, never let it be forgotten that she was a member of the first family of Elm. She had eleven children of which five sons grew to manhood; her favorite, named Nicklaus, was my father.

Compared to the Latin-blooded Kublis, my mother's family, the Otts from Schwanden, the town at the fork of the Canton Glarus "Y," were sober, pious burghers given to large families, hard work, and longevity. John Jacob Ott, born in 1799, migrated to New Glarus with his family in 1849. One of his sons, Anton, married Verena Jenny von Sool, also an immigrant, had thirteen children, was the first church secretary in New Glarus and lived into his ninetieth year. His oldest son, John Jacob, was my grandfather.

The records ended with the births of Lila Marie Kubli, my sister, and Herbert Oswald Kubli von Elm, myself. I brought the archives up to date with a memorandum of my sister's marriage and the births of her four children.

It was only five o'clock when I said goodbye to Dr. Winteler-Marti, but the shadows of the mountain had already darkened the valley. The sky from the great Glarnisch Alp, rising like a black sphinx before me, to the Schild Alp, behind me, was like a pale blue canopy stretched between two walls. Roses spilled from bushes, hedges, and trees—I counted twenty-four large red blooms on one stem—and rose petals covered the surface of a pool from which a fountain spurted water fifty feet into the air and cast rainbows in every direction. My reveries were interrupted by a wild clanging of church bells. It was the Saturday afternoon "prayer ringing" which the mountain walls echoed into a cacophony so torturous that a prayer did not seem possible.

I went into a restaurant, the Löwen, for a supper of *Bratwurst, Rösti* (fried potatoes) and salad, and a flask of dark

beer. I had looked forward to a lively Saturday night, such
as those customary in New Glarus, but when I asked my
waitress where I might find yodeling and dancing, she seemed
surprised. With condescending impertinence she said the
Glarners who had gone to America had been of the lower
classes and so, she supposed, liked that sort of thing. While
I was eating, three large red-faced women in the black uni-
forms and straw bonnets of the Salvation Army, and a wiz-
ened little man toting a drum, entered the place and sang
When the Roll Is Called Up Yonder. It was a far cry from
yodeling.

Outside in the dark deserted street, I threw back my head
and saw, high above the black walls of the valley, a white
ceiling of moonlight, and it was like looking up out of a well.
I had a mingled feeling of exhilaration and depression, and
I understood why people living so intimately with mountains are often despondent and prone to suicide.

At five o'clock the next morning I was awakened by the
excruciating bells. When they rang again at six, there was
nothing to do but rise. After a breakfast of sausages and
eggs, I went to the station to take a train for Elm. Though
it was not yet eight o'clock, the station was jammed with
Sunday mountaineers. The ruddy ladies from the Salvation
Army were moving through the crowd with their drummer,
still singing *When the Roll Is Called Up Yonder.* As we
pulled away from the station some youths in the open-sided
car began to yodel, drowning out the lachrymose trio on
the platform. I rode the train only four miles to Schwanden
where the canton divides into two valleys, known as *Grosstal*
and *Kleintal.* Here I switched to a red electric trolley that
was as bright and gay as a toy. This was the *Kleintal*—small
valley—train, traveling from Schwanden to Elm, the last
village up on the meadows of the Hausstock Alp. We started
to climb at once, through an abyss so narrow that the same
passage served as train track, auto road, and footpath. The

[1] Wilhelm Tell farm. "Men must have roots like a tree."

[2] The grandparents. Grandmother was an Elmer-Elmer von Elm.

[3] My father with his grand-daughter. The eyes were the barometer of his temper.

[4] In native dress with my mother. What we were seeking was an identity.

[5] My cousin, Gilbert Ott, as Wilhelm Tell. "Tell is the kind of man every Swiss would like to be and knows he cannot."

[6] The ancestral church in Elm. My name was on three tombstones.

[7] Kubli cousins from Elm. "They might have been born there and you here."

[8] William "Fuzzy" Pfarr. An allergy to college men. *(Drawing by Henry Major)*

[9] Sunday in Appenzell.

[10] Lötschental: the valley of the masks.

[11] "Ironic parodies of all the afflictions of the flesh."

[12] Her parents were raking hay but she knew the prices.

[13] Lötschental: She carried the bread lovingly, kissing it like a doll.

[14] At the end of the Lötschental. Just under the glacier there were Edelweiss.

conductor told me that the pass frequently filled up in winter, isolating the villages above.

The valley widened into a sunny plateau of vegetable gardens and small fields arranged about clusters of dark brown buildings. The heavens shook with the roar of waterfalls, scores of shimmering cascades on both sides of the valley emptying a thousand feet or more from the snowfields above. The sun was warm, but the air was brisk and biting and the light was blinding to my eyes. Ahead of me rose the formidable snow-covered *Zwölfhörner*, or twelve peaks, and I recognized a vent in one of them as *Martin's Loch*, through which, each November 11, the day of St. Martin's feast, oblique rays of the sun shine for a few minutes on the spire of the Elm church, two thousand feet below.

The car came to a stop at a small wooden station above which the village of Elm stretched another half-mile upward. I started walking, feeling as Rip Van Winkle must have felt, moving through a place I'd never seen, yet felt I had, where everything was familiar at the same time that it was unfamiliar. The village was empty as a ghost town, and many of the dark chalets were shuttered. Finally, I met an old man carrying hay, who told me that everyone was either in the hayfields or in church.

The *Kasbissensturm*, or "cheese wedge tower," of the 700-year-old church where my ancestors worshiped, was familiar to me from many old pictures. On the church wall there is a large plaque which tells of a great avalanche which wiped out more than half of the village in the year 1881. Among the names of the victims posted there are a Peter Kubli and forty Elmers—my grandmother's family—and I thought with a shudder that if my ancestors had not left Elm before the catastrophe I probably would never have been born. In the crowded graveyard I found the same names with which I had grown up in New Glarus: Babler, Rhyner, Zentner, Disch, Freitag, and the same devotion to a small number of first names: Kaspar, Nicklaus, Oswald. The mixed black slate and white marble tombstones made an eerie effect and I felt some of Rip Van Winkle's terror when I saw my own name, Oswald Kubli, on three of the stones.

Entering the church was, I imagine, rather like entering a seventeenth-century meeting house in Puritan New England. The interior was like the cemetery outdoors, a stark counterpoint of black on white. The church was unadorned white and the dress of the parishioners, unrelieved black. The women wore black bonnets uniform in design; the men's black stove-pipe hats stood upside down in a row on a shelf. The minister wore a black robe with a crossed white collar. The parishioners turned to look at me. I was wearing a short-sleeved striped sports shirt without jacket or tie. In embarrassment I slipped into the nearest pew and discovered that I was seated with the women, separated by the center aisle from the pews of the men. The minister, bearing in mind no doubt the haymakers in the meadows, was warning against the sin of not keeping the sabbath. When he finished, the congregation sang vigorously, *A Mighty Fortress Is Our God*. The people hurried away, speaking to one another in hushed whispers. Not even the minister greeted me. I stood in the begonia and geranium-covered graveyard, lonely among tombstones bearing the names of Kubli and Elmer.

Men, wearing loose-fitting cotton "hay-shirts" with hoods to keep chaff out of hair and ears, were carrying the hay down to the barns in huge bundles tied to their backs. One was passing the cemetery. From under the hay peered a grizzled, beard-stubbled face.

"You carry it well," I said.

"There was a day when I carried it better," he replied.

"The preacher does not approve of your working on Sunday," I said.

"The preacher does not have a hayfield," he said. "If the Lord God sends two weeks of rain, and sunshine on a Sun-

day, He cannot be too surprised to see people making hay."
And he trudged down the road into the village.

I walked after him, passing a bottling plant for *Elmer
Zitronenwasser*, the Coca-Cola of Switzerland. The factory
built over some mineral springs is owned by a Kubli who
lives in Glarus. I also passed several inns, patronized in
summer by mountaineers and fishermen from Zürich, in
winter by skiers. I entered the Elmer Hotel and asked for
a meal.

"Mother is in the hayfield," said a young girl in attendance.
"There is only some smoked ribs and green beans."

As I ate, I asked the girl if she knew any Kublis.

"How can one help but know Kublis?" she replied.

"I should like to meet some. Any Kublis."

"An old grandmother Kubli lives across the street," she
said. The house she pointed out was low and ponderous, and
gray with age. I crossed the road and knocked on the door.
As I stood waiting, a man appeared from between some
buildings and, standing in the middle of the road, watched
me silently. He was thin and middle-aged and his skin was
burned dark.

"I guess there's no one home," I said.

"I guess not," he repeated. "The old lady is making hay."

He started walking down the road and I walked beside
him. "Can you take me to her?" I asked.

"I can," he said and we walked on. "You are a stranger.
Swiss?"

"American," I said. "My name is Kubly."

He stopped and looked at me. "My name is also Kubli,"
he said. "Jacob Kubli."

"Are you related to the old lady?" I asked.

"Yes, we are related," he answered in a dry voice. We
walked another hundred feet or so. "She is my mother," he
said. He stopped and turned to stare at me. "What are you
called?"

"Herbert Oswald," I said.

"Oswald, naturally. My grandfather and my father were named Oswald. So is my first boy an Oswald."

"We are many Oswalds in America too," I said.

We climbed up into a meadow where two women, a pale youth, and a flaxen-braided freckled little girl were raking hay. The women, who were wearing the Glarner black skirts, embroidered vests, and white stockings, were Jacob's mother and wife. The sad young man who walked with a limp was my cousin Oswald and the little girl who wore a blue and pink apron, was his sister, Nonni.

"Someone has come to see us," said Jacob slowly and without expression. "Oswald from America."

The younger woman, Jacob's wife, dropped her rake. "Is it possible?" she asked. The old woman leaned on the handle of her rake and studied me. She was white-haired, strongly built, and handsome. "Are you the son of Hans Ulrich or Fridolin?" she asked, naming two of her husband's brothers who had emigrated to America in the 1890s.

"Grandson," the younger woman said. "Can't you see how young he is?"

Suddenly Grandmother dropped her fork and began to move about with excitement. "One can see that you are my nephew," she said. "Look at you! Exactly like my husband." I tried to tell her that while we were no doubt kin, the relationship was not so close, but she did not hear me. "The eyes are the same," she said. "Your hair is his. You have his voice. When you speak I can hear him." Her eyes filled with tears and she embraced me. "And now you have come all the way from America to see an eighty-three-year-old woman befores she dies."

Suddenly the child, Nonni, began to jump up and down on a cock of hay.

"Stop!" her father ordered. "Have peace!"

"I can't!" cried Nonni, leaping like a dervish. "Oswald from America is here and I feel just like a wild little goat."

"Was it you in church this morning?" Jacob's wife said.

"It was him, it was him," Grandmother said, and the two women rocked with laughter.

"The schoolmaster's wife said it was *schrecklich*," Grandmother said. "A crazy man, improperly dressed, came to church just before it was over and sat with the women. Then he made photographs of tombstones!"

I picked up Grandmother's rake and began to work.

"I have heard it will rain tonight," I said. "The hay must be under cover." Jacob was of the same opinion. "Is it possible?" Grandmother asked. "He comes from America and he knows how to make hay?"

Jacob's wife asked what work I did in America and I told her that I was a professor. "*Herr Gott!*" said Grandmother. "A professor of Elm and we let him make hay!"

"Are you married?" Grandmother asked, and I replied I was not. "Of course!" she said. "There are no Swiss girls in America and you have come home to Elm to find a wife." She told me of her two granddaughters, working as waitresses in Zürich. "Trudi is right for you. She has a happy character and is a good worker." I started to say that since Trudi was my cousin, marriage with her would be ill-advised, but I remembered that in a family which had been marrying itself for 400 years, the argument would not carry much weight.

Word that I was in Elm seemed to have spread over the village by a sort of telepathy and now a small procession of persons was arriving to meet me. I was introduced to men named Disch, Elmer, Freitag, Babler, and Zentner, all with the first name of Oswald, and six Kaspar Rhyners, ranging in ages from twelve to seventy years. Not only the names but the faces were those of New Glarus. After the first moments of shyness, men and women began to ask questions about America.

"Is it true that in America farmers have machines to do their work?" a man asked. I said that even with machines, farmers worked hard. "But not women," a buxom wife said.

"I have heard even farmers' wives have servants in their houses." I told her that my mother and sister not only did housework but often operated tractors in the fields. "Women running tractors!" the woman exclaimed. "What will it be next?"

Was it true, someone asked, that Americans were rich enough for every family to have an automobile?

I replied that not every family had a car, but that many families had two or three. An old Oswald Zentner slapped his right fist into his left hand and danced a sort of jig. "*Herr Jäger, au!*" he cried. "I wish my grandfather had emigrated." A grizzled old Kaspar Disch said, "If the people of New Glarus are so rich they must have earned it by hard work. In America, no more than in Elm, do fried pigeons fly into the mouths of men."

I noticed that some of the Swiss words I was speaking were lost to my listeners. Sometimes only Grandmother seemed to understand. I used the word *dichamal*, a New Glarus expression meaning "now and then."

"*Dichamal!*" Grandmother repeated, rocking with laughter, shaking her head. "That is a word I have not heard since I was a girl."

Slowly it became apparent to me that the dialect I was speaking was no longer the language of Elm, but was an archaic nineteenth-century patois spoken today only in New Glarus, Wisconsin. My feeling of juxtaposition in time and in space grew when, after the haying, some of the men invited me to a *Gasthaus* for some beer. Three men were playing *Yass*, just as men might have been playing the same card game in New Glarus. The music coming from the phonograph was not yodeling as it probably would have been in New Glarus, but the horns of Tommy Dorsey and Harry James. Beside me, cousin Oswald was humming *Just One of Those Things*. Young people were dancing and when I tried to show a girl how we danced *Ländlers* and polkas in New Glarus, she laughed and said, "*Du tanzischt altväterisch.* You dance old-fashioned."

I was invited to supper in the Kubli house, four centuries old and deep and dark as a cave. We ate cheese, cold veal sausage, bread and strawberry jam, exactly the Sunday night supper I might have had in New Glarus. Afterward Grandmother and I sat on a grassy slope behind the house, watching the evening shadows fall across the valley. She was one of the last survivors of the great avalanche, and now she told me how she escaped death that dark night. "I was visiting a school friend in a house outside the village," she said. "We were playing our zithers and suddenly the roar was so loud we could no longer hear the music which our fingers were making. Those of us who did not die lived in sorrow for years and no one thought laughter ever would be heard again in Elm."

In the eighty-three years of her life, Grandmother had been away from Elm only twice. "Once when I was a girl I went to Zürich. *Ach,* such a big noisy town! The drinking water tasted bad and I did not like Zürich at all." The second time was ten years past when a boy's bicycle collided with her and broke her leg. "I was taken to the hospital in Glarus in an automobile," she said. "It was the only time I rode in an automobile." She told me there were four automobiles in Elm, one of them a jeep used to haul milk and cream from Alpine pastures. "But lately automobiles come here from outside the valley," she said. "It used to be restful here in Elm, but now it has become very dangerous. On Sundays an automobile goes by almost every half-hour."

Grandmother's lame grandson shuffled from the house, still humming *Just One of Those Things.* "*Ach,* it is no different between you two Oswalds," she said. "He might have been born there and you here. It would have been the same. The young do not understand that peace comes not from where one lives but from how one lives."

The time had come for me to go to the station and mount

the little red trolley that would take me down to Glarus. Grandmother walked beside me, proud and straight, and the little goat girl, Nonni, danced around us like a wood sprite. Behind us, with his wife and son, walked Jacob, solemnly sucking his pipe, and behind him some of the people I had met in the afternoon. A few bleating goats trailed at the end of the little parade. "Take our greetings to your people in New Glarus," they said as I shook hands around the circle. When the trolley rolled away, they waved and called "*uf widerluege*," which is *Schwyzerdütsch* for *auf wiedersehen*. The trolley rattled pell-mell down the mountain. Gray rain clouds appeared over the western peaks, filling the valley with night. A blond boy on the seat beside me told me he was eighteen, that he lived in Schwanden and worked in a weaving factory. Like Grandmother, he had been out of Canton Glarus once, for a trip to Zürich, a city he didn't like at all. "We in *Glarnerland* are not accustomed to big towns," he said. "We are happiest when we stay at home." Looking backward a century, I thought how much more courageous than the boy sitting beside me had been the eight young people who became my great-grandparents, and for this I was glad.

three

WHERE ARE YOU, HAZEL HOPKINS?

When I am in Wisconsin I am homesick for the woods and on each visit I try to make at least one trip to the north. I begin every journey with the same anticipation of adventure. The attitude goes back to my southern Wisconsin childhood when north was a synonym for sin, for drunken Indians, trigger-happy gangsters, brawling lumberjacks, wild-wild women, and red-jacketed hunters, some of whom returned as dead as the buck deer on the fenders. God's Country! Man's Country! They mean the same—a male eyrie as much in fantasy as in geography—perilous, lonely, and remote, especially from the society of women.

One summer's morning I pointed the yellow sports car north and, top down, pretending in my middle years to be eighteen, I roared in four hours from the 93 degrees in the shade at my Wisconsin home on Illinois' border to seventy-three in the sun near Superior's banks. My compass is our continental divide from which the west-flowing waters cascade down the whorled Wisconsin to the Mississippi and east-flowing waters push up the businesslike Fox River through Green Bay. On Highway 49, I pass through the unincorporated hamlet called Northland (between Scandinavia

and Norskie), and see ahead the primordial gray-granite
barrier where the north begins.

"Ymer's Eyebrow," Norsemen call the disorderly Stone-
henge which swings across the land at about the forty-fifth
parallel. They say it was built from the eyebrow of a fallen
god to separate the southern world of light from the northern
world of mists. Lumbermen have their own explanation: the
stones were gathered by Bunyanesque troglodytes to bar
bustling mice-men of the south, like me, from the land of the
giants.

Myths and legends? Our north is the home of the tall story.
The granite belt—according to geologists—is a glacial deposit.
Men have fashioned the stones into houses and barns, piled
them into fences or simply heaped them like Druids' altars
in the fields. They are still there, endless, unconquerable,
bitterly backbreaking. Geologists credit the same glacier
with scooping out Superior and all our smaller lakes, but a
northerner will tell you that Bunyan scooped out Superior
to make a waterhole for Babe, his ox, and that Wisconsin's
9000 lakes are Babe's hoofprints, filled by thaws during a restless spring.

The light is icy bright, the forests dark. In the high
northern wind the conifers sigh like sleeping women and
balsam is in the air. I head for muskieland in Oneida County.
Turning at Deer Lake into the driveway of the Northernaire
Hotel, I slow down to miss a pair of fawns. As I draw up,
two fat otters slide out of the water, bowing and scraping
as if they were rehearsing for Disney. A tame raccoon climbs
in beside me and unpacks the glove compartment. In half an
hour I am in a boat trolling lily pads under which I suspect
a muskie hides. In another quarter-hour I hook what seems to
be an old stump. My rod goes into convulsions and the
flogged water boils. The muskie is the fiercest of fresh-water
fish and mine makes a threshing show, standing on his tail,
six feet or more, whipping up a typhoon. The shore audience

cheers as if I were fighting a bull. A slip clutch on my reel frees me to gaff him—after forty-five minutes.

The malevolent-eyed fish was measured (fifty-one inches) and weighed (thirty-five pounds), according to custom, in the Northernaire's night club. The hotel's bass fiddler, a Staten Islander named Jim Blake, doubles as hotel taxidermist. "All a taxidermist needs is to be a good fish man," he says. "For a dollar an inch I'll mount anything."

Over 40,000 muskies a year are caught up here. The largest on rod and reel weighed just under seventy pounds, but one weighing 102 pounds has been netted. In Pelican Lake a sportsman named Clarence Bodenhaugen had a season's take of fifty-four, and other fishermen threatened to withhold their tax payments unless he was banned from the lake. A fisherman named Clifford Isley from my own Green County hooked two sturgeon simultaneously on two rods and landed the larger, a seventy-pounder. When we tell our fish stories we don't exaggerate.

Architect Cy Williams, former Phillies home-run slugger, designed the Northernaire Hotel like a ship, painted it in pastel colors and set it on the shores of Deer Lake, where it sits like an Italian liner in dry dock. Expensive for humans, it is free to animals. Deer and fox roam the carpeted lobby, a bear wanders through the night club and a beaver swims in the indoor pool. Out on the golf course an enterprising raccoon picks the balls out of the cups and carries them into the woods.

This peaceable if somewhat chaotic kingdom of man and beasts is the creation of one of the north's legendary characters, the hotel's owner-manager, Carl Marty. A former cheese dealer who looks like a merry Buddhist monk, Marty operates his inn like a penny-shrewd Swiss concierge and befriends animals like a medieval saint. "Without exception," says he, "the animals of the forest reach out for human friendship. It is the humans who are not conditioned for such friendship."

There are no cages. The animals live in the forest and trail like a Noah's caravan through the "pet portal" fitted into the bottom of Marty's office door, coming for food, affection, and medication. There is an animal kitchen supplied with refrigerated milk, nursing bottles, canned infant formulas, vitamins, suppositories, "lollipups," and Swiss cheese for fawns which, on this special diet, grow the largest antlers in the forest. Hotel guests have learned tolerance, though popular prejudices against skunks and porcupines are sometimes hard to overcome and most patrons think Marty goes too far when he recommends his beasts as bed partners. Leslie Carroll, a pretty blond dancer in the night club, roomed one summer with a red fox, and Marty has shared his own abundant warmth with bears, beavers, raccoons, and otters. Children naturally love the Northernaire. "Without our animals our profits would be halved," says Concierge Marty, while St. Francis Marty adds, "I have never seen a dumb wild animal."

The Saturday night town in this area is Rhinelander, a paper-manufacturing center named for the New York family. Paper is the north's leading industry and the spillway of Rhinelander's Boom Lake is a mountain of logs, as many as four million of the "weed trees" ignored by the old loggers: the spruce, fir, balsam, and tamarack, as well as the beautiful birch which gives Wisconsin landscape its melancholy Chekhovian shimmer. On Brown Street, saloon doors swing and in Nick's City Bar at least once an evening lumber workers and their gals join the musicians in *When They Cut Down the Old Pine Tree*. The rendition is unforgettable.

Three miles from Deer Lake lies Nicolet National Forest. The log-cabined citizens of these 53,000 primeval acres are "Kaintucks," Kentucky immigrants whose moonshine during the 1920s was the mainstay of Capone's Chicago. It is an unforgettable spot. Old logging trails lead into deep wilderness. Shafts of sunlight fall through the timber on to shoulder-high bracken. Bushes sag with ripe blackberries and blueberries. Guideless explorations are dangerous, for the trails wind miles with only bird cries and the rippling of water to break the silence. One must be attuned with himself to bear it for long.

Somewhere in these woods is Butternut Lake, one of the most remote and beautiful in the north, famous for its bass and thieving black bears. Nearby are cranberry bogs, neat and symmetrical as Sumatran rice paddies. During blossom-time in July they look like vast pink quilts. The growers flood them in September, the fruit floats on the waters like red manna and is gathered by powered rakes. At about the same time silent Indians sliding through marshes are shaking the brown grains of wild rice into their canoes. In the north the past and present are always side by side.

Real Indians? There are 12,000 in Wisconsin. Their six reservations are not what tourists expect: no tepees, no beaded hunters, only an empty second-growth wilderness. I crossed Lac du Flambeau reservation and didn't see a single Indian until the village of Lac du Flambeau (pop. 542), where they live beyond the sumacs in gray clapboard shacks with out-houses, flapping laundry and roves of slant-eyed children. The enterprising Menominees are the exception; they manage their forests so efficiently that some of them are prosperous. In 1961 their reservation became an All-Indian Menominee County—Wisconsin's seventy-second county. A drive through it on Highway 55 follows the rapids of the Wolf River past neat cabins with TV aerials spreading wider than the roofs supporting them. On a trail into the woods I found Mike, a chunky, moon-faced Indian who is custodian of a waterfall over which Coca-Cola-colored (from iron and mulch) water boils and foams. At the edge is this sign:

> Big Smoky Falls Menomenee Indian Reservation many years 1925. There was no road with which people could get into this place in order that tourist could come and see the wonderfull waterfall we build the road and bridges and you come here view the falls also beautiful surrounds it this is why I charge 10 cent each admission
>
> MIKE.

I was drawn toward the outposts of my youth so I turned north again, toward Wisconsin's sin-across-the-border town of Hurley. The rowdy reputation of this northland Tiajuana goes back to the logging boom of the 1880s. When lumbering collapsed so did Hurley—but not her reputation. Prohibition was her renaissance; she became a haven for rum runners and gangsters. On the surface Hurley seems a peaceful village. Her silhouette on the horizon, with a Romanesque courthouse tower and the Gothic spire of a Catholic church, might be the Christmas card profile of a New England village.

The gentleness is a deception. Hurley's six-block Silver Street is jammed with fifty-six saloon fronts and looks in its gawdy neon like flats from a TV horse opera. A winding creek, presumptuously named Montreal River, separates Hurley (pop. 3034) from the larger town of Ironwood, Michigan.

I wandered up and down the blocks, searching for a place called The Dew Drop Inn where I had made my first raffish foray at sixteen, but it seemed to have disappeared, or at least changed its identity. The joints, aswarm with girls, were named Blondie's, Augie's Rainbow, Shorty's, and Gold Nuggett. Signs, crudely scrawled in chalk, offered "Wine—Booze—Rooms to Let—Floor Show." A Hurley floor show means one thing: women undressing. No comic routines, no live music, just a dreary never-ending procession of tired girls jogging to-and-fro to phonograph music under garish lights on bar tops, usually behind cash registers. I joined a row of iron miners, lumber jacks, tourists, and salesmen, climbing a high stool like a boy in a soda fountain, and watched Polish and Mexican women shimmying. A dusky Indian, dead-pan, molted red and orange feathers to *Indian Love Call* on the phonograph. Doll-like Orientals quivered (*Flower Drum Song*) and a voluptuous Negress rotated her parts absent-mindedly. The record ended and the girl waited like a broken Keystone Comedy, with upswung arm, zipper half-drawn, for the music to resume. Garments were dropped in a heap at the bar's edge. As soon as she finished, the girl picked up the dismal little bundle like laundry and slumped off, naked, sagging, with it under her arm. My companions on the stools laughed. Sometimes there are raids and the saloon owner coughs up $500 and reopens in the morning. Five years ago a man convicted of biting off an adversary's ear in a barroom brawl appealed his case to the United States Supreme Court. The spirit of Hurley is Rabelaisian, and why not? Paul Bunyan, after all, is kin to Gargantua.

Two saloons later a fat Salome with black oiled hair was dropping seven kerchiefs (*Scheherazade*). A big Swede, triple chinned, double-stomached, whirled herself like a Bendix. Two very young girls in street clothes slipped in beside me. "I'm Livia," one whispered, and the other, "I'm Lidia." Small, sullen, dark, they were by far the prettiest girls I had seen that evening. But I was no longer sixteen and I had watched thirty women undress that evening. Furthermore, though I'd had fifteen Old Grand Dads, I was cold sober. It is no secret that the "top-shelf" I had been drinking was low-grade watered stuff in short-measure glasses.

Wisconsin's northernmost north is the red-sandstone archipelago stretching out into Lake Superior, that is known as the Apostle Islands. One morning three friends arrived at Deer Lake in a little Cessna, its wingspan hardly wider than one of Paul Bunyan's mosquitoes, to fly me there. My companions were members of the Friends of Hazel Hopkins (her name is a fiction), a prankish and restricted society of nostalgic university classmates perpetuating the memory of a certain gregarious sorority nymph known to all of us twenty-five years ago and now, perhaps fortunately, passed into oblivion. The first island we saw on Superior's waters was a floating one, brown and in the shape of a tear, being towed by tugboat into Chequamegon Bay. It was a boom of pulpwood a third of a mile in diameter, 60,000 "weed trees" being floated into Ashland harbor for railroading to paper mills.

Ahead twenty-three Apostles rose from the mists like

shadows of clouds on the water. We picked the largest, Madeline, and gave it a warning buzz. There was a green strip cut through the forest and, like visitors from outer space, we descended gently into a serene Arcadia. A blond Indian youth helped tie down our plane. There are still twenty-five French-bred Indians on the island, some as blue-eyed and fair as Norman Sicilians. Madeline belonged to the Ojibways who called her *Moningwunakauning*—"Home of the golden-breasted woodpecker."

One day and evening we navigated in and out of the islands on a cabin cruiser. Colors were bold and crisp. Prussian blue waters, burgundy cliffs one hundred feet high, green conifers, white birch, yellow beaches. Circling Madeline we passed bleak deserted farms, like Edward Hopper paintings, forgotten plots where man had battled nature and capitulated. In other places tendrils of smoke rose straight up from the forest. They might have come from Indian fires, but actually they were from fishermen's smokehouses. Blond-bearded fishermen came from Norway, Finland, and Lithuania to harvest Superior's trout and white fish. The seemingly everlasting supply ended suddenly in 1950, destroyed by the pernicious villain of northern waters, the lamprey eel. When I was there only two commercial fishermen remained: Ever Bodin, a sixty-four-year-old Norwegian, and John Hagen, a rheumatic eighty-four-year-old Finn who had fished Superior for sixty years. In early sailing-boat years John caught a thousand pounds a day; now he took in less than fifty. But the old man looked forward to the day when fishing would be good again. The government-supported Great Lakes Fishery Commission has been fighting lampreys with chemicals and electrical fences, and has restocked Superior with a million young trout.

As we cruised eastward, Madeline's forests grew thicker, her solitude deeper. We passed a sunken scow with birch trees growing from its deck, a tilted fish shed nearly collapsing from the weight of gulls jostling on its gables. A dark eagle circled over a Norway pine. The white gulls broke rank and scattered over the waters.

We turned into rough open waters toward other Apostles: Michigan Island with its two lighthouses, connected by a shoal to tiny (three acres) Gull Island; Stockton, second largest and loveliest island, known for a beach which, by a curious acoustical phenomenon, sings as you walk over its sands; Outer Island with its wailing foghorn; Cat, Otter, and Bear Islands, twin North and South Islands, and finally the northernmost Devil's Island, named by the Indians for the deep caverns washed into its sand cliff, looking from the distance like the arches of Roman bridges. Afterward there were only water and the far horizon of the Mesabi Range, lodestone of Pittsburgh wealth, now a source of low-grade taconite ore.

At twilight we anchored in a forest lagoon and built driftwood fires for a beach picnic of grilled lake trout, roasted corn, potatoes, and blueberries. Later, chugging gently over silent waters in the soft mist-silvered night, we lay on deck, singing softly. On the blue hills beyond the waters the lights of waterside hamlets twinkled and for a moment I believed I was on Mediterranean waters, looking at Spain and the lights of Algeciras. Suddenly the northern lights exploded, lighting up the night, making a fiesta in the heavens. The brightness revealed still another dark, tear-shaped island of logs floating to the lumber mills, as silent as a funeral cortège in Venice. At that moment one of my companions asked the familiar question, the one we had been asking forever through the years: "Where are you, Hazel Hopkins?"

On my ear fell *wah-hoo-oo, wah-hoo-oo,* over and over, the eerie lonely keening of the loon on his evening flight. Though the night was warm I felt the chilling solitude that draws men to the north. I took a draught of whisky, sent

the bottle on another round, raised my eyes to the flashing
sky and thanked the universe for the blessed strength to endure loneliness.

Most beautiful, most festive, and most melancholy of Wisconsin's seasons is the sportsman's long Indian summer. One
golden sportsmen's morning three of us put on our fringed
buckskin jackets and flew back to sportsmen's country. Behind me Cousin Ray, owner of the Cessna, studied aeronau-
tical charts while the pilot flew us as steadily as a flock of
migrating mallards which we met; it being October, we were
flying in opposite directions.

Suddenly, after a hundred miles we were blinded by the
brilliant reflection of the Wisconsin; by an illusion of refraction, it seemed suspended in the western sky like quartzite.
Below, the forest was a stained-glass window. Autumn turns
its brightest face to the sun; seen from above the orange
maples, tangerine ash, purple oaks, and yellow birch might
have been blazing zinnia beds. Balsam and pine in the lowlands, tamaracks in the swamps, were like crescents of ferns.
We soared over the island town of Minocqua, passing from
Oneida into Vilas County where the lakes are so thick that
the picture from above is of a sea filled with floating green
islands. There were no houses, no garden patches. Sparse
habitations are camouflaged by nature and the primeval
wilderness reaches to the brooding dark cliffs of Superior.

"Must be time for a drink," Ray said. So Perry lowered us
gently into a clearing of brown rustic halls, like a Hapsburg
hunting lodge in the Carpathians. This was King's Gateway,
a resort so close to Michigan that its golf course is divided
between two states. Natives boast of the summer of '46 when
five Eisenhower brothers—Ike included—came to fish. Before we could land we had to buzz a herd of deer from the
airstrip. We moored in a row of Cessnas, Beechcrafts, Piper
Apaches, and Comanches and glass-nosed converted bom-
bardier trainers, all painted bright as birds.

As we trudged through the sand we heard the rat-a-tat-tat of gunfire. We were interlopers at a shooting fête. Outside the hotel a steady stream of captive pigeons were squirted into the sky by compressed air and dropped immediately by a gaggle of absurd gunmen and gunwomen into a meadow carpeted with bird carcasses. It seemed a depressingly disadvantageous contest.

Indoors at first glance the hotel appeared to be host to a taxidermist convention. But the animal skins and heads hanging heavily from gables and beams are standard northern décor. The bar was packed with sharpshooters discussing their pigeon scores. An elderly Chicago lady, a former champion unable to compete this time because of a toothache on her shooting side, told us that 10,000 pigeons—city birds trapped in Chicago and New York—would be shot in five days. I thought of the waste in food and expressed my shock at the number of birds. "Yes," the shooting lady said, "it's a helluva job burying ten thousand pigeons."

While we lunched on Chicago filet mignon and whisky sours (Perry observing his flying quota of one beer), an afternoon grayness was settling over the forest. Returning to the plane, we discovered the track of a bear.

As we nosed west over pines through cloud banks into a blue-and-gold ascension sky, Ray tuned in to the World Series. Whenever there was a break in the cloud bank, lakes appeared beneath us. These were the headwaters of the mighty river Chippewas called Wees-Konsan, "the gathering of the waters," a name spelled *Ouisconsin* by the French and changed to *Wisconsin* by President Jackson when he established a territorial government in 1836. Pious seventeenth-century Jesuits, believing themselves on a short cut to China, were told by Indians that the prodigal forests were "earthly paradise." The familiar story of human avariciousness followed: Astor's American Fur Company came for pelts; the Carnegie and Frick companies in Pittsburgh mined ore for their furnaces; Rhinelanders and Weyerhaeusers plundered the lumber. The state was cleared of timber in forty years. Next came wheat farmers, burning up the soil with successive crops and moving to the more fertile Dakotas. When the Indians got the land back, paradise was a barren and lawless tundra. Lumbermen called it "tougher than hell and a lot livelier." But today the northern migration is bigger than ever. Reforestation and fire control have raised a second timber from the ashes. Wise conservation has returned game to the woods and fish to the waters. The wealth flow has been reversed; and pleasure-intent aliens are returning it in dollars.

At Boulder Junction we buzzed the black bears in the town dump and chased two wolves from the airstrip. Boulder Junction is one broad avenue of sporting stores, boating shops, souvenir stands, and gas stations. Three miles in the forest is Dairymen's County Club, a luxurious private retreat, not for Wisconsin farmers but for well-heeled butter-and-cheese men, mostly from Chicago. They rough it luxuriously with private golf and tennis, 6000 virgin acres of protected wild life and ten private lakes leaping with fish.

To let Perry properly enjoy the evening we grounded ourselves for the night. A hired station wagon was waiting. We made regulation stops at a pair of man-and-wife-operated forest saloons known as Johnnie's and Jessie's, and Shrimp's and Clara's. Clara Wilfer, *wirtsfrau* of the second, is our north's Wife of Bath. Her insults and whooping ribaldries, impossible to bowdlerize, draw a devoted sporting clientele, including those tired tycoons on fishing trips where no one fishes. The bar is a taxidermists' heaven of several thousand dead animals and fish which have the curious effect with me at least, of increasing beverage consumption.

Twenty forested miles west we entered a German fairy-tale woods. Hidden inside on the shore of Little Star Lake is the most famous hospice of the north, Emil Wanatka's Little Bohemia Lodge. Emil was waiting. Within a half-hour we were Lucullan senators dining on wild duck, wild rice, and red cabbage, appropriately orchestrated with a light

Liebfraumilch. The peerless menu of game and fowl is modeled after the old Hotel Continental in Pilsen, Bohemia. Emil is a dark, sinewy little Slav in his seventies with leathery brown skin and beetle-black eyes. In his favorite costume, a red wool shirt and cowboy necktie, he looks like a wary fifty-year-old Indian from the Lac du Flambeau reservation across the lake. A great talker, he repeated for us the curious Horatio Alger success story which has made him a living legend.

"So in 1906"—he began—"I am seventeen when I land in wonderful New York with a dollar-ten and no suitcase. I come to Chicago and get a job as a boxer trainer and I meet a lot of boys. I get a job in the bar of Little Bohemia restaurant. Then Prohibition starts. I make a lot of money and buy Little Bohemia. I feed a hundred people a day and maybe more. I pay police seventy dollars a day and every night someone is killed. I dodge fifty bullets. Then the St. Valentine's Day massacre kills my customers. It's nerve-racking, killing my good friends. So I sell Little Bohemia and come up here. I do O.K. Now if I want goldfish milk I can buy it—all I want."

Some of his Chicago customers—those still alive—followed Emil north to Little Bohemia Lodge. Late one April afternoon in 1934 three autos arrived carrying six men and four women.

"They say, 'Hi, Emil.' They know me from Chicago. I pick up a bag and fall over, so heavy it is. I'm suspicious. They can't be hardware salesmen. Then at night when we are playing poker and I see two .45s on the shoulder straps of the familiar-looking guy reaching for the money, I know it is John Dillinger. Also Tommy Carroll and Homer Van Meter and Baby Face Nelson I am playing with. Very cold night. April is still middle winter up here. Baby Face and Tommy Carroll go to a cottage with two girls and Dillinger goes upstairs. In the morning the girls make breakfast, one makes toast, another fries bacon, another irons dress and we

all eat around the kitchen table. Dillinger asks me am I
afraid. I said, 'Every undersheriff in America is looking for
you, why don't you do me a favor and get out?' Dillinger
takes me by the shoulders and says, 'Emil, I'm hungry. I'm
tired. I want to sleep and eat a few days. I'll pay you well.'
What could I do?"

The wintry idyll was ended abruptly on the evening of the
third day by the barking of Emil's dogs. "It is the FBI. Three
of my customers are leaving the place and the FBI mows
them down, killing a CCC boy from a camp nearby. I go
into the cellar with the girls and listen to the shooting.
Fifteen, twenty minutes after it starts the fellows escape by
dropping fifteen feet from a window. I get out through a
basement window and drive my truck to Koerner's Resort
and there is Baby Face holding the place up. In my place there
is nobody left but those poor girls in the cellar and all them
G-men shooting up the place until six o'clock in the morning."

It was Dillinger's last skirmish before he was shot in
Chicago three months later. Emil has preserved the bullet
holes. On his walls he has hundreds of photos of Dillinger,
Nelson, Hitler, Milwaukee beer barons, U. S. Senators, a
governor of Wisconsin, James A. Farley, and several Eisen-
howers. In the forest Emil has built a Dillinger Museum.
With a flashlight he led us out to it, a rough clapboard shed
filled with macabre Dillinger memorabilia—shirts, suits, ties,
toothbrushes, playing cards, tear gas bombs, all perpetuated
as lovingly as saints' relics in an Italian church.

"No one claimed the baggage," Emil said. "Nelson was a
small man, his suits fit me tailor made. But Dillinger was an
inch taller. I drove to Indiana to visit Dillinger's father. He
had the bloody shirt that John was killed in and I had the
suitcases, so he came up and we made this museum. He was
very polite, a church member, never drank. Fifteen, twenty
times a day he would make a speech on crime doesn't pay,
look what happened to my boy and he would cry and John's

sister would sing. Everyone did a lot of crying and each
ticket was twenty-five cents and when they took a picture
they gave us a dollar and I made quite a bit until the old
man died."

Outside, Emil flashed his light on a sign: "Receipts go to
Father Flanagan's Boy's Town. Thank you."

"Why not?" said Emil. "I made mine. I got all the goldfish
milk I can drink. You only can do this in America. God
bless America."

Wisconsin was playing Purdue that weekend and we flew
back to Madison on Friday for the game. Saturday began at
the hour of six in a duck blind one hundred feet out on
Lake Mendota. Decoys bobbed on chilling Prussian-blue
waters. Our prefabricated hideout, furnished with electricity,
telephone, radio, and television, was as warm as home. While
we passed time with TV news broadcasts, John, an insurance
executive who was our host, cooked bacon and eggs. I expressed amazement at such Texas ostentation in Madison and
John said, "When the ducks aren't flying I take care of my
office calls. No time lost, you see."

Beyond, the city, a dumbbell-shaped isthmus deposited by
a glacier between Mendota (Indian for "evening gathering
of the waters") and Monona ("morning spirit"), was a gray
silhouette in the red dawn. At opposite ends of the two-mile
wedge the sun's first rays glittered on domes, the capitol
dome of government on the left and the dome of academia,
the university observatory, on the right. I thought of my
first views of the capitol years ago, usually on a summer
Sunday morning. We would leave our New Glarus farm
after morning chores, my father driving the open Buick
northeastward through towns with Italian names: Basco,
Paoli, Verona. Some time after Verona we reached the crest
of a hill (countryside then, but crowded suburbia now) and
all of us, Father, Mother, Sister, and I, cried out together,
"Lug, dat ists!" Father stopped the car and like a family of

Boetian peasants approaching Athens, we gazed on the white dome rising over the forested hills.

The distance by road between New Glarus and Madison was short, only thirty dusty miles, but the distance in spirit might have been measured in light-years, as I found out later when I came to Madison to stay. I was the only one from my class in our provincial high school to enroll at the university; for permitting this my father was laughed at for a fool. A relative asked my mother how old I was and when my mother replied, eighteen, the cousin said, "*Herr Jesus Gott!* And still going to school. He must be a dumb one.*"

We passed the morning with coffee and bourbon, respinning with middle-aged bravado, our Rabelaisian myths of Hazel Hopkins. Symbol of our lost youth, at that moment I felt her there in the duck blind with us, palpable and real. She was pale and delicately cast with beautiful gray eyes (she was the first person I'd ever seen wearing harlequin glasses) and billowing copper-colored hair, the soft texture of which I could still remember. I could even hear her voice, softly rapturous, her warm heart throbbing through it, and I remembered her smile, winsome and a little sad, as if she were pitying us, or perhaps herself. The word "no" was not on her tongue—as we found out when, unable to turn down a friend, she made separate prom dates with three of us, Joe, Dick and me, all good friends.

We were, I think, the last carefree generation, late perpetuators of the collegiate myth born in the Prohibition twenties, documented by Scott Fitzgerald and all his imitators, and believed in until World War II, our war. We were dancers, devoting at least two nights a week to orchestra parties, or driving to Club Hollywood, Cuba Club, or the Chanticleer, which our elders referred to as "roadhouses." We drank spiked beer (three were quite a load) at "Pop" Lohmaier's on campus, or in an abandoned brewery known as The Malt House, and afterward danced *La Cucaracha* all the way down Langdon Street with sorority girls. We went to shipwreck parties dripping from a shower, wrapped only in towels. We made our own "gin" from blackberry syrup and medical alcohol, and when the ice melted in the prom punch we went, in white gloves and tails, to harvest more on the frozen lake.

There was a high excitement in our studying too, for we were taught by great and sometimes eccentric individualists like William Ellery Leonard, a poet whose agoraphobia imprisoned him within a two-block radius of his apartment; anthropologist Ralph Linton who guided us through Fiji burial ceremonies and Madagascar fertility rites; philosophers Alexander Meiklejohn who taught us to love Plato and Max Otto who taught us to scorn Plato; and economist William Kiekhofer who each October during Homecoming telephoned the police when we smeared the stone fence around his house with paint and the next morning was greeted at his lecture with a hero's "Sssss . . . booommmm . . . ahhhhh!" skyrocket.

Today Wisconsin's faculty complains of "intellectual quiescence." A literature professor said, "Students are accustomed to the passive role. They hesitate to use their intelligence. It's almost as if they were painted on the wall." It couldn't have been said of us. We were activists who joined the Young Progressives, the Hoofers (a hiking and sailing club), the Players, and a variety of other earnest and foolish societies. We debated idealism and pragmatism as if they were political confessions. In Helen White's creative writing class I wrote endless short stories, and outside class Hazel Hopkins and I wrote lurid confessions of imagined adventures which we sold to Bernard MacFadden's magazines. One bitterly cold Armistice Eve I led a torchlight parade down State Street, carrying a placard which said—just why, I no longer remember—"Down with Hearst!" After graduation my first job, which I held for five years, was as a reporter on a Hearst newspaper.

With undergraduate gusto we were simply entering into the polemical climate of the town. Madisonians are tetchily opinionated and almost always in a turmoil of controversy. The tradition goes back to the great orator, Robert M. La Follette, Sr., who with fire in his eye and bells in his voice aroused friends and foes to strong opinions. In Madison, politics is the basic storm center as one would expect in a state which in three decades has swung from La Follette's Progressivism to the demagoguery of the late Senator McCarthy and back to both a liberal Democratic mayor and governor.

These days, the chief stirrer of troubled waters is La Follette's old friend, newspaper publisher William T. Evjue. A small man with a bombastic voice, eighty-year-old Mr. Evjue is a major stockholder in Madison Newspapers, Inc., which owns both of Madison's newspapers, the conservative morning *Wisconsin State Journal* and the liberal afternoon *Capital Times*, of which Evjue is editor. They are written in the same building—by different staffs—and printed on the same presses, and they maintain a snarling antagonism on every issue. On the subject of McCarthy, the *Journal* was pro, the *Times* con. Since those dark years, Madison's loudest and longest hassle has been over Wisconsin's most famous native, the late Frank Lloyd Wright. Anxious to build a public monument in his own state, Wright designed a civic auditorium to jut out over Monona's waters. After eight years the exhaustive political battle over Wright's "marriage of lake and city" still breaks friendships and splits families, and no one knows whether the auditorium will ever be built.

The journalistic Guelphs and Ghibillines who stoke the furnaces of public opinion maintain their hostilities even in their common hermitary, the nearby Congress Bar. Hard-talking, hard-drinking *Times* men, wearing baggy tweeds, huddle dourly at one end of the ninety-foot bar, and neat, pin-striped *Journal* men muster at the other, and no words pass between them. "You're damned right we're sincere in our feelings about each other," said an editor. "We may keep our hands in each other's pockets, but our fists are in each other's faces."

With all their love for contention, it is really as Brahmins of the Midwest that Madisonians fancy themselves. An elderly gentleman, greeting a visiting Boston dowager at a party, told her, "I think you'll feel at home in our city, since Boston is the Madison of the east." Madison's version of Boston's Athenaeum is Mad Lit (short for Madison Literary Society), a monthly levee at which sixty members averaging sixty years of age (neither number nor age has varied in eighty years) sip nonalcoholic spiced cider and listen to papers on *The Pursuit of Happiness in the Middle Ages* or *The Art of the Possible in Politics.* The literary Wednesdays —with tea and scones—in the shadowed lakeside salon of Gertrude Slaughter, ninety-plus-year-old novelist and biographer, are also Bostonian. Mrs. Slaughter is one of the indestructibles. When I was a student she jitneyed herself around campus in her Detroit Electric auto with the lofty regality of the White Queen.

There is a reason for such cultural earnestness, because Madison, an infant as cities go, is New England's child. The first families were patriotic New Englanders who named the settlement for James Madison who died in 1836, the year the city was born. They named streets for Signers of the Declaration. As the town grew, the gentry settled on Langdon Street, which follows the curve of Mendota. In the twenties, when the university began its move up Langdon, ruffled society made an exodus around Mendota to Maple Bluff, and fraternities and sororities moved into the mansions. But one of Langdon's grand dames, Mrs. Ada Sumner Moseley, lived out her life on the street. Once, before her death in 1959, I got her to reminisce of the days when Madison's population was hardly more than 10,000 and life was as gracious as an invitation to a ball.

"Our houses were wainscoted in walnut and in them we had lovely times," said Mrs. Moseley, a patrician blue-eyed beauty, at eighty-four. "Of course we knew everyone. Afternoons we sent for our carriages, took our white gloves and our card cases and went calling. We were very dressy at formal teas and dinners, and for student dances high necks were proper. The boys went down to Music Hall early in the day to walk the wax into the floor for the waltzes."

Across the street from the window at which Mrs. Moseley was sitting, some youths were rumbling metal beer barrels into the front door of a fraternity house for a pajama party that evening. They wolf-whistled at passing sorority girls wearing plaid Bermuda shorts.

"We had no liquid refreshments at our dances," Mrs. Moseley said. "I understand they don't dance any more, but *listen* to their music. I must say it seems quite lazy of them. A pajama party. Imagine!" Mrs. Moseley's voice turned sad. "We grow up and we change. Now when I go into town I meet hardly anyone I know."

It is, alas, the face of America that is changing. Wisconsin, clinging to her pastoral image of dairying, is actually an industrial state and has been since the war. A new parkway reaches out to New Glarus, leaving no more magic for country boys, and sociologists speak of a great urban expansion that will absorb the little Italian-named villages and eventually include even my home town. Twenty years have increased Madison's area from eight to thirty-seven square miles, doubled her population to 130,000, and added 6000 students and 110 buildings to the university.

"Remember the night Hazel left the Alpha Delt formal in a canoe with Tom Plout?" Joe, a lawyer, was saying. "The canoe drifted away . . ."

Our black-and-white retriever tensed and began to whine. We heard the vibrating hum for which our ears were cocked, and saw swift shadows pass over the water. Opening the sliding panels on the sectional front, we set ourselves, leaned forward and aimed our 12-gauges. In a half-hour each of us had his limit of two canvasbacks.

We packed, loaded our gear in a Chris-Craft, and headed into the swell toward the city, passing other duck blinds hidden behind cattail islands and rousing white-breasted gulls on an inland holiday from Lake Michigan. In my day the shores were a jungle of virgin forests which in earlier times had been especially loved by the Winnebagos who built villages of umbrella-shaped bark and skin houses, preserved the forms of their totems in gigantic burial plots and left a litany of Indian names for Madison's lakes and streets: Waubesa, Wingra, Kegonsa, Nakoma, Nagoosa, and so on. Now one sees roofs of houses everywhere, for Madison has grown around her five lakes and there is no wild land left. The sad fact is that people are contaminators; the waters in late summer are choked with algae, inseminated with bacteria and no longer pleasant for swimming.

We made for Mendota's glittering mile—the university and fraternity shore. The red turrets of the gym pointed out of the trees like Bavarian King Ludwig's Neuschwanstein Castle, and the steel-and-glass hulk of the university's Union theatre shone like a new ship. In the Union, art shows, symphony orchestras, opera companies, art movies, Broadway plays and restaurants, where students are served Milwaukee-brewed beer, are housed in labyrinthine disorder. In the summer the terrace is bright with students in bathing costumes sunning on the grass or lunching *al fresco* under candy-striped umbrellas. Madison has an aquatic culture, and town and gown share equally the joy of living with water. Like Zürich's bankers who swim in their lunch hours, Madison's businessmen and professors can step from office into lake. The magnanimous waters provide not only recreation but food. Madison fishing is a never-ending Biblical draught that is measured in tons instead of pounds, and Friday night's perch fry is as much an institution as Saturday's beans are in Boston.

In our boat we passed rows of fraternity piers, and the mansions of the Sig Chis, Delts, Phi Gams, and the Chi Psi's gray bastion housing the heirs of Milwaukee's brewing aristocracy. Except for a canoe or two it was desolate now, with discarded beer cans shining like zircons beneath the waters. But I felt Madison's great quality, her harmony with the earth's turning, her delight in the pleasures of strong northern seasons. Scenes passed through my mind's eye like calendar lithographs—biting cold winters freezing the breaths of skaters, thousands of fishermen squatting on ice like Eskimos. In February, Mendota, a natural propagation lake in which fish overpopulation is a nuisance, is the setting for The Percharee, a fishing contest in which 4000 fishermen, from ages two (pulled on sleds by zealous mothers) to eighty, chop holes through which they fish for perch and bass to compete for three hundred prizes. Bands play, lady skin divers submerge in rubber suits, and a queen is crowned. The two-day take is about 25,000 fish, which flop once on the ice and freeze instantly. Later, tossed into a tub at home, the fish thaw in two minutes and swim about fully restored.

Spring in Madison, usually late, literally explodes. The lakes rumble like thunder as the ice-covers break and floes piled on shore sizzle like seltzer as they melt. Trees bud, forsythia blooms and a chartreuse haze of pollen hangs over the town like a cloud. Finally, when the first co-eds sun their white bodies on the piers and the two hundred varieties of arboretum lilacs drug the atmosphere with fragrance, the summer season of water and boats, and love and games is on. Then the piers creak with their burdens of flowing-haired sirens and golden-skinned tritons languidly drinking beer. Coveys of sailboats circle, and canoes slide past to their own radio music. Riviera cruisers—gaudy rafts with striped awnings and bars—carry gay cargoes to picnics and beer busts. Occasionally one may even see a dark-spectacled Lorelei reading a book.

It was nearly noon now and behind us the silver dome of

the university's most romantic spot, Observatory Hill, was flashing like a beacon. Johnny Burke, an alumnus from the twenties, immortalized it in a collegiate moonbeam song. I hummed the tune, trying to bring back the lyrics.

> *We'll learn what astronomy is for,*
> *We'll learn what the stars can have in store,*
> *I know in advance, the moon may mean romance,*
> *When it's dark on Observatory Hill. . . .*

We docked and drove to an old haunt, Jennie Justo's on University Avenue, on the edge of town. Petite, youthful-appearing Jennie is Madison's reassuring landmark, not only for my generation but for the nostalgic old-timers from a decade before who drank beer, wine, and gin in the Justo cellar on Spring Street when Jennie was the famous "queen" of Madison's Prohibition. In the club she opened after repeal Jennie greets alumni by their first names and joins grayhairs and baldies in tearful laments, often in song, for the dear dead days. After we had eaten steaks, she sat down with us for a sentimental brandy and told how Fredric March, in town for his thirtieth class reunion, burst into her kitchen, greeted her old Sicilian mother and wiped a few dishes. "He was just like you fellows," she said, starry-eyed. "As plain as anyone."

In the game that afternoon Wisconsin won the fast vigorous battle and Purdue's "golden girl" majorettes won the intermission band contest legs up. When our own band played *Varsity*—schmaltzed up with celeste and cymbals—and I sang with 50,000 others, my eyes clouded as they never had a quarter of a century ago.

That evening, long after midnight, leaning on a bar, one of us asked, for the dozenth time that day, "What ever's become of Hazel Hopkins?"

My classmates and their wives, who were classmates, too, laughed, and I realized that, though we would continue to ask the question whenever any of us were together, no one except perhaps myself really wanted to know the answer. A moment later one of the wives, with chilling intimations of mortality, chose to remember that the Club Hollywood, where all of us had danced with Hazel Hopkins, was now a rest home for old people, called Agehaven. Because I, the restless one who came and went, was leaving in the morning, I offered a toast. "To Wisconsin!"

"Wisconsin, Wisconsin," sing-sang one of the girls. "What is Wisconsin?"

"An idea in the mind of God," I said. "One of his best."

four

RENAISSANCE IN A COMPANY TOWN

The plane flying west followed the glistening silver ribbon of the Monongahela below. The air was pure and bright. We descended gently, toward forested hills so green it was like coming down on County Limerick. We glided over the runway toward a new five-decker terminal, modern and hygienic as a biscuit factory. Waving from the observation platform was my long-time friend, Mary Shaw Marohnic.

My visit to America's traditionally most ill-favored city was a kind of homecoming, like a man returning to make peace with his people. Though a Wisconsin native, I am often tempted, when asked where I was born, to reply, "Pittsburgh." It would be an untruth truer than true, for spiritually I *was* born here. I was an unfledged college graduate when I came to Pittsburgh for my first job, as a newspaper reporter. I stayed five years, and though since then I have lived in many other cities I have never learned to know one so well, nor to love and hate one so much. Now I was returning for a birthday—Pittsburgh's two hundredth—and to see for myself the renaissance that was turning the old "Mellon Patch" into "Mellon's Miracle."

For me, Mary Shaw symbolizes Pittsburgh. She is a large, hearty woman descended from pioneer families, the English

Irwins and the Irish Shaws, both of which have streets named after them. She married a first-generation Croatian whose family came with the great tide of Eastern European laborers to the mills and mines. "The blood was running thin in my group," she says, "and those Slavs had such straight backs." She is an artist who paints the hills and mills, the rivers and buildings of her city with relentless affection. One summer vacation she sent her son to work in a mill. "No young man has a right to live in Pittsburgh without at least once making steel," she told him. "I want you to understand your roots."

As she drove me over a new parkway toward the city, I remembered, too vividly for pleasure, my first arrival from a Wisconsin farm. Awe and panic were my emotions then, as the train clicked up the black, malodorous canyon of the Ohio River toward the old brown station. A doctor had warned me of evils that stalk youths in cities, so I went straight from the train to a room at the YMCA—around the corner from roaring Diamond Street (now Forbes Avenue), a casbah of low bars, burlesque, and girls. In the morning I reported for work on the police beat of the *Sun-Telegraph*, and met assistant city editor William "Fuzzy" Pfarr, a mercurial old-timer with a robust allergy to college men.

One evening that first week I saw an explosion of flames in the night sky and ran to a phone to report a very big fire. "Gee whiz, thanks," said Pfarr, after I'd explained where the blaze seemed to be. "Hop a cab and get right over there." I raced to my first big story—and found that the volcano in the sky was a Jones and Laughlin blast furnace. Pittsburgh in those days was a sooty Klondike of blackened buildings over which a pillar of smoke hung by day and a pillar of fire by night. The "Golden Triangle," named for its concentration of banks, was golden only to those few who amassed their gold under its clouds. To the rest it was, in words attributed to Charles Dickens, "Hell with the lid lifted."

Like many of my other *Sun-Tele* colleagues, Fuzzy Pfarr
was dead now. The road rolled down green hills into a dark
valley of cinders and piled-up railroad cars. We wove our
way through a tangle of bridges under which lean, unpainted
houses reached into air and light like thin yellow plants
growing in a cellar. Their top-story windows followed us
like eyes of misery. "No place to hang out a wash," said
Mary Shaw, and I remembered what Herbert Spencer said:
"A month in Pittsburgh would justify anyone in committing
suicide."

We were approaching a new tunnel built under Mount
Washington—the former Coal Hill in west Pittsburgh—but
Mary Shaw with happy abandon took the road over the
mountain instead, through the German colony with its
square, painted houses and geranium boxes.

"Prepare thyself," she said, as if reading from a roadside
religious poster. "The sound of the riveter is heard in the
land and the old ball swings." On the summit she turned into
Grandview Avenue and stopped.

I blinked, and blinked again. Nothing I had heard or read
had prepared me. Four hundred feet down was the Point,
that sharp confluence of the Allegheny and Monongahela
rivers that is the birthplace of the Ohio. But where I remembered an abysmal jungle of crumbling railroad sheds and
blighted buildings, I was looking on a broad green park of
hawthorns and maples and polished lawns. From gardens beyond, a new white city of steel and aluminum rose up. Mary
Shaw identified the unfamiliar buildings: three Equitable Life
"Gateway" buildings, dazzling green from their thousands
of Venetian blinds at half mast, the aluminum Bell Telephone
Building and a blue laminated State Office Building. The
most spectacular was a forty-one-story stainless-steel monolith, the Mellon-U. S. Steel Building, and rising in front of
them all was a new Golden Triangle Hotel for which Conrad
Hilton had promised golden aluminum walls. The commuter
traffic of late afternoon moved swiftly over an intricate lace-

work of bridges, parkways, and interchanges. Pleasure launches glided on rivers which in the old days floated only smoke-belching towboats. On riverbanks remembered for their pollution, children played on sidewalk esplanades.

"You need a drink," said Mary Shaw, speaking gospel truth. She took me one block to the Tin Angel, a glass-walled eyrie with an urban view that only San Francisco's Top of the Mark can match.

Gazing over the ocean of mountaintops humped like waves, I couldn't help wondering how a city was ever built on such untractable terrain. Yet the one who chose the site knew what he was about. He was a twenty-one-year-old Virginia scout, Major George Washington, who on November 23, 1753, wrote in his journal: "The land in the fork I think extremely well suited for a Fort, as it has the absolute command of the rivers." Warring Iroquois controlled the area and the meeting point of the three rivers was ruled by a formidable queen named Alaquippa. Young Washington wooed the vigorous ruler with a fur coat and a bottle of rum and the next year the British built a fort which was destroyed by the French who built their own Fort Duquesne. This skirmish began the French and Indian War. In 1755, a British Army under General Edward Braddock attacked the French, but Braddock was killed and his subordinate, Colonel Washington, led the retreat back to Virginia. Three years later, in 1758, Brigadier General John Forbes, assisted by Washington, led the winter march on Fort Duquesne and routed the French. General Forbes gave the newly captured point the name of England's Prime Minister, William Pitt. When the British captured the river gateway, the civilization of the New World was changed from Latin to Anglo-Saxon. Pittsburgh's backbone has been cast-iron Calvinist ever since.

The first product was whisky which the Scotch-Irish settlers swapped for furs with the Indians, or sold for thirty-five cents a gallon. Iron ore was discovered in 1780, and four years later coal was found on Mount Washington, on the site where the Tin Angel now stands. By the time Washington was President, western Pennsylvania had fourteen furnaces and thirty-four forges and was the iron center of America.

Behind the Golden Triangle, on the highest crest of the city, a three-mile ledge of 7000 public-housing units extended from river to river, a red-brick band veiled by green trees. Through the filigree of the "three sister," identical bridges crossing the Allegheny at Sixth, Seventh, and Ninth Streets, I could see upriver to the steel- and glass-manufacturing towns of Millvale, Etna, and Sharpsburg. Up the Monongahela lay the Polish and Slav south side and the dark, convoluted profile of Jones and Laughlin, the only big steel mill left inside the city of Pittsburgh; in the distance were the industrial boroughs of Homestead, Hazelwood, Braddock, and Rankin.

Rising from the Jones and Laughlin stacks were wispy clouds, pale coral in the evening light. "Smoke," I said triumphantly, for it was the first I had seen.

"Hush," said Mary Shaw. "You just said a bad word. What you're looking at we call *ore dust*, and someone is spending a million dollars for precipitators to eliminate it. I wish they wouldn't. Can you imagine Pittsburgh without *any*, er—ore dust?"

Behind us the brown waters of the Monongahela and the green waters of the Allegheny flowed side by side, unblended bands, down the Ohio, past the steel and chemical towns of McKees Rocks, Coraopolis, Ambridge (named for the American Bridge Company) and boatbuilding Neville Island. As far as the eye could reach, it was Allegheny County, the "greater Pittsburgh" of 129 municipalities, 730 sloping square miles from which more wealth has been beaten and more millionaires sprung than from any other tract its size on earth.

Pittsburgh is a company town, the largest in the world. Her unceasing wellsprings of coal and iron begged for stewards and the nineteenth century produced three: Andrew

Carnegie, son of a poor Scottish weaver whose American address was Barefoot Square, Slabtown, Pennsylvania; Henry Clay Frick whose father was a Swiss immigrant in the coal fields south of Pittsburgh; and Thomas Mellon, a Scotch-Irish immigrant whose first American home was in Poverty Point, Pennsylvania.

Impelled by the stern Calvinist ethic that it is a sin to be poor and a virtue to be rich, this astonishing trio of Horatio Algers set out to harvest gold in Pittsburgh. The stealthiest was Mellon. A farmer's son who did not want to farm, Tom Mellon apprenticed himself to a judge and when he had saved $1500 he became a moneylender, obtaining on each note a mortgage and judgment bond. For his wife he chose the daughter of a land-wealthy family, Sarah Jane Negley. He wasted no time on courtship. "If I had been rejected," he wrote, "I would have been annoyed at the loss of time." The "transaction" of marriage was closed on August 22, 1843. When two girls died in childhood, he wrote, "Girls who die young need not be greatly lamented." He built a special school for his five sons because, "for businessmen it is unnecessary to waste much time on classics and special sciences." When one of the sons wanted to enlist in the Union Army, Judge Mellon wrote, "I had hoped my boy was going to make a smart, intelligent businessman and was not such a goose as to be seduced from his duty . . . it is only green-horns who enlist." Pittsburgh's furnaces, glowing day and night, furnished the munitions, and after the war turned out rails for trains on the Western plains. In the panic of 1873, Moneylender Mellon attributed the hunger riots to "vicious classes," and so vigorously did he sweep the broom of fore-closure that he was able to found the largest family fortune in America. Inevitably, "Caeser of Steel" Carnegie and "King of Coal" Frick had become partners, and when Mellon took a first mortgage on Frick's coke company, Pittsburgh's trinity of entrepreneurs were at last united.

In 1892, when union-hating Frick ordered a hired army of

guards and Pinkertons to fire on orderly strikers, he set off the most famous labor battle of all time, the bloody Homestead steel strike. At the time Carnegie, then the laird of Skibo Castle, was wandering through Scotland founding public libraries. Frick stabbed by a strike sympathizer, dictated in an ambulance: "I do not think I shall die, but whether I do or not, the company will pursue the same policy and it will win." He lived, and ultimately he cabled his absent partner: OUR VICTORY IS NOW COMPLETE AND MOST GRATIFYING.

Unions destroyed, Frick sent agents into southwestern Europe to recruit cheap labor. They lured impoverished Poles, Slovaks, Yugoslavs, Ukrainians, and Hungarians to a Promised Land of peonage in smoke-smudged company towns with clapboard shacks and muddy lanes. Presbyterian Pittsburghers believed Catholic "Huns" and "Hunkies" were inferior clay deserving no better.

The joyfully welcomed Spanish-American War brought a boom in armor plate, shells, and rifles. In the crash of 1903 and in each succeeding depression the Mellons collected bankrupt steel mills, coal companies, banks, railroads, and hotels. When aluminum was invented the Mellons assumed financial control of its production and when Texas turned into a Klondike of oil, the Mellon-owned Gulf Oil Company bought up the biggest geysers and became a leading oil producer of World War I.

After Frick and Carnegie died, both in 1919, Pittsburgh became increasingly a one-family town. Its boss was the favorite and frailest of Thomas Mellon's five sons, Andrew W. Mellon, a Croesus to whom three Presidents entrusted, as Secretary of the Treasury, the finances of the nation, and whom one of the Presidents, Harding, called "the ubiquitous financier of the universe." It was an opinion Mellon must have concurred with himself, for he ran his empire like an Olympian god. As Secretary of the Treasury his legislation abolishing excess profits taxes and reducing income assessments saved the Mellons' millions. When his wife sued for divorce he had the Pennsylvania Legislature change the state's divorce code. In 1931, Mellon-owned companies evicted Pittsburgh's unemployed from their homes and when Governor Pinchot went to Washington to borrow relief funds to take care of 1200 destitute families, Mellon declined. Charity, he believed, weakened the moral fiber of its recipients. He died in 1937, after which his nephew, Richard King Mellon, became head of the clan and guardian of its $8,500,-000,000 holdings.

It was twilight now and the city's cleaning women, turning lights on and off as they moved through the buildings, made the skyscrapers flicker like the Milky Way. A small white tender churned up the Ohio, pushing sixteen barges of black coal. "Did you know that Pittsburgh is America's largest inland port?" Mary Shaw asked. I was vaguely aware of river traffic, but it was always so unobtrusive. "Suez and Panama are millstreams compared to muddy old Monongahela," she said.

Driving east over Bigelow Boulevard, I was grateful for such familiar landmarks as the Heinz "57" in green lights across the Allegheny and—a touch of Venice—the three green domes of the Church of the Immaculate Heart of Mary. During my Pittsburgh years I had lived in the Oakland area "civic center," and there I settled now, in an apartment in a garden on little Mawhinney Street, one block long and pretty as an English mews. I arrived right in its "pink" season—Pittsburgh claims more Japanese flowering cherries than Washington, and all were in bloom.

To the left was forested Schenley Park, green and lush as Constable's paintings of Hampstead Heath, and the campus of the Carnegie Institute of Technology; on the right was Mellon Institute, a columned approximation of the Parthenon, and rising above it all, the forty-two-story University of Pittsburgh skyscraper known as the Cathedral of Learning.

This controversial monolith has been called a masterpiece of modern Gothic, a phallic monstrosity, and a frozen confection melting like treacle in the sun. Entering it next day, I felt the old claustrophobic panic, for the vertical piling of classrooms has inadequate elevators and echoes like a river canyon. But my spirit soared in the lofty, Gothic common room on the ground floor, and in the quadrangle surrounding it I made my reconnaissance of the nineteen rooms presented by Pittsburgh's nationality groups. The gold-leafed Syria-Lebanon room is shadowed and cushioned like a seraglio, the Norwegian room is a peasant cottage, the Greek room a miniature temple. The English room is modeled from the House of Commons, the German after the great hall of Heidelberg, and the Italian room after a Tuscan convent.

The price of progress, I learned, can be high. The university's sky-aspiring young chancellor, Edward H. Litchfield, talked of plans to reclaim commercial and residential property for a 1600-acre common campus for Pitt, Tech, Mellon Institute, and Carnegie Museum. Little Mawhinney is probably a doomed street.

Lying in the morning shadow of the Cathedral is the Schenley Hotel, a damask and crystal landmark that was a glory of the old Pittsburgh. Six years ago the hostelry and its adjoining apartments were purchased by the university for student housing. The elegant suites in which Lillian Russell was married, and a goddess died, are now towel-and-sock strewn dormitory rooms. I found a revered lost plaque, wiped away the dust with my handkerchief and read:

> Eleonora Duse, world tragedian of the Italian Theatre, in the glory of her immortal art, answered the last curtain in Pittsburgh, April 21, 1924.

The landmark with the heaviest nostalgia for me was also the closest to my door. Looming across narrow Mawhin-

ney was Carnegie Museum, a black-walled fortress that has
been since the 1890s the setting for the famous Carnegie
International art exhibitions. These have made Pittsburghers
extremely knowledgeable about painting, and in my time
the first-prize winners always whipped up a tempest of controversy. The year Georges Braque's semi-cubistic *The Yellow Cloth* was chosen, Fuzzy Pfarr assigned another reporter
and me, with photographs of the painting, to harvest a series
of man-in-the-street opinions—derisive, of course. The day
was so smoggy the street lights flickered at midday, and our
task was so depressing that we spent the afternoon in a bar
composing jewel after jewel of journalism, like:

> Plumber, Lower Smithfield Street: "Nothing but a dirty
> rag to me."
> Hairdresser, William Penn Hotel: "Some table. I guess you
> glue the cloth on to keep it from sliding off."

To a callow Wisconsin farm boy twenty years ago, the
halls containing copies of Greek sculpture, and the perma-
nent collection of predominantly nineteenth-century paintings upstairs, seemed full of marvels. Now I found the collection pitifully slight. Pittsburgh's only great painting seems
to be Georges Rouault's masterpiece, *The Old King,* but it
is so much on loan that Pittsburghers seldom see it.

The art tragedy of Pittsburgh is that her collectors be-
queath their paintings elsewhere—Henry Clay Frick to New
York, Andrew Mellon to Washington, where he built the
National Gallery, the Arensbergs to Philadelphia. At present Pittsburgh's curators are sweating out the eventual disposition of two important collections, one owned by H. J.
Heinz II and the other by G. David Thompson, a steelman-
stockbroker. Thompson's hoard of twentieth-century art,
seen by only a few, is said to include the largest group of
Paul Klees anywhere.

To reacquaint myself with Pittsburgh's most unusual art
treasure, I crossed the Allegheny to the steelworkers' com-

munity of Millvale and climbed a knoll to St. Nicholas Croatian Church. It is a drab, yellow-brick structure on the outside, but inside it is frescoed as splendidly as a Balkan cathedral. Filling the apse is a monumental Madonna with Child in Croatian dress. On the right, miners and workers with their priest offer her the Church of St. Nicholas, which they hold in their hands; on the left a Croatian family bows in prayer near some cows in a field. The arched ceiling is crowded with saints and apostles, done in the romantic-mystic style of Blake, and the walls are painted with contemporary social themes. The artist, Makso Vanka, was born in Croatia and lived in Bucks County, Pennsylvania.[1] The frescoes were an ex-voto gift to the land of his adoption and he painted them in Millvale because the good friend of his youth, Father Albert Zagar, was priest there.

Father Zagar, my own friend for twenty years, is a gentle little Franciscan with flashing dark eyes and a bald head, with impish tufts of hair growing up from his ears to make him look like a benevolent satyr. "Tourists come from all over the United States to see our church," he said to me, "but Pittsburghers do not even cross the river. They don't know that in a hundred years St. Nicholas' will be the most famous church in America." We were drinking altar wine by a great picture window in the new parish house, which the Father was blessing that afternoon. Across the river we could see the span of Pittsburgh, all the way from the Golden Triangle to Etna and Aspinwall. "Is it not wonderful, my view of a new city rising?" said Father Zagar.

Pittsburgh is a nationality center, thanks to great waves of immigrant labor that flowed to the mills and mines from 1880 to 1914. One evening I went to Syria Mosque, where twenty nationality groups were united in a jubilant folk festival sponsored by Duquesne University. On the stage upstairs there were music and drama from the Old World; on the

[1] He drowned in Mexico in 1963.

half-acre basement dance floor people whirled in ancestral
rhythms. Chinese girls floated through butterfly dances to
plaintively wailing reeds. Green-bodiced Irish girls jigged to
an accordion. Mexicans in gaudy serapes leaped over hats,
and Swiss youths in black velvets, their girls wearing hats
like lacy white wings, rocked through schottisches. Greek
men in ruffled white fustanellas and tasseled red caps coiled
and uncoiled harems of girls with eyes like purple pansies.
Carpatho-Russian millworkers, wearing coq hats, embroidered blouses and flowing sashes, danced squatting on their
haunches, possessed devils barking like dogs. Slovak men,
with flower gardens on their heads and sweat-shining faces,
polkaed with women beribboned as Maypoles. Croatian men,
virile Pierrots in lacy white pantaloons, and girls like quilted
dolls snaked through a kolo to *tamburitza* music.

The dance floor was surrounded with food booths, and
here visitors ate themselves around the world. Polish *borscht*,
Swiss *fondue*, Greek *dolma* (stuffed grape leaves), Indian
thandai (almond milk), Italian lasagne, Ukrainian *mediwnik*
(wedding cake), Serbian *strudla*, and Lebanese rose water
and so on. As the evening progressed things grew confused
on the dance floor. Sombreroed Mexicans were jigging with
Irish girls, the preening Carpathians were swaying in a languid Lebanese courtship dance, some Chinese were caught
up in a schottische. Suddenly the festival turned into an intoxicating and delirious Babel with twenty nations scrambled
in rough-and-tumble rock-n-roll. A gray-haired woman in
black watched with tear-glistened eyes. She was from Croatia,
visiting her American daughter, and she said, "I haven't seen
such happiness since I was a girl."

Not surprisingly, the greatest sight in Pittsburgh is her
steel mills. Wearing a steel helmet, I entered a gallery of the
open hearths with which Jones and Laughlin has replaced
its old Bessemers. Rows of furnaces gave off blinding white

light and roared like a hurricane. Screaming sirens cleared the way for overhead cranes, their loading hooks and magnets swaying like trunks and moving with elephantine deliberation. To protect my eyes I was given purple cobalt spectacles which turned everything to violet. Through these glasses my guide, a company press officer, determined by its color the temperature of the metal inside—3300 degrees Fahrenheit. The climax of a visit is the tapping, a spectacle familiar to television viewers of the U. S. Steel Hour; a steady-nerved visitor is occasionally invited to throw the firing key. Workmen in aluminumized suits, silhouetted in the brightness like outer spacemen, took a sample of the incandescent liquid, like a housewife testing a cake in the oven. Then they put the *bazooka*, or jet-tapper, into place, a signal whistle blew and I pressed the key.

Whoosh! I was surrounded by a great explosion, as if I'd been caught inside a volcano. Fiery liquid spurted into a giant ladle, accompanied by the most marvelous fireworks I'd ever seen. Luminous metal cascaded like a fountain and spattered around us in a waterfall of stars colored rose, orchid, purple. The molten metal swirled and churned in the 280-ton ladle like hot pink milk and the overflow gathered in glowing magenta lakes around its smoking base.

From the black ladle the metal was "teemed"—poured—into ingot molds by a muscular Negro named Jimmy Whyle, who, my guide said, "is a legend like John Henry—the best steel pourer in the business and the best bartender at steelmen's parties." We followed the ingots to the yards outside, where they would remain red for three or four hours, and then went on to the "blooming mill" where other ingots were reheated to a uniform temperature and, with great thunder and clatter, rolled and manipulated into shining ribbons of steel flying through space like silver demons. In two hours I had seen metal changed from ore to finished sheets and rolls. I emerged like a salamander from a shattering inferno.

Among the joys of Pittsburgh are easy excursions into the beautiful western Pennyslvania countryside. Drive on almost any road out of town and you will come to rhododendron forests, tumbling mountain cascades and the man-made lakes that hold back the waters of the Allegheny and Monongahela, which used to flood Pittsburgh so disastrously.

With Mary Shaw, I made a sentimental reconnaissance to one of these reservoirs. Young Lake lies over the sites of three villages, one of which, Somerfield, used to be my favorite mountain retreat. We drove south, past rows of old coke ovens overgrown by forest, then followed the old National Pike—U.S. 40—until we came upon a great lake spanned by a concrete bridge. There was no familiar landmarks to guide me out of my confusion, but across the bridge I found a familiar face, that of Carl Cornish, of the old Cornish Arms Hotel.

In his cabin cruiser, Cornish took us over waters surrounded by forests. Newly leaved trees and blossoming dogwood cast chartreuse and white-lace shadows by shores where deer came to drink. But as we skittered over the water my mind was 160 feet below, in a lovely eighteenth-century summer village, with wisteria-covered farmhouses, steamy meadows bright with sweet william and tiger lilies, and blacksnakes twisting around limbs of trees to rob the nests. It had seemed like a painting of Eden by Rousseau.

We were passing over the site of his old hotel, said Cornish. Soon we were over the old red Endsley house, in which Mrs. Endsley had died—from will power, they said—just before she had to move away. A moment later we floated across the old Great Crossing Bridge, built when Monroe was President, and under which I remembered summer's-night bathing in the moonlight. The stone bridge had not been removed, and during autumnal low tides, said Cornish, often around Halloween, its Roman-style arches appear, undulating like ghosts in the depleted waters. A chill shot through me. I was passing over the grave of my youth, and I thought again how terrible can be the price of progress.

For three weeks I wandered like Rip Van Winkle through a Pittsburgh both familiar and strange. Demolition and construction side by side, the thunder of swinging headache balls and the rat-a-tat-tat of rivet guns made the hills ring like a battlefield. Demolition squads tore away blighted blocks while construction crews built bridges, parkways, and towers. The backyard slum known as Lower Hill had disappeared, but before its snarl of 1400-odd buildings could be removed, half a million rats were exterminated to keep them from migrating to the Golden Triangle. Now the ninety-five acres were being tilled for trees and parks, for apartment houses, and for an auditorium with room for 14,000 people and with a dome 415 feet in diameter—largest in the world—that can be opened to the stars on summer nights by the touch of an electric button. I began to collect columns of figures— $100,000,000 for the university, $150,000,000 for slum clearance—but it was obvious that no man could tell how much it was all going to cost.

As to how the bills will be paid, no one wonders. Pittsburgh's citizens share the faith of a certain little girl in Sunday school who, when asked by her teacher "Who led the children of Israel out of the house of bondage?" answered brightly, "The Mellons."

The people of Pittsburgh talk lyrically of their renaissance as a flowering of Jeffersonian democracy, and there is certainly an idealism about it. But as everyone, perhaps even the little girl, knows, the two great movers are a pair of kings: capital's Richard King Mellon and labor's David "The King" Lawrence, Pennsylvania's former governor and Pittsburgh's mayor during the first thirteen years of the renaissance.

Until Lawrence's first election as mayor, in 1945, he and Mellon were political enemies who had never met. Both men are of Scotch-Irish descent. But the Protestant Mellons have worked the Scottish side of the fence, and Lawrence, who still takes up Sunday collection in the Point's St. Mary of Mercy Church, is a professional Irishman. Lawrence was born on the Point and grew up in the Hill, two slums which he, as mayor, wiped away. Mellon, princeling of wealth, grew up in the family's town mansion and at Rolling Rock, its fox-hunting barony in the Westmoreland County Hills. In forty years of noncombative association with the United States Army he has risen to the rank of major general and is known around Pittsburgh as "The General."

Lawrence, a politican now for fifty years, came to the foreground in the Depression when the powerful CIO United Mine Workers moved into town, turning Pittsburgh into a capital of big labor as well as of big capital. Politically, Pittsburgh is a monument to Franklin Delano Roosevelt. In 1932 she had been solidly Republican for twenty-four years. Since then she has been uninterruptedly Democratic. Lawrence is a Democratic boss molded in F.D.R. clay. He shares the master's social philosophies, shrewd political know-how, indefatigability, steel-trap memory for names and faces and, when angry, a capacity for salty Democratic language. In his long life in politics he has known gall and wormwood. He was twice tried—and both times acquitted—on charges of conspiracy and violation of election laws. In 1942 his two sons, aged sixteen and thirteen, were killed in an auto accident. Pittsburghers believe that he plunged into power politics to quell his grief, that suffering turned him into a lonely uncommunicative autocrat who rules by harsh respect instead of human affection. Around Pennsylvania he is known by a variety of epithets: Mr. Dem, King David, Frosty, and Granite Face.

Whichever Lawrence may be, I discovered him a man hard to track down. I caught him in City Hall one noon, lunching alone on sandwiches and milk—a ruddy-faced, white-haired, sturdy man with icy blue eyes. A moment later he was in the washroom, in his undershirt, braces down, lathering up to shave for a ground-breaking ceremony. He told the story of his partnership with Mellon.

"The war had left Pittsburgh a dying city, the dirtiest slag pile in the United States, smothering under a blanket of smoke. Young men who had seen other cities during the war were not coming home, and industrialists were planning to move plants elsewhere. Something had to be done. One day General Mellon crossed Grant Street, walked into City Hall and offered me his family home and grounds on Fifth Avenue for a park. Mellon Park was the beginning of the renaissance."

At their historic meeting the two kings discovered two qualities they held in common—a strong identity with their city and a personal sense of destiny. Instead of heeding Frank Lloyd Wright's advice to abandon Pittsburgh, they plunged into a crash program to halt its decline.

A soft-coal prohibition and the dieselizing of railroads wiped the smoke from the skies. In the cleared horizon miracles appeared everywhere. Among their Golden Triangle skyscrapers the Mellons built a $4,500,000 park of fountains and gardens, modeled after San Francisco's Union Square, and under it a six-level subterranean garage for 1000 automobiles. Slums were hauled away and housing projects made to mushroom. On the eastern edge of the city, near old Poverty Point, there sprouted Monroeville, a new community of scientists, staffing fifty-eight research laboratories. A complexity of new hospitals and laboratories rose in Pittsburgh's Health Center, a Mellon pet which gave the world Dr. Jonas Salk's polio serum.

Authorities, councils, and commissions working on renaissance projects were co-ordinated by the Allegheny Conference on Community Development, a voluntary group of civic, industrial and political leaders who work with religious fervor. But nobody worked harder than the two kings, who operate on the premise that all Pittsburghers are, like themselves, energetic supermen. "We can't help being a teeming town," Lawrence said. "In the last century Pittsburgh drained off the strongest and best workmen of Europe. Vitality is in our blood."

Socially, Mellon and Lawrence are ill at ease with each

other, meeting largely at ground-breakings and on the banquet dais. Their conferring is by telephone. Formally, they remain political opponents; in each of Lawrence's successful campaigns, Mellon has made a token contribution to the Republican ticket. But hardly anyone ever wondered who he hoped would win. Pennsylvania's GOP bosses despair over the never-ending spectacle of Lawrence publicly applauded for improvements bought with Republican money, and they remember with horror the time just before an election when Mellon praised his partner at one of their cornerstones. Lawrence calls it "enlightened self-interest." "The Mellons are still good businessmen," he said. "Every dollar they've invested has increased the value of their holdings."

After a fortnight of negotiations, word came like a command from court: "The General will see you."

In a stainless steel elevator, swift and smooth as Elijah's fire chariot, I was floated to the top of the Mellon-U. S. Steel Building, and discharged into the walnut-paneled offices of "T. Mellon & Sons," corporate name of Grandfather's bank now used to front the vast network of Mellon philanthropies. It was a hushed place of softness: soft rugs, soft lights, soft-toned family portraits on the walls—even the telephones whispered. Titles on the bookshelves included *Public Finance*, *Corporate Finance*, *Money and Banking*, and Mortimer Adler's *Fifty Great Ideas*. I waited apprehensively, trying to piece together my hearsay impressions of the man inside. He was modest and self-effacing; he was an imperious Napoleon accustomed to commanding; he was—said one of his friends—a frugal man who commuted daily fifty-five miles to and from his farm in order to save the cost of an apartment in town; he never let his personal checking balance slip under seven million dollars—said a despairing bank clerk—and he paid his minutest obligations with checks; he was taciturn and hated interviews. . . .

A nervous attaché came to warn me that the General was somewhat tense, and then ushered me in.

Facing me across a desk was a ruddy, large-headed man, not tall but trim and vigorous in body. I thought at once of Ibsen's *Master Builder*. From his clear desk and sparsely furnished office it was obvious that he was a neat and methodical man. Together we looked down on the city spread out so far below it looked like a museum model. Uneven walls of rising buildings, cranes like insect mandibles swinging their demolition balls, half-finished bridges projecting over the rivers, the orifice of a new tunnel—all seemed like toys. The man who had watched and planned spoke slowly, but with young enthusiasm. "I can hardly keep up," he said. "Suddenly one day there's a new skyscraper. I have to think— it's the Porter Building. I wonder what will be next. The Hilton Hotel and then Gateway Center Number Four. We're building for the future, and we never build an airport large enough or a highway wide enough. We're not halfway through."

The General seemed a warm man, anxious to communicate. I asked him where in Pittsburgh's hills had been the place called Poverty Point. He replied curtly that he did not know, and I realized that the subject was of no interest to him. Then, as if to show me he was a man of humor, he spoke of the Negro families which had been displaced by the Lower Hill demolitions. "They disappeared," he said. "We lost them as citizens. No one knows where they went. They simply loaded their televisions in their pink Cadillacs and drove away." He seemed to want to minimize his own part in the renaissance. "We've got things organized so the work will continue as long as there's a need for it," he said. "It's all a joint project. Politics are a secondary consideration. By George, look! We get things done!"

Did the General think of the renaissance as a family philanthropy? "Let's say selfish interests are involved," he said. "We have a lot of property here. We can't very well move our banks." Were there, in his estimation, great men in Pittsburgh? "Great men? We've got one. Jonas Salk. He's so modest he won't even let us name a building for him."

The firm of T. Mellon & Sons has, at this writing, five vice-presidents and four assistant vice-presidents. These are the so-called Mellon Knights. Their Round Table is an upstairs penthouse decorated with a springtime burst of floral wallpaper and bouquets of fresh flowers. In this lofty eyrie the Knights lunch together on carefully counted 340-calorie lunches and theorize on the new world they are building.

The Knights do not disband. When they are not mapping the future in their club above the city, they live in the past at Rolling Rock, seventy-five minutes from Pittsburgh. Here, in houses leased or sold to them by the General, they rusticate in feudal fellowship. Wearing the costumes of English squires, they greet the dawn with drums and horns, riding to hounds which follow the scent of fox urine soaked in rag and dragged through the forest by a horseman. On special occasions, purchased foxes are chased over the rolling hills, and the General is master of the hounds. Every October sportsmen and horses arrive from England and many parts of America for the Rolling Rock Steeplechase, one of the most fashionable race meets in the nation.

Pittsburgh society is based on money and power, not pedigree, and it is constantly changing. In the beginning of the century, fashion was centered on Ridge Avenue in Allegheny City, now part of Pittsburgh's north-side slums. The summer colony was in the hills behind Sewickley, a borough twelve miles down the Ohio. Hostesses of the epoch were Mrs. William Thaw, Sr., and Mrs. William Thaw, Jr., mother and sister-in-law of Harry who shot architect Stanford White in Madison Square Garden over the model Evelyn Nesbit. In those days Pittsburgh's heiresses married foreign counts and earls who demanded cash settlements, occasionally in the church foyer, before the ceremony. In the last three decades —no doubt because of the lack of domestics—society has

settled in modest early-American-style brick houses in the
green hills of Fox Chapel beyond the Allegheny, or clustered
about the Mellon hermitage in Rolling Rock.

Pittsburgh is a club town. Because blue laws prohibit public
sales of liquor after 1 A.M. and on Sundays, every Pitts-
burgher who is not abstentious, bedridden, or under age
carries a wallet of membership cards for a variety of the
726 curious organizations registered in Allegheny County by
the Pennsylvania Liquor Control Board. These range from
the fashionable Pittsburgh Golf Club (which has no golf
course) and the Pittsburgh Athletic Association, to such
esoteric affiliations as the Sand Scratchers, the Swiss Singing
Society, House of Lords, Bamboola Club and the Sonny
Boys Athletic Association. The clubs give Pittsburgh some
of the rakish adventurousness of the Prohibition 1920s—one
is always ringing buzzers and being scrutinized through peep-
holes.

The most coveted club in town is the Duquesne, a sanctuary of the steel and finance aristocracy. The somber old
marble clubhouse, a museum for portraits of Carnegie, Frick
and deceased Mellons, is a must for executive luncheons.
Corporations maintain dining suites for V.I.P.'s, tables in
banquet halls for V.P.'s, and company cars for transporta-
tion. "I know exactly where everyone is, at what table,"
said my host. "I can get my business done like that"—snap
of the fingers—"and don't need to bother telephoning. Few
major decisions in this town are made outside this building."
Until recently members had to be of Republican persuasion
and preferably Protestant. Lately a few respectably affluent
Democrats and Catholics have been elected to uneasy membership, but David Lawrence is not one of them. "Of course,"
said my host, a young Gulf Oil Company executive, "if the
governor wished to lunch here there would always be *someone* who would be delighted to have him as a guest." The
problem is not likely to come up. When in Pittsburgh the
former governor lunches at the YMCA where he showers

and works out on the Exercycle. At seventy-seven his energies are considerably more and his waistline considerably less
than those of most members of the Duquesne Club.

Pittsburghers like to compare their renaissance with that
of Florence centuries ago, and the comparison is not inapt
since the great Medici builders were also bankers. But Pittsburgh is Florence without Lorenzo. Her Medicis are builders, not dreamers, with a Calvinist mistrust of the humanities
and arts. The tradition goes back to Grandfather Thomas
Mellon, who in his autobiography wrote on education:
"Young people are led to believe that its end is to enable
them to live without work." Carnegie (who later was to
endow 1400 libraries and fifty-one colleges) said, "A man
with a university education is lost to commerce."

In the mid-nineteenth century a Pittsburgh editor noting
that his city had no theatres, wrote, "We think that this
speaks well for the good taste and morality of our inhabit-
ants." Even now drama fares little better in Pittsburgh. The
beautiful old Nixon Theatre in which I saw my first professional plays, was closed in 1950 with a curtain speech by
Mae West after a final performance of *Diamond Lil*, and
torn down to make way for the Alcoa Building. There is
the local amateur Pittsburgh Playhouse, and road companies
appear occasionally at a former movie house now named
the Nixon, but the best theatre is at the Carnegie Tech drama
school, where I saw superb productions of *Measure for
Measure* and *Under Milk Wood*.

Orpheus is more nobly served. The celebrated Pittsburgh
Symphony Orchestra plays forty home concerts a season.
Conductor William Steinberg's progressive programing of
contemporary music occasionally irritates the more conservative of the orchestra's 3000 contributors, but I heard a performance of Mahler's Second Symphony, *Resurrection*, in
which the orchestra and a chorus of 350 brightly robed youths
seemed, aurally and visually, like a celestial choir.

Pittsburgh's best-known dreamer was America's greatest
song writer, Stephen Collins Foster. The composer was no

child of poverty—his father was mayor of Allegheny City
and his brother a builder of the Pennsylvania Railroad. But
he was a non-materialist who had no contribution to make
to industry, and both his family and city rejected him. He
was only thirty-eight when he was found on the Bowery
one January night, naked, cut, bruised, and penniless, and
was taken to Bellevue Hospital to die.

Today the city is more hospitable to its troubadours. As
evidence there are my friends, composer Nikolai Lopatnikoff
and poet Sara Henderson Hay, Pittsburgh's most distinguished
couple in the arts. Nikolai was born in Russia; Sally (she is
Sara only on book covers) is a native of Pittsburgh who
moved away and came back. We sat one afternoon in their
garden, soothed by lilac fragrance and dappled by chartreuse
light filtered through maples. Nearby was Schenley Park
and, beyond, the vast arc of the city.

"I remember stumbling to school each morning through
darkness, with the city smelling like a tunnel," Sally said.
"I never wore light-colored dresses or white collars and gloves.
Each morning my mother had to wipe the coal dust and
steel chips from the window sills."

When Sally was ten her mother, a Southern lady who
found gray Pittsburgh especially uncongenial, took her
children back to the climatic civilities of Alabama. "I was
overwhelmed by the flooding hot sunlight," Sally recalls.
Ten years ago she returned to Pittsburgh as Nikolai's bride.
"I found sunlight as bright and yellow as Alabama's," she
said.

Nikolai, a native of St. Petersburg who has lived during
his wandering life in Helsinki, Karlsruhe, Berlin, London, and
New York, came to Pittsburgh in 1945 as a Carnegie Tech
music professor. "Friends warned me I could not bear it
more than a year, that I must keep my apartment in New
York," he said. "How mistaken they were! I am a city-bred
man and Pittsburgh is what I have sought all my life. It
has the advantages of urban life with the rural calm and

tranquillity necessary to creative life. I never thought I could live in a city with trees and a garden, in peaceful co-existence with wild rabbits and squirrels. Pittsburgh is the perfect city and will remain forever my home."

In an exhibition of Mary Shaw's paintings I saw one canvas in which Pittsburgh, seen from above, explodes upon the brooding black night like a gushing furnace in the mills. To show me this view of the city, Mary took me to Stony Hill, a bleak belvedere looking down on the confluence of the Allegheny and Monongahela, a mile away. The night was cold and windy. Pulling our coats close, we sat on a sheer ledge and looked. The two boulevards following the rivers flickered like a necklace of diamonds and the illuminated towers glowed over the town. The cone of the Gulf Building beamed orange-red to prophesy fair weather, and the flashing red signals on the Grant Building spelled—as they have for some thirty years—"Pittsburgh" in Morse code. The roof of the Koppers Building was a shimmering sulphuric green. To the south, red pillars of fire rose over Jones and Laughlin, and in the distant shadows, behind the dark hills, the silhouette of the Cathedral of Learning flickered like a Gothic ghost.

We were looking over the site of labor's bloodiest wars, and we marveled that, less than half a century after Homestead, capital and labor could unite to create what we saw. This is the real miracle of Pittsburgh.

The sky was black, and so was the wide Ohio beneath us. After a time, flecks of salmon light appeared in the east and the profiles of the towers grew sharper. It was so quiet we seemed to hear the fog move down the rivers and rise in opalescent clouds to blanket the city. The colors in the east turned brighter. As daylight gathered strength, spires began to pierce the clouds, and then the fog crept silently back into the rivers. The city unfolded slowly to our vision, and suddenly the sun rose and there was Pittsburgh glowing in the dawn.

five

ROME'S LIVELIEST QUARTER

For three years in the mid-fifties I lived on Rome's loftiest hill, the Janiculum, a silent place of tall pines and wisteria gardens. In the villa of a Pope's nephew a shepherd boy watched his flocks graze on buttercups in January. My favorite walk, shared by nuns and seminarians flapping to and fro in pairs, was by the Passeggiata del Janiculum to the equestrian statue of Garibaldi. There the religious, like members of some Fra Angelico paradise, would gaze down on the city, slightly convexed, as if the domes and spires were molded to the curve of the earth. Between Garibaldi's statue and the river lay Trastevere, the quarter "beyond the Tiber."

Halfway down from these sanctified premises, at the Fontana Paolina, the silence is shattered by a hubbub of men and machines from below. At the head of a flight of steps, the noises are irresistible. Suddenly you are plunged into a maelstrom of passionately worldly people.

The steps are grass-tufted and slippery with moss. You meet no one coming up, except young couples climbing part way to make love on the steps. At the foot you enter Via Garibaldi, one of the widest and straightest streets in the area, where your ears are assaulted by exploding scooters, shouting women and braying donkeys. The Trasteverini love their noise. The medieval disorder of winding streets makes the quarter seem larger and more crowded than it is. You need not fear getting lost: the Tiber is less than a half-mile away.

The wet wash is strung across the streets like ropes of ships' pennants. Gasoline vapors, festering garbage, and frying foods fill the nostrils. Layers of political posters peel from the ancient walls like skins. The complex of architecture—Romanesque towers, Gothic spires, baroque façades —is a précis of history. If it is summer, entire families are in the streets eating pasta and drinking Frascati. Children, their faces fevered from the wine, run shrieking around the tables, gathering food morsels and kisses.

In some ways Trastevere is reminiscent of Naples. The difference is that Neapolitans, being southerners, externalize their emotions and tensions. In Naples one knows when a conversation is friendly or quarrelsome, but not in Trastevere. The Trasteverini's passions are more deeply rooted and more dangerous. Watch, for instance, a group of street loiterers playing their finger game, *Morra*. Nothing, seemingly, could be less inciting than counting an opponent's dancing fingers. Yet the antagonists gesticulate so violently that they seem to be possessed by diabolical passions. Their frenzies fire them to disputes which have been known to end in murder. Like thieving, murder is more common in Trastevere than in any other part of the city. It is no accident that Rome's murky Carcere Regina Coeli, the Queen of Heaven Prison, is in Trastevere. The Trasteverini are unruly, hasty, vengeful, and vigorously liberty-loving. Their community is the center of Roman Communism.

But underneath their braggadocio and violence the Trasteverini are generous, affectionate, and fun-loving. The name they call themselves means "young men of Trastevere," and every male, no matter how old, thinks himself a youth and a satyr. They boast that they are the true descendants of the ancient Romans—and there is physical evidence to support their claim. Tom Dahill, a Boston artist who spent three years sketching and painting the Trasteverini, found them like Roman statues, short-legged with strong arms and chests and wide, handsome heads. Their skin is dark, their hair and eyes brown. Their characteristics are preserved because they seldom marry outside their quarter. Despite their low-slung bodies, the young women are lovely, with high chests and luminous Roman faces with occasional wens for beauty spots. Raphael's beloved mistress, La Fornarina, was from Trastevere, and so were Caravaggio's equally adored cata-mites. Children are fat and blond with the crafty, knowl-edgeable eyes of the aged. Dahill painted some pudgy blond *bambini* living in a tarpaper shack and later found identical cherubs in the frescoes of the fifteenth-century church of St. Cecilia in Trastevere.

The Trasteverini's pride stems from a medieval guild chauvinism, for they are the traditional *carrettieri*—the cart drivers—of Rome. Their passion for beasts of burden has been transferred to the automobile and its parts and tools. In the Viccolo dei Panieri—the Little Street of the Bread Bakers—the rows of dwellings with arched entrances are former stables. Other stables have been turned into automo-bile repair and accessory shops.

Sometimes cars being stripped in the streets have a dubious origin. An American sculptor whose tools were stolen bought them back the following Sunday at the Porta Portese flea market. The market is a kilometre's length of sleazy junk, faked and bad art, old radios, clothes, crockery, puppies, and purple-and-orange-dyed birds. Here one August morning I met two children selling *stecchetti*, plastic collar stays. Both were wearing long buttoned overcoats, giving the impression they had nothing underneath. Their blond hair was matted with filth; it was hard to believe two children could be so dirty. The larger had a sharp evil look; the younger was cherubic and innocent. I assumed they were brother and sister.

When I met them again in a month both were wearing baggy corduroy pants. They told me they were brothers, eight and seven years of age, named Primo and Secondo. It was about as much as they would say. Instead of addressing prospective buyers they weaseled through crowds, tugging at elbows, poking into flesh to catch attention, then, by lowering their eyes and heads, they would look as pathetic as possible. I saw them frequently that autumn. Primo's pathos was chronic, almost malevolent. But Secondo had a happier disposition with a natural smile which he flashed when Primo wasn't looking. Almost always Primo would catch him at this and poke him, whereupon Secondo's face would reassume its forlorn expression.

Trastevere's clanship extends especially to its feasts. *La Festa di Noialtri*, "The Feast of Us Others," is their big spree, and it goes on from July 15 to July 31. It is like a Thanksgiving extending over the hottest two weeks of the summer. Chairs and tables in the streets turn the quarter into a great café. The famous restaurants—Alfredo's and the Galeassi on the Piazza Santa Maria in Trastevere, and the Cisterna, a popular ancient wine cellar where waiters wear red sashes and flowing ties—are for visitors with fat wallets. To celebrate with the natives, one must follow them into the little streets to the family *trattorias*, where papa or mamma cooks, the older children wait on table and the *bambini* dance around the chairs charming patrons.

The Trasteverini sit for hours around barrels from which the Frascati flows deep amber and slightly foamy (the lighter-colored tourist variety is probably watered, and just as well). To no one's surprise, the Trasteverini are Rome's champion drinkers. They interrupt the Bacchic flow from time to time for a bowl of *pasta*, a joint of the traditional *abbacchio arrosto*—roast lamb—or a slab from one of the *porchetti*, whole roast pigs turning on their spits. The men follow with glow-

ing eyes a tight-skirted girl's triumphant maneuverings over
the rough cobbles on thin high spikes. "What natural grace,
what glory!" a robust gray head says, chomping on a piece of
pig. "She is young, a virgin," his stout wife replies, sighing
for fleeting beauty. Eating and childbearing cause Trastevere
women to grow most of their lives. Uncorseted matrons with
strategic buttons missing thump noisily over the stones on
wooden clogs. Grandmothers, so heavy they cannot move, sit
outdoors in wicker chairs, tending chestnut roasters until dusk.

The feast is an outrage on the ears. The ever-present street
singers would be ingratiating if they were not lost in the
battle of loudspeakers from every establishment, outblaring
each other with popular ballads. On street platforms costumed young people dance the *saltrello*, or compete in the
singing of *stornelli*, improvisations of love, praise or insult.
Insult is a cultivated art. Fashionable society from across the
Tiber crowds the *trattoria* Qui Sta Cencio on untidy Vicolo
del Cedro to hear three brawny brothers sing bawdy lyrics
and mamma shrilly accuse patrons of lechery, cuckoldry, and
bastardy. The insulted guests think it's hilarious.

In smaller places, in the mellower hours, men recite poetry.
The Trasteverini love the sound of their dialect, which, they
tell visitors proudly, is the purest Roman spoken. Etymolo-
gists have doubts. The plebeian vocabulary is so filled with
vulgarities that an ordinary street conversation is unprintable
in English. The names of fruits and vegetables, for instance
have sexual meanings and are spoken with full round sounds
which in themselves are suggestive. Listening attentively to
two men who seem to be reciting a list of country produce,
one suddenly discovers that they are really describing a well-
favored woman. An American archaeologist who learned to
speak from the natives wondered for months why he was
not accepted in Roman society like other Americans.

The local poems probably derive from Trastevere's own
poet, Giuseppe Gioacchino Belli. He died in 1863, but his
spirit is still very alive in Trastevere. A statue of him in

top hat, facing the Garibaldi Bridge, makes him look like a stodgy Johannes Brahms. Actually, Belli was a literary Daumier whose savage Roman sonnets, ridiculing the Pope, helped overthrow the Papal State. He was and is a poet of the cafés, quoted and misquoted more often than read. Since he was a master of the double meaning, he is difficult to translate and to print.

A gentler occasion in the Trastevere calendar is the feast of St. Cecilia, patroness of church music, on November 22. A softly keyed choir sings Palestrina in the Church of St. Cecilia. Trastevere's greatest art glory, a Last Judgment fresco by the thirteenth-century painter, Pietro Cavallini, is in the church convent, but the painting is almost impossible to see. When I finally got permission to look at it, I was pushed through by a dwarfish little nun who kept ringing warning bells for her sisters to hide.

Trastevere's passion for noise reaches a climax, fittingly, on New Year's Eve. I passed one there with two other Americans and a Roman princess. The evening began quietly in Galeassi's with dinner and Asti spumante. In the quarter-hour before midnight everyone on the streets crowded indoors. "To be in the street," said the princess, "would be dangerous to your life."

I have no doubts. On the stroke of midnight there was an explosion of gunpowder and the clamor of ten shivarees. Lights blinked out and women held their ears and screamed with pleasure. Outdoors the air was thick with flying objects, zigzagging from open windows like demented birds. Wine bottles, fluorescent-lighting tubes, dishes and especially chamber pots crashed and shattered on the cobbles. The objects had been saved for a year, the princess explained, and the smashing chamber pots were necessary symbols of good fortune. The din continued for half an hour. It seemed like the bombing of a city.

The feeling was even stronger when we went out. The sulphuric smell of gunpowder filled the air and across the square the façade of Santa Maria in Trastevere was only dimly visible in the rising smoke. The empty streets were covered with broken glass and crockery, making foot passage perilous and auto passage impossible. Here and there a red fire smoldered like a dying incendiary. We made our way up the twisting Viccolo del Bologna, as if we were the last four people on earth.

But we weren't. Around a corner we came upon some youths with a supply of chamber pots which they were blasting into the skies, one by one, with torpedo firecrackers. Squatting low, a youth reached out with a match to light a fuse and then joined his pals crouching against a wall. "Sputnik!" they cried, holding their ears. Brr-ooo-ooo-oo-mmmm! The vessel rose like a rocket from its launching pad and exploded in the night above us. We heard the pieces rattling over the roofs like echoes. "Sputniks!" the youths shouted, rolling with laughter. It was like a scene I had seen in an eighteenth-century lithograph entitled "Popular Amusements."

Suddenly I became aware of other presences in the cold night, of two scavengers poking like rats among the debris for bits of precious metal or a piece of leather. Then I recognized them. They were Primo and Secondo dressed in thin trousers shot through at the knees and shoes from which toes poked. Secondo flashed his smile and said, *"Buon Anno."* Primo scowled and Secondo looked his saddest. I returned the New Year's greeting, passed them some lire and then walked toward the steps to the hill. Everything was silent, as if Trastevere had finally satisfied its mania for noise. But only for a moment. Another "Sputnik" exploded in the night.

six

AMBIVALENT ADRIA

The gateway to Adriatic Italy is Bologna, town of gastronomy and drunken towers, landlocked in the center of Italy, but sea-minded enough to dedicate her most famous fountain to Neptune. The fountain and everything else in town—food, towers, paintings, women—are overwrought and overwhelming, a setting for a colossal Olympian romp.

Bologna is the hedonist capital of a region containing Italy's richest farmlands and Europe's longest riviera, a fair Eden which takes in two provinces—Emilia-Romagna and Marche—and forms a triangle bounded by the Po, the Apennines and the Adriatic. To its eighty-mile seaside, summer sybarites flock like migratory birds. What they come for, quite precisely, is a colossal Olympian romp.

There is a serpent present. Though it is quite possible to romp through the garden without meeting it, it is responsible for much of the farce-tragedy which at times makes Adriatico seem like a comic opera Ruritania. The hedonist provinces where pleasure is the major industry are also Italy's Red region. What melancholy old Marx would make of this is anybody's guess, but there is no ideological iron curtain to cross. Adriatic Communism is strictly Italian style—anticlerical, but not necessarily pro-Russian.

Communist of Bologna, boasting: "The Russians will invade Italy and arrest all anti-Communists."

His Christian Democrat friend, boasting: "The Americans will invade Italy and arrest all Communists."

"*Madonna mia!* Who will be left?"

"The same forty-eight million Italians."

In any case, the visitor is reassured by certain signs on the edges of these Communist-governed cities, announcing the hotel where the Rotary Club lunches on Tuesdays.

As Bologna is the gateway, so Rimini is the hub. Between them lies seventy absolutely straight miles; the Emilian plain throws no obstructions on track or road. Rimini's onslaught on the senses is vigorous and confusing. "*Man spricht Deutsch,*" window placards advise alongside *Löwenbräu* and *Spatenbräu* beer signs. The opera house is playing Lehar's *Der Graf von Luxemburg* and yellow posters herald a circus with "*Eine grosse Löwengruppe.*" Little girls with outstretched hands fugue, "*Bitte schön, danke schön, bitte schön, danke schön*" over and over like birds chirping.

Rimini's 80,000 natives entertain some 300,000 visitors a summer, of which half are Italian and most of the others German-speaking tourists from Germany, Austria, and Switzerland. Bargain prices attract a minority of English and French and in the last years some explorative Americans. They call it the third Gothic invasion—the first being the conquest of Italy in the fifth century by the barbarian Theodoric, who made his capital in Ravenna, and the second being the German occupation during World War II.

Today in Rimini, the golden-haired, lush-bosomed Rheinmaiden and the walnut-skinned, dark-curled satyr lolling on the sands are probably a Düsseldorf shopgirl and a government clerk from Rome. Here men and women haven't lost their sexual identities. Unabashedly, they like each other. It's the affinity of opposites, male for female, north for south, dark for light, that has been simmering ever since the first barbarians marched down from the Alps.

The night foments this polar chemistry in moonlit out-door clubs where young and young-in-heart, wearing any-thing from white tuxedos to blue jeans, crowd the tables under the canopies of sycamores. Music includes xylophones, Congo drums and a buxom singer warbling *Auf Wiederseh'n* or *A Woman in Luff*, learned phonetically from a phonograph record. Flocks of *pappagalli*—parrots, the name given to eager local males from eighteen to forty-five—roam the shadows seeking out tables of ladies.

"*Darf ich bitten?*"

"*Ja, gern!*"

"You dance?"

"I don't mind." In a Midlands accent.

Each bird gathers a pink-faced, two-days-in-the-sun Lorelei in his arms and tangos, waltzes, or gyrates in a rock-n-roll or twist, as the music dictates.

Hours later, when the musicians stop, couples seek the shadier streets or wander to the sea, which covers their poly-glot murmurs with its own. Since many parrots wear wed-ding rings, enduring intimacies are seldom born in Rimini, but the girls have memorable holidays and the parrots pre-serve their illusion that the Italian male is the world's most indispensable to women.

Sea, moonlight, and the summer's romantic high spirits are powerful leaveners and in the ensuing warmth no one re-members that Rimini was three-fourths destroyed by Ger-man occupiers and British raiders, nor that the old Piazza Giulio Cesare, on the site where Caesar addressed his troops between the Rubicon and Rome, is now the Piazza Tre Martiri, named in honor of three young partisans executed by the Nazis.

Undeniably, red is a color that has soaked through the area's many-layered history. In its gloomy clutch of medi-eval castles and dungeons, ducal blood spouted from severed necks like red spumante from uncorked bottles. Through a tempestuous Renaissance, the ruling families Este of Ferrara, Polenta of Ravenna, Malatesta of Rimini, Sforza of Pesaro, Montefeltro of Urbino, and Borgia of Romagna, married, chopped and poisoned one another with astonishing alacrity. From our own century there are new fields of white crosses, harvest of some of the most brutal battles of the last war.

"Do you want to see girls?" a city official asked me a half-hour after my arrival. I did, of course, and he taxied me to the posh Grand Hotel where a solemn committee of movie directors and local dignitaries were selecting "Miss Cinema." It is every Adriatic tourist official's unchallengeable conviction that there is no scenery so breathtaking as the young female form. To keep sightseers happy they sponsor pageants for the selection of Miss Italia, Miss Europa, Miss Mondo, Miss Universo, and Miss Anything Else that an enterprising promoter may think up. The contestants are invariably all Italian—but who can quibble in a land where they all look like Sophia's younger sister? Every event whips up a press hullaballoo of photos and interviews and ends with a white tuxedoed functionary congratulating the winner— after which the decks are cleared for the next contest.

One thinks of Atlantic City, of course, and Jones Beach: gregarious, middle-class, cozily family and always riotously Italian. Greater Rimini, a category including a dozen suburban villages, has nearly a thousand seaside hotels and pensions invariably named, with optimistic chauvinism, Danubio, Basilea, Bavaria, Zurigo, Piccadilly, Vienna. The beach of fantasy-colored umbrellas and awnings blossoms like a riotous flower bed ten miles long. Scanty bathing costumes permit unembarrassed enjoyment of one's own body as well as everyone else's. No one minds the naked children. It is all as active as a René Clair film run in double time, and even Italians go along with the Teutonic bustle of gymnastics, calisthenics, soccer, and generally abandoned exuberance. Multicolored sails wing over the water like exotic water fowl, and pontooned *pedalo* boats creak after them like quacking ducks. A pair of troll kings approach carrying a life-sized elephant and zebra. They are photographers and they set their papier-mâché beasts against the tent of a palm reader —"Prof. Karaiki of the Academies of Occult Science of Paris and Egypt."

Running parallel to the sea is Viale Vespucci, avenue of hostelries plain and fancy, and a carnival of shooting galleries, mechanical ball games, photo shops, and beauty salons. Pavement cafés offer *Schinken mit Spiegeleier* and "tea like mother makes"; night clubs advertise in three languages, "Special prices for all tourists." Special prices, I discovered, are 600 lire for an *espresso* and 900 lire for a native cognac, together more than one day's room and board in a good second-class pension. "They're supposed to be Reds," an astonished English companion said. "Bloody free enterprisers, I'd say."

So that no one need suffer a quiet moment, there are American jukeboxes, most of them out of doors and all of them amplified. From a corner on Viale Vespucci I heard snatches of Elvis Presley's *"Don't Be Cruel,* Frankie Laine's *Cool Water,* Belafonte's *Banana Boat,* an unknown white voice singing *The Holy City* and a Negro voice hoarsely rasping, "She's got it, she's got it, she's got it . . ." on a record which was labeled *Gangster Cerca Moglie* ("Gangster Searches Wife"). At an outdoor bar across the street a jazz band was playing *The Birth of the Blues.* It was a heartening capitalist cacophony.

Some say it is the blinding silver light, others the never-ceasing offshore winds that charges the atmosphere with adrenalin. A more logical explanation is that the hedonists bring their stepped-up thyroids with them, that the momentum is everlastingly renewed by unloading trains and Volkswagens. My own theory is that some of the acceleration comes from the sea itself. I can never speak of the Adriatic without pronoun difficulties, for this tempestuous and vigorous arm of the Mediterranean seems to me a male sea, a northern triton—with *his* magnetism for drawing northerners —by some accident ensnared in the gentle south. Fishermen and anyone else living intimately with the Adriatic think of it not as a soft woman but as a belligerent adversary.

"The Adriatic is perfectly safe for children," travel brochures say, and on calm days this is true, for the beaches are flat and so gradual in their slope that the diving towers are set a third of a mile out in the water. The tide seldom varies more than eighteen inches. But the Adriatic is green with silvery lights, like the eyes of a jealous devil, and that is warning enough. In winter it turns gray, churns like soap, and is unsafe for navigation. Up and down the coast, I asked the same question: Why is the Adriatic green and not blue like the Mediterranean of which it is a part? From fishermen, travel clerks, and waiters, I drew a variety of fanciful answers. Green was the color of Adriatic light which the sea reflected; or the color of the vegetation beneath the waters; or subterranean volcanic furnaces exploded sulphuric minerals into the water. A city official at Riccione offered the most logical explanation. "It is a matter of light refraction," he said. "The Adriatic is green because it is shallow. Halfway across, it is hardly more than a hundred feet deep, but over on Dalmatia where the rocky coast is steep, it is as blue as any sea in the world."

One charm of Rimini is that no one fusses about sightseeing. There are three monuments, all conspicuous enough to be unavoidable. Two—the Arc of Augustus and the Bridge of Tiberius, which is still a thoroughfare over the Marecchia River—are splendid souvenirs of Imperial Rome. The other is the temple of Malatesta.

The Malatestas of Rimini were a tribe equal in bloodiness to their neighbors, the Borgias. Founder of the house was Malatesta da Verrucchio, who lived a hundred years. It was one of his sons, Giovanni the Ugly, who married Francesca da Polenta of Ravenna and then killed her and his brother, Paolo the Handsome, when he caught them in a lovers' embrace. Lustiest of all Malatestas was the fifteenth-century Sigismondo, a dissolute voluptuary who married Ginevra d'Este and probably poisoned her in order to marry Polissena Sforza—whom he strangled to marry Isotta degli Atti on whom he had already conceived several children.

It was to provide a tomb for Isotta that Sigismondo rebuilt a Franciscan church into a pagan pantheon. The temple, destroyed on January 21, 1944, was one of Italy's great art casualties of the war. Paintings, including some by Giotto, were lost, but the richly detailed stucco interior of Agostino di Duccio has been restored. Sigismondo had no interest in swooning pietas nor saccharine madonnas. Instead, he had engraved, hundreds of times among the statues, balustrades, pilasters, and cornices, the interlocked initials *S* and *I.* The symbol—which resembles an incompleted dollar sign—indicates beyond doubt that the real deities of the temple, which pretends to Christianity, were Venus and Mars.

For gourmets the shrine of Rimini is the Ristorante Giardino, where the tables are set under plane trees in the yard. The President of Italy named the Giardino's Bruno Barosi a *Cavaliere* of the Republic simply for his artistry in cooking fish. "No! No!" wailed this magician of fish in despair when the Milanese journal, *Oggi*, praised his *fritto misto*. "Never, *never* once in my life have I fried a fish!" Bruno is a round-faced man in his middle sixties with long white hair like a music maestro's. He led me and my companion, a young lady from Switzerland, into his kitchen where ten charcoal broilers were lined up like a row of old gasoline drums. Bruno has no bill of fare. He interviews his guests, exploratively as a tailor at a first fitting, and when he has decided what you should eat, he goes to the kitchen to supervise its preparation. He sent us a fish antipasto—lobster, crayfish, clams—served with lemon oil of a special delicacy from Spoleto. Next a steaming *zuppa di pesce*, after which my young lady begged for mercy. Silly girl! Bruno himself delivered the "roast," a great silver platter which he carried high, like a steward serv-

ing a king. On the platter were buttered lobsters, sole grilled
with lemon and rosemary, and a skewered shish-kabob of
squid, shrimp, crabs, and oysters. The wines, too, were
Bruno's selections—Stella d'Oro, Cupramontana, and the
great white wine of the Adriatic, cool spicy Verdicchio.

From Rimini the inland foothills are a cloudland out of
which on bright days three mountains rise like a trio of
sphinxes. As one approaches the mountain named Titano there
emerges from the clouds a cluster of crenellated fortresses
and castles, like a movie set for a romance by Ariosto or
Walter Scott. They are the towers of San Marino, the world's
smallest (23 square miles) and oldest (fourth century) republic. The 14,000 San Marenesi have their heads in the clouds
and their feet on solid rock. During my visit they were in
the midst of one of their revolutions, busily overthrowing a
twelve-year Communist government with no casualties other
than a few wounded feelings. "You see, we're all related,"
said an anti-Communist. "It just wouldn't do for anyone to
get hurt. The memory would stay too long."

San Marino is a place loved by winds. A cyclonic gale, the
garbino, ripped awnings, hurtled metal furniture and television antennae through the skies like kites, and billowed nuns'
habits like parachutes. The wind made the vertical vistas even
more dizzying than ordinarily and tourists jammed shops to
buy local ceramics and postage stamps which are printed in
London, and cafés to munch *Torte San Marino*, an airy waffle
of chocolate and almonds and drink the local sweet Moscato
and Sangiovese. The eerie wind whistled into the evening,
lashing at power lines so that the lights of the town sputtered
below us like candles and each man felt a little mad as if he
were watching the lights of the world flick away.

The strange and noisy world of Adriatico also has its quiet
places. Ferrara for instance. Driving on a foggy morning
north across the valleys, I remembered that Goethe preferred
it to all other Italian cities, that it was a peak on the cultural
grand tour until the late nineteenth century, when the rumor

spread among Victorian travelers that it was unhealthy. The unhygienic conditions were corrected, but travelers never returned. The town is on a horizonless plain, spread in dismal flatness around some castle turrets. Soon I was walking over handsome streets, passing ducal palaces with dart-and-bead cornices and exquisite doorways, marveling how designers had brought grace to a square town simply by curving a street or rounding a palace. I wandered like one bewitched through a world of *cinquecento* sweetness, with rippling fountains, tinkling bells, sunny gardens of roses and pomegranate trees and soft-footed nuns jealously guarding beautifully frescoed little chapels. How had it come there, this *città di silenzio,* so finely jeweled.

Ferrara rose like an Undine from the River Po. Young as Italian cities go, her first towers appeared out of leech swamps in the seventh century. Wealth flowed to her on the river, firing the avariciousness of the powerful Guelf house of Este whose soldiers came down from Paduan hills and sacked the people's democracy for their own. The Estes built a gigantic fortress with a hundred dungeons in which, for two gory centuries, they liquidated papal Ghibellines and each other in their battle for power. A sort of peace came finally in the fourteenth century with the reign of Niccoló d'Este III.

"*Molto prolifico,*" said a local bookseller, nudging my ribs with his elbow, directing my gaze with lewd pride across the municipal square to Niccoló's statue high on a column. "He had many women and even God could not count the children." Niccoló recognized thirteen from a variety of mothers and his subjects danced to a song,

> *On both sides of the Po*
> *All are children of Niccoló.*

His lusty breeding set the stage for a succession of fratricides that continued for five generations. The bloody sequence was begun by Niccoló himself when he chopped up his young wife, Parisina Malatesta, and his oldest son, Ugo, for behavior unbecoming a boy and his stepmother. Niccoló was succeeded by two of his bastards, first Leonello the Noble, who patronized literature and art, and then Borso the Just, a pompous, kindly egomaniac whose courtly splendor is remembered as Ferrara's "golden age."

Borso's processions and pageants can be seen still in the "Schifanoia months," probably the most remarkable non-religious frescoes of the Renaissance. Of all the Este palaces the summer Schifanoia on the edge of town was the most pleasant. The name means "shun care" and this is precisely what Borso demanded of the Ferrara masters Tura, Cossa, and Roberti, whom he commissioned to cover the walls of his banquet hall with a calendar of twelve paintings. Seven, from March through September, have survived. The central theme of the cycle is a celebration of Borso, and the panels are filled with the details of his daily life. One sees him, an overfed little man with a ponderous nose, double chin, and gray hair, smirking with self-satisfaction as he bestows gifts, picks cherries, receives ambassadors, and hunts, phalanxed always by a coterie of cavaliers. The most astonishing of the frescoes shows April's flowery garden of love in which youths and maidens woo with ribald innocence, while at their feet amorous and fertile rabbits are doing exactly the same. In this picture Borso, a misogynist who disdained women, is hawking herons with his knights.

When Borso's nephew, Alfonso, was married to the Pope's daughter, Lucrezia Borgia, the nuptial buffoonery continued for six days and nights. Lucrezia, already twice widowed at twenty-one, turned into a decorous Duchess of Ferrara who ran the government in her husband's absence and died after childbirth in penance and grace. Her tomb is still guarded by Clarissa nuns who collect a fee from visitors. Ferrara respects strong women, and after negotiating with nuns and old wives to open the locked doors and bolted gates to Etruscan and Renaissance treasures, I had no doubts who

were the custodians of the town. It was no surprise to learn
that the mayor was a lady.

"Housekeeping matters are for women," say the local
barons of business who gather on any warm evening at café
tables on the piazza where the night air is pungent with the
odors of the *castello* moat (the water, they joke, is original
Este). Like caricatures of capitalists, they push their hats back
on sweating bald heads and, their round stomachs straining
at trouser buttons, eat baroque pastries filled with cream and
drink endless coffee while they hassle over market quotations
and the price of sugar beets. I asked a grain and wine broker
the name of the mayoress. He puzzled a moment and turned
to a companion.

"*Come si chiama la sindachessa?*"

The companion pulled at his ear and finally asked why I
needed to know. The question traveled from table to table
and I received a variety of uncertain replies. Treboni? Don-
chati? Balbini? No one was sure. The next morning a pretty
secretary in the tourist office told me the Mayoress was
Signora Luisa Balboni, a mild-mannered high school *profes-
soressa* of English. Communist, of course.

Back toward the sea. Red brick barns, corn shocks, plow-
ing tractors, flocks of turkeys, trees bent with ripe apples
and pears and autumn's blue smoke hanging over it all like
September at home in Wisconsin. But there were differences.
Huddles of black-robed women were hand-husking corn and
retting long white fibers of flax pale as witches hair, exactly
as in the Schifanoia frescoes. My destination was the Abbey
of Pomposa, where medieval monks collected a great library
in the middle ages and Guido d'Arezzo invented modern
musical notation. Here the brothers were as industrious as
they were learned. They drained moors and operated farms
on which the Ferrara dukes fished and hunted boars and
wolves. After a thousand years the monks were betrayed in
the sixteenth century by the capricious Po. A series of floods

ruined their land and leeches and malarial mosquitoes drove them away.

The waters receded, but the monks never returned. Pomposa stands in haunting desolation among pines and poplars, its copper-colored Romanesque tower gleaming like a lighthouse over the fields of wheat and hemp. On spring evenings the solitude is filled with the song of hundreds of nightingales which nest in the warm, damp meadows. Echoes whine like ghosts through the great halls and refectories. The damp has faded some of the Giottoesque frescoes but the Last Judgment is still bright, its Heaven and Hell as alive as insect colonies. In a neat, well-ordered paradise angels blow golden trumpets while tight rows of benign souls sing roundelays of joy for having made the team. Below is an inferno unrivaled in grisliness. Serpentine monsters torment writhing souls, and devils impale human bodies like oxen skewered for roasting. During all of my Adriatic wanderings I have never been quite free of that awesome work, finding in the contrasts through which I was moving an uncomfortable closeness to both that heaven and that hell.

The sea beyond Pomposa was turquoise and silver like a sea on the moon. An hour's drive through desolate marshes, down the loneliest shore of Italy, brings one to Ravenna. The day was gray, and the bell in a leaning tower was knelling the minutes as regularly as a buoy on the sea. It was altogether fitting to find a tolling bell in *la città morta*, a birthplace, deathbed and sepulchre of Roman civilization. For Ravenna, the southernmost city of Cisalpine Gaul, entered history in 50 B.C. when Caesar mustered his forces to cross the Rubicon and conquer Italy. Augustus made Ravenna the Empire's naval center and in the fifth century Honorious made it the capital. It remained so until the imperial tragedy was concluded by the Barbarian Odoacer, first King of Italy. Odoacer was followed by Theodoric, who ruled the Roman-Gothic kingdom wisely for thirty-three years. But the forces of new Rome on the Bosphorus were directed on Ravenna and after five years of murderous Byzantine wars, Justinian was Emperor and Ravenna was for a second time capital of the West.

But the long decline had begun. The Po, fed by two hundred tributaries, deposited its alluvial silt, the sea withdrew and Ravenna stood high and dry, like Pisa and Ostia on Italy's western shore. In the Middle Ages the violent Polenta family took over the tired city. One of the evil band, the fourteenth-century Guido Novello who brought Giotto to Ravenna and extended hospitality to the troubled Dante, was known for his goodness. In his house Dante finished his *commedia* and died.

A *portière* told me that the bell tolling so sorrowfully was observing the anniversary of Dante's death. I walked across the town, to the "zone of silence" around the poet's tomb. On the steps a golden-haired young woman shouted, *"Ruhe! Ruhe!"* The crowd hushed and she said in German, "Driven from his home by the vicious Florentines, the poet found refuge in the warm hearts of Ravenna. . . ."

The young woman spieling on the steps wasn't German at all, if you please, but a native Ravennisi, Signora Wanda Gaddoni, surely one of the most beautiful guides in Italy. "Our tourists are almost all German," she told me. "They consider Theodoric their own and Ravenna their first capital. They come like Mohammedans to Mecca."

Ravenna's thousand-and-one-nights glory, her mosaics, must be seen in the morning light and only on sunny days. The earliest is the tomb of Galla Placidia, sister of the Emperor Honorius. To enter this plain, cross-shaped little building is like plunging into death's darkness. But in a moment the eyes adjust and slowly a radiance of light shines from the dome and walls. Figures emerge: Christ, saints, and wondrously decorative arabesques, until every inch of space shimmers like jewels. It is possibly the most astonishing monument of the fifth century. From the Gothic period there is *St. Apollinare Nuovo* with its long processions of virgins and saints, so serene and exultant they might be singing a Bach chorale, and the richest fragment of all Ravenna's mosaics, the gift-bearing Magi *running* after the Christmas star. Finally, there are the sophisticated Byzantine mosaics of St. Vitale with Justinian and Theodora in glum and regal grandeur, and out in the country in St. Apollinare in Classe, a green-and-gold apse that is as fresh and bright as springtime.

The Renaissance which brought Ferrara and Florence into glory bypassed Ravenna. From the sixteenth century she has one curious relic which has an extraordinary appeal. Appropriately, it is a figure of death, Tullio Lombardi's reclining statue of the fallen warrior Guidarello Guidarelli.

As I entered the small chamber in the Accademia where the statue lies, I met a sobbing young woman being escorted out by a guard. Inside, looking down on the image of the warrior, laid out like a corpse on a catafalque, I felt a deep melancholy, as if I were at a wake. The visor of the armor was raised on a romantic face with long lashes and languid lips, a face hollow from weariness reposing as if in sleep. "The Rudolph Valentino of marble," it is called, and with good reason. Byron and d'Annunzio wrote poems about it. Its visitors are women: women dressed in mourning, women collapsing into hysteria, women begging permission to spend a night alone in the room. The white stone face was flecked with tears, the lips stained with lipstick, until five years ago when the statue was enclosed by rope and women were no longer permitted to enter alone. Still an American woman sent flowers to the statue every day for a year. "The romantic ladies are Italian, French, and American," said Signora Gaddoni. "German ladies come and look—but quite truthfully, they prefer Italian men alive."

Is the city really dead, as they say? The Via Cairoli is a little Via Condotti of fashion and luxury, and to its left is a street of banks. The money comes from the surrounding countryside of grain fields and herds of meat and leather-producing cattle. Toward the sea, a double file of tankers and freighters from Newcastle, Dubrovnik, Trieste, and Panama moves down the Corsini canal. The ships cast their shadows on aluminum-painted oil refineries and a new synthetic rubber plant built with American capital.

The seaside road leads through a green and silent wood. This is the *pineta*, a forest of long-trunked umbrella pines which forever extends itself as the sea retires farther and farther from ancient shores. I stopped and walked through vertical shafts of light dappling the crocus carpet under my feet, crossing a canal over which graceful fishing nets called *padelloni* billowed like spiders' webs. A clearing in a grove marked by a marble column, the *Piazza di Dante*, is the site the poet selected for his earthly paradise. A tree frog croaked above and bells tinkled on some distant sheep.

The pines continue, off and on, almost to Rimini. Halfway, the pleasant seaside resort of Cervia is built among pines. Here I stopped to inquire for the Rubicon; I did not wish to cross Caesar's stream without properly organizing my emotions for the momentous passage.

The Rubicon? Two of a dozen or so people in Cervia had heard of it, but neither knew where it was. Since it drained into the sea I was sure to pass over it. After seven miles I came to a dark algae-filled little canal flowing sluggishly seaward through a field of vegetables. I asked the farmer hoeing among artichokes what the stream was called. He shrugged. "It has no name, it is just a ditch." Rubicon? "What is that?"

I looked into the dark little channel, so narrow a youth could have leaped across, and tried to imagine Caesar, preparing to seize the lordship of the world, crying out, "Let us go . . . the die is cast!" Either the stream had shrunk or the budding emperor had been rhetorical.

I struck out south toward Ancona, over a road that hugs the sea most of the way. Long stretches of beach were empty and desolate. The Adriatic was high with wild waves roaring to the highway, covering me with spray. I closed my car windows against the strange sea and felt as if I were shutting out a friend. After the bathing towns of Riccione and Cattolica I crossed into Marche where the road rose suddenly to Mount Gabbice, a jut of rock which interrupts the flow of sand. On the summit stands the formidable medieval fortress of Gradara. Built by Malatestas in the twelfth century and admirably restored in ours, the fortress was, according to Dante, the setting for the love tragedy of Paolo and Francesca. Outside, bazaars offered ceramic representation of the anguished love scene and fratricide, and bottles of *"Liebeselixir von Paolo und Francesca."* Inside torture chambers, lime cisterns and trap doors impose a *Grand Guignol* atmosphere which the madonnas and crucifixes are unable to sweeten. In Francesca's bedchamber the linguistic young guide, anxious to slight no one, summarized Dante:

> "Paolo lieben Francesca and knows key for sleeping to Francesca. Grand amore. Un Duell zwischen fratelli. Morte. Kaputt tutti e due Paolo und Francesca. Finish!"

Inland, about thirty miles, is Urbino. No other town on the Adriatic dominates its lands so magnificently as the birthplace of Raphael and Bramante. The Romanesque spires of its ducal palace pierce the blue sky like needles. All of Urbino is a Renaissance museum, unaltered from the days when its powerful dukes were exuberant and jealous art collectors. The piazza is lonely as a church on Monday, the streets are silent corridors. When it was built by Federico da Montefeltro, the palace was the ideal of princely residences. Today it is a gallery for Raphael, Titian, Paolo Uccello, and Piero della Francesca, whose *Madonna di Senigallia* with her small wide-set eyes, prominent nose and blond hair is a type of woman still familiar on the Adriatic.

At the southern end of the long beach Ancona, like Bologna in the north, is a gateway. On its curved wharf stand two welcoming arches, a Roman one built for Emperor Trajan, and an eighteenth-century one for Pope Clement XII.

A Doric city founded by Spartans, Ancona is built in the amphitheatre style of the Mediterranean, on hills sloping down to the sea. At the summit, like an entrance to paradise, stands a noble Romanesque cathedral, built in the fifth century on the foundations of a temple to Minerva. The cathedral piazza is a belvedere below which the city spreads like a map of itself. Sunset is Ancona's noblest hour. Then the red-and-white granite of the cathedral glows like a living flower. In the harbor, ships of every size and shape—flat tankers, round-bellied freighters, graceful yachts and crescent fishing schooners—jostle for space. Shipyard cranes sway like the sensitive mandibles of insects, and acetylene torches light up the black hulls with a bluish light. Rising from the city below are the smells of oil and smoke and tar, and the shrill sounds of locomotive whistles and sharp hammer blows from foundries and shipyards. Ancona is the railroad center of the Adriatic and, next to Livorno, Italy's second biggest commercial port.

The *Anconetani* are a blend of north and south with, especially in the upper regions of the town, the northerner's stature and dignity. There are strikingly blond men and women, tall and fair with dark Mediterranean eyes and lashes, who stand out in the southern population like Arcadian gods.

In the human flow fishermen are the most easily identifiable. Fishing franchises are handed down through centuries from father to son, and the families are an inbred species. Fishermen are short, broad-shouldered, strong-chested and low in the chassis. They wear a common costume, pants, tricot shirts, berets, everything blue, and they are frequently barefoot. Their women, too, are low with a round full softness.

I was on the fishing wharf the evening of *Lascia o Raddoppia,* Italy's television *Double or Nothing,* which in the year of 1957 for an hour each week stopped normal activity from Como to Agrigento. The boats had not gone out at dusk as usual, and the bars and billiard rooms on the wharf

were packed with rows of chairs. For a half-hour before the
broadcast, grizzled, brawny fishermen padded into the tiny
improvised theatres and took their places. The silence was
reverential as they watched the screen. A girl contestant
wrinkled her brow, wrestling with a question. Suddenly the
audience cheered. She had answered correctly.

The program over, the fishermen padded to their boats
with hardly a sound. Lamps flickered in the cabins, muffled
motors began to chug softly, and boats, one after another,
slid out to sea. Soon the harbor was empty of everything but
the petrol fumes and a dog keening because he was left behind. The next night and for five nights after, the boats
would leave at dusk and the dog would not be forgotten.

My host in Ancona was Dr. Carlo Ulisse, a lawyer whose
warm affection for Americans goes back to the war, when
he was interpreter for Allied troops. The doctor's formula
for a memorable tour was a proper balance of sight-seeing
and gastronomy.

One afternoon we drove to the summit of Mount Conero,
a rugged granite pile which rises vertically out of the sea.
Here the wild winds sighed and whistled about still another
Romanesque church, the eleventh-century San Pietro al
Conero. With sickening vertigo we peered from the edge of
the mountain 1700 feet down to the water. Milky turquoise
and shining green whorled into one another like a sea of
marble; far beyond lay a shadow which Dr. Ulisse said
was Dalmatia. An abbey on the mountain, abandoned by
monks in the nineteenth century, was turned into an inn
twenty-eight years ago by Signora Marianna Meloppione,
now seventy-six years old. We dined on her famous speciality,
pollo in potacchio, young chicken cooked in oil, garlic,
rosemary, white wine, and hot peppers, and we drank Fior
di Bacco, which a native cookbook accurately describes as
"eternal glory for a magnificent marriage with food."

It was night by the time we emerged from Bacchus' flower
bed. Across the Aspio Valley we could see silhouetted in

lights, glowing like a holy city, the dome and spires of Loreto, Italy's greatest pilgrim shrine. Loreto's famed relic is the Holy House in which, it is believed, the Virgin Mary was born and her son Jesus lived until his thirtieth year. The story of how the house came to Loreto has been carefully documented. According to printed histories, on May 10, 1291, when Palestine was invaded by Moslems, the house was flown by angels to Tersatto in Dalmatia for safekeeping. A popular version of the story relates that the Dalmatians did not sufficiently venerate the shrine; whatever the reason, on December 10, 1294, the angels descended a second time to move the house across the Adriatic into a forest near Recanati, seven and a half miles from Loreto. But the woods being full of bandits, the Holy House was moved again, this time only a half-mile to a farm belonging to two brothers. The brothers quarreled over the proprietorship of the house, and the angels made the air transfer a fourth time, carrying the house into a laurel grove which gave Loreto its name, and there it has remained. Because of the Holy House's air-borne history, the black-cedar Madonna which stands inside is, among other things, the protectress of aviators.

The heavenly illumination in Loreto was in celebration of the feast of her Nativity. The next day I went there with Dr. Ulisse and some friends. Until twenty years ago pilgrims walked to Loreto, some needing two or three weeks for the journey. Now they were traveling mostly in chartered buses, and all traffic leading to the city on the hill was a slow-moving caravan of blue. A casbah of bazaars filled the streets. The piazza outside the basilica, which was built to encase the Holy House, was a crowded gipsy camp of pilgrims wearing country costumes of central and southern Italy. Under the board arches of stately double-decker loggias they ate, drank, slept, and socialized. Wide-hipped old women, wrapped in the shawls of Lazio or the Abruzzi, sat sleeping on stones, their bare feet stretched before them. Men in rustic moleskins leaned against columns drinking wine. Young women holding tiny mirrors combed their hair, and children curled in sleep in a sea of suitcases, boxes, and bottles in which pilgrims carried their provisions.

Inside the sanctuary it was even more crowded, and the odor, a mixture of stale bodies, goats, cheese, and old incense, was so strong that the ladies in our party soaked handkerchiefs in eau de cologne and covered their nostrils. Pilgrims squatted everywhere, and in a small chapel a woman was washing her tired feet in a basin. The center of the basilica is taken up by a white marble structure with richly sculptured walls. This is the covering to the Holy House. Around it an endless line of pilgrims crawled slowly on their knees toward the entrance, guided by two ruts cut into the stone by their predecessors over the centuries.

They were almost all women—the men were either sleeping in the piazza or whooping it up in the wine shops. Young women hobbled with babies on their arms and old women helped themselves along with walking sticks.

We stood against the rear wall of the Holy House and watched the line pass. The room was a rectangular, arch-roofed patchwork of brick and stone, black from centuries of candle smoke, and steaming from the heat of thirty golden oil lamps. Glowing in a small apse were the shiny ebony faces of the Madonna and Child. The sight of the figures, armless in their garment of gold-and-silver filigree, moved the pilgrims to hysterical weeping. As we watched, one fainted from emotion and many begged for time to pray. But the line was endless and guards pushed them on, allowing none to linger. Some rejoined the line outside and began the long crawl again, perhaps for a third or fourth time.

Outdoors a lorry loaded with watermelons drew into the piazza and hundreds pressed up to buy the fruit and quench their thirst on its scarlet flesh, dropping the seeds and rinds about everywhere. Groups of pilgrims sang *La Bella Madonna di Loreto*, and the song was like a sorrowing fugue that might go on forever. As the shadow of the church fell across the piazza, pilgrims opened bags and boxes and began to eat salamis, chickens, and joints of roasted kid, and to drink deep from dark red bottles. As they chomped and guzzled, they watched with curious eyes a trio of well-dressed visitors, a man and his wife and daughter, who were arguing loudly in English. They were from Buffalo and the women's anger was directed at the father's Italian relatives who had brought them to the *festa* without arranging for beds. "You and your trip," cried out the girl to the unhappy father. "Will I ever be glad when I get back to the U.S.A. again!" The mother, weeping, sobbed out, "I'll kiss the American soil, that's what I'll do, I'll bend right over and kiss it and I'll never leave it again, not as long as I live, I won't. . . ."

Night came, and with it the hour of the *grande spettacolo pirotecnico*. Bombs screeched into the skies, bursting graceful tendrils of pink and purple stars which floated down toward the shrine and flickered away. At the climax the heavens lit up with the words *Ave Maria*. I thought of the hundreds who would sleep happily on the stones that night because they had seen a miracle.

In the morning the pilgrims seemed lost, like sheep without their shepherd. Children wailed and mothers nursed babies on the church steps. Old men, washing at the fountain, spoke longingly of home. Bodies were sprawled everywhere, sleepers curled about one another in a clutter of melon rinds, chicken bones, papers, and bottles.

Groups of women began to sing in strange minor-key wails. They were waiting for the recessional of the brides; Loreto's Madonna is also patroness of brides and this was the marriage hour. An air-force band in white played arias. The new brides and grooms emerged and were met at the portals by boys who gave them handbills from a furniture store. The band swung into a brisk military march and brides, grooms, and pilgrims looked heavenward. There was a deafening roar and twelve jets in V-formation zoomed through the skies. On the loggia balcony a red-robed cardinal waved

his hand, offering the Madonna's traditional blessing to all
planes and airmen. The planes buzzed the sanctuary a second,
a third time, and the old cardinal feebly waved his blessings.

From inside the church the organ boomed. A huddle of
bearded and tonsured young Capuchins appeared. Gloriously
arrayed bishops, Knights of the Madonna, *carabinieri* and air-
force officers formed a procession. Music and colors were
fair and bright; the spent pilgrims rose to their feet and, with
shining eyes, followed the procession into the sanctuary. A
teen-aged peanut vendor, sitting on the church steps with
his merchandise piled between his legs, shouted merrily, "Big
Sale! Closing out! Last chance! Must vacate premises!"

I thought of the painting in Pomposa, the heaven and hell
which had such reality on the green sea's shores. Buses loaded
with weary human cargoes were rolling down the hills
toward the plains. We fell into the blue caravan, passing on
our way the local cinema which was showing an old Graham
Greene film, *La Fine dell' Avventura.*

seven

THE PASSIONS OF SARDINIA

I n the museum in the capital city of Cagliari there is a
pregnant Bronze Age statue with the whole world in its
belly. There is no more perfect symbol for this lonely, cut-
off island forced by desperate necessity to be self-sufficient
in all things of body and spirit. Sardinia is a fierce Apocalyptic
landscape of sea and rock, a world of wind sculptures covered
with the patina of gray-green lichen. The evening music in
the villages, the singing to pipes and guitars of sad shepherds'
songs, seem to have floated over from Algerian deserts. Silent
eyes follow the visitor everywhere. Unlike the chameleon
eyes of Sicilians, which are apt to take on the complexion of
the moment, Sardinian eyes are large, smoldering pools always seeming on the edge of tears. It is the eyes that tell
most eloquently of loneliness and the bleak blood hunger for
human fellowship.

I arrived in Cagliari on April 30, the evening the Sards
begin the celebration of their patron, St. Efisio. Looking at
the statue with painted goatee and mustaches and a corpulent
abdomen, one could see at once his relationship to the pregnant statue in the museum. "Efisio pampered his belly," Sards
say with pride, and who can blame a people accustomed to

centuries of poverty and hunger for worshiping the full belly, for venerating a sybaritic glutton?

The saint's feast was a Scheherazade explosion. Like flocks of exotically plumaged birds, Sards in native dress descended on the city from all over the island. They were gathering for the food fair, to marvel at stars and pinwheels shaped from fruits and vegetables; at waterfalls of peas and miniature football fields with beet and carrot players and onion-stalk goal posts; at breads in the shapes of conch shells, flowers and saints, polished like mother-of-pearl; at tanks of fish and crustaceans; at beef carcasses filled with flowers; and freshly slaughtered lambs and kids lying in beds of green ferns. The grotesque comedians of the show were scores of baby pigs painted scarlet in their own blood, festooned like Christmas tree baubles so that they seemed to be running races up and down trellises like mischievous cherubs in a baroque church.

Such a flowering of the earth and the sea is intoxicating. Crowds danced and an orchestra played *Yes Sir, That's My Baby* while a frail and aged bishop, phalanxed by police guards, tottered through the maze of stalls as he swung his censer, and covered it all with holy water and incense.

Four days of earnest eating followed. In the morning, Efisio rode a gold-and-glass sedan carriage drawn by flower-garlanded oxen, beginning his annual journey to Nora, the town of his birth. Behind him moved a caravan of pilgrims on foot, horses, bicycles, and scooters, and out on the sea fishermen accompanied him in their boats. The distance to Nora is only twenty miles, but the round trip took four days because of the lavish feasts served in villages and at wealthy estates on the way. A modest breakfast included spaghetti, beefsteak, cheese, artichokes, fruit, and wine. At Efisio's welcoming dinner in Nora the plates were stacked ten deep before each diner, and waiters had only to remove a plate after each course. This raised the second course of soup to chin level, an angle from which spooning it was hazardous. It took three hours to work down to table level, through antipasto, sole *al parmigiano*, roast lamb, fried brains with artichokes, eggs, chicken *al diavolo*, green salad, cheese, fruit, cream pastries, and coffee. A different wine irrigated each course.

After dinner, I followed the saint down to the sea, to the ancient city where, according to legend, Efisio became a Christian convert and was martyred. The ruins, part of which have sunk into the water, are one of the archaeological wonders of Sardinia. Ancient columns undulate beneath the shimmering turquoise surface like sirens among sea ferns; mosaic floors of patrician villas are jeweled sea beds.

Two nights later the people of Cagliari greeted the return of Efisio's torch-lit procession with bells and sirens. Men and women, tears like stars glistening in their eyes, stampeded the saint, kissing him as if he'd been gone for years. Fireworks lit up the sky until midnight and an old man said the rockets reminded him of the bombs which destroyed much of the town in 1943. By morning pilgrims had spread out over the island in silent caravans and the city was quiet. It was the end of feasting and, for the Sards, a return to more frugal fare.

Sards are such small people that anthropologists used to believe they were descended from a race of North African pygmies. Their reduced stature, which extends also to their donkeys, cattle, and horses, is the result of centuries of adaptation to Sardinian climate, geography, and diet. Mainland Italians despise the island as an outer limbo. They have no taste for its wild megalithic landscape and they have been afraid of Sardinia's traditional dismal trinity of evils: disease, poverty, and banditry. Two thousand years ago when Quintus departed Rome for Sardinia, his brother, Cicero, warned "Take care, my brother, of your health," and forty years ago when D. H. Lawrence made his querulous winter's journey across the island, he suffered such arctic discomforts that the Sards seemed to him to resemble Eskimos. "Sardinia is like nowhere," he wrote. "It lies outside; outside the circuit of civilization."

So it was, through the last war. The Germans, retreating
from allied advances in 1943, flooded the lowlands to en-
courage the breeding of malarial mosquitoes. The next year
there were more than 78,000 malaria victims, including many
Allied soldiers. On the heels of the armies came civilians with
foreign aid. The Rockefeller Foundation, working with
UNRRA and ECA, declared a four-year war on the
anopheles mosquito, a siege which employed 26,000 men and
cost $11,000,000. Since 1950 there hasn't been a single new
case of malaria on the island.

Sardinia is named not for the fish, but after the Greek word
for a sandal, which it resembles in shape. A little larger than
Massachusetts, it is divided into three provinces: Cagliari in
the south, Nuoro in the mountainous center, and Sassari in
the north. Ninety-two per cent of Sardinia's 1,200,000
people live in small villages. Their loneliness has made Sardinia an island of hosts, and the keynote of a Sardinian
journey is an effusion of hospitality which no one who has
lived through will ever forget. A young Swedish doctor and
his wife arriving by boat at Santa Teresa in the north, met a
cork-grower who entertained them in his mountain home of
Tempio for two days, then sent them on to Sassari with a
letter to an archaeologist who, after three days of wining and
dining, dispatched them to an artist at Oristano, who introduced them to a businessman in Cagliari. In this way the
Swedes encircled the island, never without a native host.

April and May are the best months to visit Sardinia, but
October and November are lovely. In the autumn the island
may be scorched brown and dusty, but the golden days are all
exactly alike and the nights are warm and silvery. Spring
ripples with green wheat splashed red with poppies, and the
mountains are covered with the white bloom of asphodel so
thick that sheep get lost in it.

The most beautiful entrance to Sardinia is on the Naples
boat to Cagliari. Cagliari is a shimmering golden city hanging
from a hillside, always about to plunge into her bay. Above

the city the heavens are the softest blue, a color which increases in depth as it approaches the sea, so that at the point where sky and water blend both are of the same deep blue and there is no horizon at all. One feels as if he were looking on a celestial city suspended in the sky. The bay, as beautiful as Naples', is fittingly known as Golfo degli Angeli, the Gulf of the Angels. Watching over the harbor from a seaside chapel is the Lady of Bonaria, a beautifully jeweled Madonna who, according to legend, in the year 1370 rose from the sea holding a lighted candle. Her nautical delivery, like the origins of the Sicilian Madonnas of Tyndari and Trapani, is a Christian adaptation of the pagan myth of Venus' aquatic birth.

In contrast to the softer Sicilians who are partial to such female patronesses, Sards ordinarily favor male saints, and the foppish Efisio notwithstanding, the manlier the better. The saint that interested me most was St. Francis of Lula, the patron of bandits. But my determination to flush him out in the wild tumultuous heart of the island was frowned on by the Sards, unhappily concerned over the world's association of their island with crime. A police official in Cagliari denied there was any such saint, so I showed him my *Guida della Sardegna* which described St. Francis of Lula as "the saint protector of *grassatori* (robbers of money), *banditi*, and *rapinatori* (robbers of animals)." The book spoke of a ten-day novena in honor of the saint, beginning the following week. The policeman shrugged his shoulders and said no more; clearly it was my affair. I took a bus.

It had a pretty hostess-interpreter, two drivers, and an assortment of saints dangling over the steering wheel for protection from road mishaps and bandits. Since buses go anywhere on the island in a day, one is never separated from comfortable accommodation. To the lazy traveler they have one fault—they are always off at the crack of dawn. But when you adjust to sleepy departures, the reward is watching the island awaken in a rosy burst of life. Our road companions

were flocks of bleating sheep and donkeys so tiny that the
boots of the men riding them stirred the dust on the road.
Donkeys and women are the Sards' beasts of burden and the
roads were filled with a procession of women carrying sacks
of wheat, bundles of wood, and tethered lambs. Carrying the
world on their shoulders makes Sardinian women, so lovely
and winsome in youth, bent, twisted, and arthritic as old olive
trees in age.

My seat mate was a finely cast blond youth with high
cheeks and arched nostrils, blood echoes of an ancient invasion from the north. In halting English he said that his
name was Fidelio Baronati and that he was a university student going home to Nuoro for a holiday with his family.
We were passing a complex of pink-shaded terra-cotta
houses neatly laid out in square green fields. Welcoming the
opportunity to speak English, my companion told me how
Italy's *Cassa del Mezzogiorno* (Fund for the South), financed
by World Bank loans, had redistributed a third of Sardinia's
arable lands into such small fifteen-acre plots. His face turned
to the window, Fidelio described how foreign technicians had
introduced new methods of soil conservation and fertiliza-
tion, had distributed hybrid seeds, had constructed roads and
built dams to provide electric power and irrigate 150,000
acres of once-barren plains. Near the village of Tonara,
Fidelio pointed to a brand-new building of white mortar
which he said was a hotel, one of a network being built with
foreign loans. "We Sards are a Lazarus people, awakening
from a long malarial sleep," he said softly. "After centuries
of rejection, we feel the civilized world is accepting us at
last."

His own province of Nuoro, said Fidelio, in addition to
being the center of banditry, also was once the center of
malaria. During the mosquito campaign, donkeys, jeeps, and
helicopters were used in the rugged mountain terrain. Country people fired on the exterminators whom they believed
to be police in disguise, and once bandits held up a payroll

truck, killing three guards and escaping with two million lire.

We were passing clusters of nuraghi, those curious pre-historic towers of unmortared stone which are the unsolved riddles of Sardinia. Were they tombs? Watchtowers? Castles for Bronze Age dukes? "The archaeological disputes go on and on and no one knows," said Fidelio. Whatever their purpose, the 3000 dark cones, rising from the land like chimneys of hell, were left by a race of kings.

The bus stopped frequently to let people on and off—country people smelling faintly of goat and wearing the dazzlingly bright costumes of their villages. In the St. Efisio procession I had learned to tell where a woman lived by her dress. Rainbow colors are used in infinite combinations. The women of Desulo wore bright red skirts and jackets embroidered in yellow and blue; those of Orgosolo wore dresses of red and blue harlequin triangles. The women of Macomer, twisting wimples about the lower parts of their faces, all seemed to have mumps, and the women of Fonni, folding their hands, under embroidered aprons, all appeared pregnant. By far the most curious were the girls of Tempio who, swathing themselves in bolts of black silk with lacy white wimples and dickeys, looked like flirtatious nuns.

The men, too, have their splendor, though with less variation. The most common male costume includes billowing white linen trousers, kiltie skirts of black goatskin, red waistcoats, and long caps which flop over the side of the head. Older men look like sedate penguins. The goatskin tunics of the men from Fonni are lined in red, and flare roguishly outward like an inverted lily. The young men of Teulada wear high Elizabethan ruffs and black skirts under which protrude dainty white lace petticoats. Perhaps their flat Spanish-type hats redeem them, for on horses they appear fiercely, barbarically male.

Looking at the faces of the aged one sees, limned by time, the uncompromising character of the landscape. Girls, pretty as small pink dark dolls with sometimes slanting eyes and black hair, grow into gaunt women, often with mustaches on their upper lips. Youths, wiry, virile, and brooding as satyrs, season like leather into a hard-brown toughness. Sards do not laugh easily, and when they do one understands what is meant by "sardonic," a word which comes from the Latin *Sardonius,* or Sardinian. The mirth is cool, scornful and never abandoned. In repose Sard faces have an inscrutability which recalled the Indians of my Wisconsin boyhood. I found no softness in any Sard, but I felt a great deal of gentleness.

Gentleness? These are the people to whom banditry is a way of life. The term is, of course, loosely used. Let me emphasize at once that Sardinian banditry has had no effect on non-Sards for more than ten years. Nor does it have a political complexion like the roisterings of Sicily's Giuliano. The banditry of the island is a never-ending internal warfare rising out of her history. Sardinian history is a long procession of invasions: Carthage (in 450 B.C.), Greece, Rome, Pisa, Genoa, Spain, Piedmont, France, Austria, united Italy. All have invaded and ruled. Strangely diverse peoples have inhabited the island. As the invasions continued, they abandoned the coastal plains for the barren mountains where they fought one another for survival. Geography and history have left a heritage of ancient feuds. A vendetta among hill tribes, a feud between shepherds—it is all banditry of a sort.

The smell of Nuoro is the smell of goats; one notices it on the bus even before arrival. Much of the architecture is in Mussolini's hideous neo-classic style. But the town is surrounded by gray granite mountains of an Olympian splendor. In his family Fiat, Fidelio drove me to the top of the most famous mountain, the Ortobene.

At its foot is the simple white Chapel of the Solitude, the tomb of the only Sard to gain international fame. She is Grazia Deledda, a plain, dark little woman whose novels about the troubled and violent Nuoresi won her the Nobel prize for literature in 1926. From the chapel the road climbed through forests of cork oaks which, recently barked, looked like lewd red-stockinged thighs. Under their low branches men and dogs battle wounded boars by day and bandits conclave by night. We ascended dizzily around hairpin ledges to the wind-swept summit where, on a jut of rock, stands a great iron statue of *Il Redentore*, Christ the Redeemer, the patron of Nuoro. It is a passionately romantic Christ, both Hellenic and Byronic, a savagely Herculean symbol of the fierce pagan-Christian soul of the island. Standing at the giant feet of Christ we looked down on clusters of villages with names beginning with "O"—Oliena, Ornani, Orune, Orgosolo—where bandits live. These were the villages I intended to visit.

"I do not think you should go to Orgosolo," Fidelio said. "The people are desperate and dangerous. Go to Oliena where the people will receive you well. You will see there a curious comedy of Lysistrata. But not Aristophanes. Our political comedies are written by priests." He explained: "In Sardinia we have three political parties: the Christian Democrats who are the party of the priests, the Communists, and the *Partito Sardo* which is fighting for a Sardinian autonomy like Sicily's. Because the men divide their votes between the Communists and the Sardos, the women, voting as the priests tell them, win the elections for the Christian-Democrats. Women are ordered by the priests not to sleep with husbands who vote against the Church. Men denied the tenderness of women feel a fierce loyalty for each other. They blame the priests for all their troubles and they do not go to church."

Fidelio gave me a letter to a barber who was his friend and the next morning, a Sunday, I went to Oliena. On the bus I was haunted by a presence of Spain. Two black-shawled old ladies were a Goya; a sad-faced shepherd boy in a sheepskin cloak was a Murillo. Some men began to sing. The leader, a basso, rumbled like Boris Godunov and the dissonant Algerian wail of his song chilled my blood.

On its mountainside Oliena seemed to be crumbling away in the morning's heat. The bus stopped on a dusty square and

there I found the shop of Antonio, the barber. He was a
good-looking young fellow with a bright and untroubled
face—a rare thing in Sardinia—and an easy and hearty
warmth. "I shall be honored if you will be a guest in my
house," he said. "Of course, it will not be American cooking," he apologized. "It will be kitchen *Sardo*." He took me
to a bar for coffee and Strega and asked what I would like
to do. I said I would like to go to Mass. He frowned and
said, "Very well, I shall meet you in the square when it is
finished."

The square outside the church was filled with loitering
men, old ones in the black-and-white penguin costumes,
younger men in green moleskin or corduroy and golf-style
caps as flat as stove lids. The church was filled with women,
dressed alike in pleated woolen skirts and black-fringed
shawls embroidered with an Oriental richness of flower de-
signs. There were only four men: myself, the priest, an adult
acolyte in a corduroy suit, and a bridegroom standing in red-
faced embarrassment beside the bride whom he had just taken
in marriage. Women gathered the collection.

"In Oliena only the women believe in God. The men do
not," Antonio said when we met. He took me to his home,
hidden behind a stone wall in a garden of pomegranate trees.
We drank wine and nibbled at the agreeably acid pomegranate berries while Antonio's wife and two aged aunts
cooked food in outdoor ovens. The table was set for three:
Antonio, his younger brother, Franco, and myself. The meal
began with *carta musica*, great discs of crisp unleavened
bread splashed with cool red wine. We ate *cosciotto di cin-
ghiale*, a wild boar marinated in aromatic wine, and lamb
roasted in thyme and myrtle which Antonio called an *Agnus
Dei*, "Lamb of God." There were wines, desserts, coffee, and
aqua vitae. When we were finished Antonio invited me to the
wedding celebration in another part of the town.

Approaching the bridal house, we could hear the monot-
onous music of an accordion and the rhythmic scraping of

men's boots on stone. In a windowless steaming room sweating wedding guests, linked in a large circle with the bride and groom, were leaping up and down and moving slowly to the left, dancing the traditional Olienesi *ballo tondo*. According to Antonio, the dance—mirthless as an Indian rite—had been going on without interruption for two hours. After a time the groom invited some male guests into an upper chamber where in the dimming twilight we gathered around the bridal bed which was decorated with two long white candles and several ears of fertility corn. Quiet-footed, lovely voiceless women served us voluptuous sweets to eat and drink. So modulated it was, so controlled. What could excite these people?

The celebration was interrupted when a boy at his Sunday games in an olive grove a short distance from the matrimonial house found the freshly shot body of a man and spread the alarm. The next day the Cagliari papers headlined another *Vendetta di Banditi*. The victim was a forty-five-year-old farmer, and the pious women of his family arranged for his body to be taken into the church. But only women attended the funeral on Tuesday. The men gathered in the square outside, muttering that the priest had taken advantage of a helpless corpse. When the coffin was borne from the church on the shoulders of women, the men fell into line and followed it to the cemetery fence, and there they watched as the priest and the women saw the dead man into his grave. "The cemetery belongs to the women," one man said. "No man goes there until he is carried."

The next day, without telling anyone, I took the bus for bandit-ridden Orgosolo. The road leading more deeply into the mountains was patrolled by guards with police dogs. About halfway a police jeep armed with tommy guns waited to escort us over the rough and narrow roads. Two weeks before a postal bus had been held up and robbed of a million lire.

The bus unloaded in Orgosolo near a police barracks. I

inquired when the bus departed and was told in two hours, at five o'clock. The dusty limestone houses were like a huddle of caves dug into a yellow mountain. There was no green anywhere. Skeletal dogs nuzzled the sewage which flowed in the streets. I had seen people get off the bus, but now as I walked up the street I saw only a pair of armed policemen with a dog. Still I had a feeling, like walking through a forest of hidden animals, that I was being closely watched. I turned about quickly and saw faces draw back into windows and doors. Looking up a narrow alley I saw some barefoot women sitting like mendicants in clouds of flies outside their doors, spinning a bit of wool or nursing a baby. There was not the sound of a single voice. I saw a sign, *Alimentari,* and entered a dark, sour-smelling cavern where a silent woman sold me some hard bread, a chunk of dry salami and a half-liter of wine. These I carried to the edge of the town, down a hill to a church and a blessed patch of grass upon which I rested and ate.

On the wall of the church seven years ago the townspeople had discovered the crudely printed names of thirty-six persons doomed to death. Despite round-the-clock patrols and curfews, the murders have continued on schedule. On cemetery tombstones I read the record:

"Give peace, Oh, Jesus/to the soul of/Francesco Cuchedda /policeman of public security/exemplary citizen/affectionate father/stolen from the affection of his wife/and of his tender children/by an assassin's hand."

"In vain the little/Luisa waits her/father Nicolo Moro's return/fallen victim/of a brother's hate."

"Prize with glory/Oh, Lord/the beautiful and pious soul/ of Luigi Peddo Cancellu/fervent Christian/earnest citizen/ stolen by a cruel hand/in his best age."

The cemetery seemed filled with the bones of men—and of women, too—who had died *tragicamente* by a *mano assassina.*

The church bell began to clang nervously and I saw that it

was nearly five o'clock. I climbed up into the town and hurried through the silent street to the police barracks. Some men and boys were gathered there to watch with interest my arrival. I soon found out why.

The bus had left a quarter-hour early. The police commandant was in a rage and seemed to blame me for my dilemma. The shadows of dusk were already falling and I knew that I had to get out of Orgosolo before nightfall. I asked the commandant if I might hire a car. He said the only car in the town belonged to the priest. I walked swiftly back down to the church. I found the priest, a Benedictine from Tuscany. Tall, lean, and bearded, in his white robe he looked like an El Greco St. Jerome. He listened and then walked back with me to the commandant. After a soft-voiced conversation between the two men, the priest told me his car was known and it would be quite safe for his driver to take me to Nuoro, a distance of about twenty miles. The car appeared, a tiny Topolino station wagon driven by a strong Tuscan youth named Hugo. As we drove away, the priest's hand reflexed to the silver crucifix on his robe and his lips moved silently.

Movement at least was reassuring, even if my chauffeur was not. "It is a favorite road with bandits," he said. Building up his own heroism, he added, "No one travels here without a police escort." I sat stiffly beside him, noting two saints on the dashboard and a Virgin on the key ring. We met patrolling policemen but the distance between them seemed agonizingly long. A man with a gun gave me a bad moment, but it was only a hunter. Finally, Nuoro appeared in the twilight like a constellation of stars beneath us, and I relaxed. Soon I was hobnobbing with the strolling evening crowds, no longer minding the smell of goat, for by this time I was smelling the same way.

In the morning I was moving again, this time in a caravan of five buses of pilgrims on their way to the shrine of St. Francis, the saint of bandits. The trip to Lula, about twenty-two miles as the crow flies, took two hours over the winding mountain roads. From the squalid village of Lula the pilgrims, carrying candles, moved up the mountain like a long and endless snake. I fell in, padding ankle-deep in dust. At the top of the mountain we crossed into a vast green-forested bowl encircled by gray peaks. A path descended gently down to the sanctuary, a plain squatting structure of stone with a red tile roof. The area was as alive as an insect colony. Around the church was a larger circle of *cumbessias*, tiny one- and two-room huts in which affluent pilgrims lived during the ten-day *festa*. Those without huts lived in tents or caves in the surrounding hills or slept in the open. Skins of lambs and kids hung about and brightly hued laundry flapped from trees and bushes. Between the circle of huts and the church were rows of beer and wine stalls, and vendors offering food, religious objects, toys and an endless variety of sweets and nuts. Musicians played everywhere and circles of men, locked in each other's arms, solemnly danced the *ballo tondo*.

Through opened doors came a priest's high-pitched voice. I pushed my way into the dark grotto-like chapel. Inside were women in the bright costumes of Nuoro, Oliena, Orgosolo, and other towns I did not recognize, and many widows in black. There were the crippled and maimed, hoping for a miracle. A miracle had been reported the day before; an eight-year-old boy, dumb from birth, had spoken his first words, *"Grazie, San Francesco,"* and the event had excited the crowds. Most disturbing were the vast numbers of one-eyed men and women, victims of the African eye disease, trachoma, which afflicts so many Sards. Many were mumbling prayers in an inarticulate monotone which rose and fell like moaning. The priest, young and dark, was angry. "There's no need to push," he scolded. "St. Francis has been here three hundred years and he's not going to run away now. So stop behaving like Communists!" A group of swarthy unshaven men in the back roared with laughter.

Not until the Mass was over could I see the saint. He was

a large burly figure in a glass case surrounded by candles and lilies. His brown Franciscan robes were caked with dust and his brutish head was thrown back in a sort of ecstasy, giving him the appearance of a deformed man, a hunchback. His beard-covered face was dark and angry and a hand bearing red stigmata clutched a cross as if it were a dagger. I tried to associate this fierce anti-Francis with the gentle Umbrian who talked with birds and "Sister Moon." Obviously, the bandits created their patron in the image which they cherished of themselves, a rough and violent man capable of brutality. Men and women were moving in a procession before the image, kneeling, kissing the glass, dropping currency offerings, weeping as if they were being reunited with an old friend.

Outside, the refreshment tents were booming. I entered one in which three young musicians were playing on a harmonica, an accordion, and a sort of Jew's harp called a *trunfa*. Immediately they played *Oh! Susanna* in my honor, and followed it with a series of bloodcurdling "Indian" yells. A gaunt youth with a knife-scarred face started to dance. Others joined him and soon the whole tent seemed stricken with a seizure of convulsions. The accordionist's veins stood out like a blacksmith's and the harmonica player fell on a table, his legs dancing wildly in the air. Some men began to sing and the words were:

> *The girls of St. Francis*
> *Go to church to find men,*
> *But they won't find men in church,*
> *They'd better come out here. . . .*

I was being served drinks which the waiter said had been paid for. When I asked to know my host I was introduced to a sober fellow standing in a corner watching. He wore the boots and moleskin trousers of a shepherd and one of the stove-lid caps. When I tried to buy him a drink, he would not hear of it. "When I am in America I will be your guest," he said. On such terms, as both of us knew, Sardinian hospitality was a one-way street. He was a shepherd named Giusto Vanni and he was camping in a cave nearby. When he invited me to eat with him I accepted, for I was ready to leave the tumult. We climbed through fields of white asphodel which covered our trousers with its sticky orange pollen. The cave under a rock bluff was dark from smoke and smelled sourly of cheese-making. My host went out and returned shortly with a freshly slaughtered carcass of a lamb. He hung the skin over the door to dry, and the white stomach, knotted at both ends, from the ceiling of the cave. He explained that he would use the stomach's contents of digestive juices and freshly suckled milk later as a cheese culture. As the lamb sputtered on the spit, we drank heavy red wine and talked of America. "Is it true," Giusto asked, "that in America men can marry more than one woman?"

"Not at one time," I said.

"But if a man tires of one he can divorce her and marry another," he said. "America is a civilized land."

The lamb was crisp and wondrously tender. As we digested under a tree, Giusto told me the history of the sanctuary below. "More than three hundred years ago a bandit was fleeing from the police," he said. "A vision of St. Francis guided him to a cave in which he hid while the policemen passed by. To show his gratitude to the saint for saving his life, the bandit built a small chapel over the cave. The church was built later."

I said I found it incredible that the mild and childlike St. Francis should be the patron of bandits. Giusto told the story of St. Francis receiving "with loving kindness" three murderous robbers, befriending them with food and drink and finally converting them into friars. Except for some minor embroidery, his version was the same as the one in *The Little Flowers of St. Francis*. "We are all God's sinners, we are all bad," said Giusto. "Thieves are sinners persecuted by men and hence especially loved by Jesus and his saints."

After the turbulent Nuoresi, the relaxed, easygoing people of Sassari province, in the northern part of the island, were a welcome relief. The city of Sassari, a center of culture and learning, is the home of Italy's President, Antonio Segni. It rests on a shining pate of a mountain, surrounded by a halo of olive groves, and the ascent is most memorably made by night when the silver olive leaves shimmer in heavenly ghostliness. Sassari has a fine museum, a university noted for its medical school, and the only skyscraper in Sardinia. The town is an excellent base from which to explore the most picturesque province in Sardinia. A short drive into a rocky wilderness took me to several *nuraghi*, and to two lonely twelfth-century Pisan basilicas. These great temples striped black-and-white like prisoners' suits and wonderfully frescoed inside, stand in isolated splendor, abandoned to bats and crows which rail at visitors from the towers.

It is a half-hour's train ride from Sassari to Alghero, a wind-swept, sea-washed fishing town settled by the Catalonians in the fourteenth century and still Spanish in character. The town and its mighty sea wall are built of glowing limestone. In the spring it is covered by a thick orchid-colored rock flower called *bella di giorno*. Then Alghero is a pink-carpeted bastion of gold rising from the indigo sea like a holy city.

From Alghero I sailed in a rented boat with a hired crew around Capo Caccia, an extraordinary peninsula of iron-red rock rising more than 700 feet out of the sea. Midway in this staggering cliff is a niche for a Madonna to which youths, inspired by derring-do as much as piety, dangle on ropes like monkeys to make their obeisance. At water level the sea has carved out an exotic underworld of grottoes. Great green stalagmites rise from the floor like tree trunks and stalactites descend from the ceiling like organ pipes. Walls of quartz glitter like halls in the Arabian Nights. Here my companions told of ancient revelries involving primitive fishermen and mermaids, and in such an atmosphere it was easy to believe the stories. We emerged from the underworld into a setting sun and, with the sea in flames, steered our boat in and out of a chain of jutting rocks with names like *"Calle d'inferno"* and *"L'ultimo"* while a convoy of angry gulls swooped around the mast. As we sailed away, the cliffs folded behind us into the twilight mists, each taking on its own shade of gray or blue. The scene was like an illustration by Doré and I was hardly surprised when one of my native helmsmen, offering me a cigarette, told me his Christian name was Dante.

The happiest Sardinians are not on Sardinia at all but on a tiny fishing island off its southwest coast called San Pietro. The five-by-three mile island is part of Cagliari province. Its 8000 citizens nearly all live in Carloforte, a harbor town which comes closer than any place I know to an escapist's paradise—for men but not necessarily for women. It is remote—getting there involves still another boat ride—and the island economy is so self-sufficient that no one concerns himself deeply with what goes on in the world. The climate is arid and sunny; the gracious crescent-shaped harbor is the cleanest in Italy, and the sloping pink terra-cotta town, covered with oleanders and bougainvillaea, has a storybook loveliness. It has an opera house and a rich and spontaneous music and art culture.

Perhaps the most amazing thing about Carloforte is that English is widely spoken. Carlofortans tell you that they are not Sards at all but descendants of a colony of Genoese fishermen. Unlike Sards, who have no taste for the sea and little interest in travel, they are rovers. A club of local patriarchs who made their fortune in America meets daily on the quay to gossip about Scollay Square, Telegraph Hill, and a street in Brooklyn inhabited entirely by Carlofortans. The most dapper club member is an old man named Saturnio who, during forty-five years of barbering in San Francisco, profitably played the stock market. Another who owns a restaurant, a fleet of boats and a street of houses, is reported to have made his fortune panhandling in New York.

My host was a professor in the high school, a cultured man who in his youth was a Sardinian football player. With some friends, he took me on an all-day sail around San Pietro, showing me marine scenery more spectacular than that of the Amalfi Coast or Capri. We explored grottoes the color of orchids, so large that our fishermen guides could navigate the sailing boat inside, turn her neatly around and sail her out with the thirty-foot mast only occasionally brushing the ceiling.

We anchored in a sheltered cove where the professor raised a hatch for a table and spread out a picnic of local delicacies. These included cheese-like slabs of *vova di tonno*, which were tunny fish eggs dried and salted in their original sac, and those dark little water porcupines so poisonous to swimmers, known as sea urchins. From the fishermen I learned how to pry them loose from the rocks, shuck them open with a knife and slurp the soft pink pulp inside. We sampled a variety of Sardo wines, including dry *Nuragha*, light rose *Luogodoro*, and golden *Vernaccia*, limpid as sunlight and twice as sweet.

The next day we jogged over rocky donkey paths in a tiny bus to an old fortress known as *Guardamora*. Carlofortans had good reason to "guard against Moors." My companions told me the story of Maria Rosso, one of a thousand islanders, male and female, captured by pirates one night in 1798 and taken to Tunisia as slaves. Intercession by Pope Pius VII and the governments of Russia and Turkey failed to free them, but in 1803 Napoleon was able to negotiate their release. But Maria Rosso did not return. She had become *la favorita* in the harem of the Bey and eventually gave birth to another Bey.

I do not doubt that Maria Rosso was happy in the seclusion of a seraglio, for even today Carlofortan women are as cloistered as nuns. A young fisherman said, "We permit them to enjoy themselves once a year at *carnivale*." I never saw a woman after dark, not even at the farewell party in my honor. The evening was nonetheless a lively one. It included a concert by a local *"maestro,"* a composer known throughout Italy, and an excellent show of paintings by a local artist. There was a hearty community sing, including the final death aria of *La Traviata*, and some lusty dancing of the local *tarbachino*, a quadrille-like whirl in which old men threw aside their canes and turned spry as colts. "In Carloforte, we are all brothers," the professor said, and indeed, watching fishermen whirling with former American capitalists, boat carpenters with shipyard owners, it seemed so.

Old Saturnio hobbled across the room, threw his arm over my shoulder and began to roar, "Ta-ra-ra-boom-da-ay. . . ." I was a boat voyage, a cross-country bus ride, and an airplane flight from Rome, but at that moment I felt very much *inside* "the circuit of civilization."

eight

ISLE OF EXILE

My embarkation for Elba was like a sailing on the Styx. The port was smoky Piombino, a little Pittsburgh of smelting furnaces and slag pyramids. The boat was called *Aethalia,* or "burning isle," a name given by awed Greek sailors to the smoldering island which lit up the ancient seas by night.

Melancholy vanished with bright sun and shimmering water. The hour-long voyage was a gay preview of life on the island seven miles out on the Tyrrhenian Sea. Dark-spectacled sirens in red shorts, snug tricot shirts, and mandarin hats clung tightly to their masks and snorkels. Walnut-skinned sportsmen carried bamboo fish-guns and black rubber fins. Peering through a hatch one could see the hold, filled with sports cars and a dozen red cows.

The passengers, so like tourists from outer space, made a bizarre cargo to be traveling backward into time. The Latins called Aethalia, "Ilva," which in time became Elba, and the fires which frightened the Greeks were the smelting furnaces of the Etruscans whose mines have been yielding iron without interruption for four thousand years. Because Elban fuel has long since been used up, ore is no longer smelted on the island and today it is the furnaces of Piombino which light up the heavens at night.

In the mists ahead the island took shape. It was a world of Genesis which the *Aethalia* was approaching, the earth on the fourth day of creation: barren mountains rising from the sea and a jagged skyline without signs of life.

A town appeared finally, Cavo, the first port of call, an elegant colony of Italian and English summer villas set in gardens around a crescent harbor reminiscent of the Bahamas. The comparison was helped by a bright fishing fleet and Harry Belafonte singing *Waltzing Matilda* on a harbor jukebox. The ship followed the shore, a green and gray virgin landscape slashed by the red bleeding gashes of open iron mines. Passengers crowded to portside, listing the ship so that the bawling cattle below had to be herded starboard for balance. The cows, alas, were the most unfortunate of passengers. I had assumed they were headed for green island pastures, but an Elbano standing beside me on the deck said they were on their way to butchers to provide meat for hotels and restaurants. Because of lack of refrigeration, meat is brought to Elba alive and eaten upon slaughtering.

Making a sweeping portside turn, the *Aethalia* suddenly faced a golden city rising from cobalt waters. This was Portoferraio, the capital city built on a cliff curling into the sea, its back wall a rock bastion topped by a lighthouse and an impregnable fort called Stella, or "star."

From the front, Portoferraio—the name means "port of iron"—was a neat and shining toy Naples. The green-shuttered houses curving around the horseshoe harbor might have been stage flats for a ballet or opera. The façade is a deception, however, as I quickly discovered by stepping through one of its arches. Behind lay a bustling port city with 12,000 citizens all of whom appeared to be living outdoors. Since the town is a concave and vertical shell sweeping steeply from blue sea to blue sky, the streets are golden staircases, up and down which the population scurries as gaily as heaven-climbers in a medieval painting of paradise.

It is a heady experience to climb up one of these golden flights to the top of the city and look for the first time over Elba's dazzling vista of sea, city, and mountains. The basic colors of Elba are the blue of sea and sky, the red of iron and the green of the mountains burned in summer to a deep live bronze. But variations and combinations are limitless. An American artist on the island was beside himself. "It's not enough to see all the colors of the rainbow," he said. "There are colors here I swear don't exist." The city glows pink from iron in stone and golden from lime in mortar. The sea changes from aquamarine to a silvery Prussian blue that becomes almost black, according to depth, vegetation and color of the bottom. Loading derricks hover over the port like the antennae of prehistoric insects, bright fishing sails ruffle lazily on a becalmed sea and from two tall chimneys of the island power plant spirals of dark smoke float like airborne serpents toward the hazy mountains beyond. Watching the changing panorama before me, I had the feeling I was in a theatre. Shifting lights caused mountains to slide in and out of the mists like flats. Though the summer sun was dazzling, a veil in the light made everything seem to be seen through a dream.

On this eyrie above sea and town in the Villa Mulini (Small Mills) lived the most famous Elban resident of all time, Napoleon Bonaparte. The ex-emperor of the world arrived on May 5, 1814, and announced at once to the curious crowds, "I will be a good father to you; be good children to me." He had done his homework well, for he captivated everyone with his knowledge of the exile kingdom of eighty-six square miles. His first act was to design an Elban flag, a white banner with a red diagonal containing three golden bees representing peace, harmony, and industry. There was no doubt that he was serious about the industry. Napoleon found the sun-drenched Elbans a *dolce far niente* people. Their mines were idle, their hills were barren, and the whole island smelled badly. Writing proclamations every night, he roused the becalmed natives to social revolution. The emperor's first order was to build latrines. He levied a cleanliness tax to pay for a sanitation system. He built roads, harbors, and forts, he improved the water supply, introduced potatoes and grains, planted chestnut, olive and mulberry trees on the naked hills, laid out salt marshes and began silk and tuna-fishing industries. The result was whirlwind prosperity. Three months after the emperor's arrival, Elbans formally celebrated his birthday with dancing, feasting, and fireworks.

While he whipped his subjects to a frenzy of activity, Napoleon studied the seas in his villa above the city, watching through telescopes the movements of British warships detailed to prevent his escape, searching the horizon for a neutral ship. At San Martino, two miles from Portoferraio, he built a country villa. On the ceiling of the salon he had painted a sentimental symbol of the empress and himself, a pair of doves tying lovers' knots with blue ribbons in their beaks.

The emperor had accepted his exile on condition that his wife and son would join him. But they never arrived, and other women came instead. Napoleon's mother, Letizia, and his beautiful and scandalous sister, Pauline Borghese, who had posed for the nude Canova *Venus*, reigned over his court in the modest Villa Mulini. The young Countess Maria Walewska also came with Napoleon's illegitimate son, but old women with searching eyes seemed to be behind every door and she was driven away within two days.

The neutral ship never appeared. Napoleon's Empress, Marie Louise, was busy singing madrigals with General Neipperg, whom she later married, and the Emperor of Austria held Napoleon's small son, his own grandson and the King of Rome, a prisoner in Vienna. It has been said that if Napoleon's wife and son had come to Elba, Waterloo would have been avoided.

During a nighttime carnival celebration in February 1815, Napoleon boarded a ship named the *Inconstant,* slipped past the British warships and went to Paris to be crowned a second time. His brief visit was the island's one moment of historical glory, and Elbans will not permit you to forget it. Hotels are named Bonaparte, Napoleone, Walewska, and Désirée. The bay where Pauline bathed is the Spiaggia Paolina and in the village of Procchio the Ristorante Renzo advertises, "Here Napoleon has never eaten."

Today's Elbans are again like the carefree natives who exasperated Napoleon. Gentle and peaceable, they fish, mine iron, quarry granite, and make wine, all at a leisurely pace. Most of all they enjoy life in their abundant sun. There are no beggars, and unlike other Italian islands, there is no crime. Police hearings are concerned with goats eating neighbors' vegetables or drunken singing after midnight. Despite their seemingly sybaritic lives, Elbans are the puritans of Italy, with a modesty easily shaken by tourist antics. They were severely jolted during a recent winter by a visit of Caitlin Thomas, widow of poet Dylan Thomas, whose self-indulgent Elban memoirs were published in the book *Leftover Life to Kill.*

The easiest way to meet these tranquil folk is to join the early-evening *passeggiata,* or walk, in Portoferraio's outdoor living room, the Piazza Cavour. A jukebox flooded the square with American popular songs. Youths and girls wore identical striped fishermen's shirts and tight cowboy pants, and on buxom female and lean male *derrières* were the labels of American manufacturers. Prancing arm-in-arm, the boys and girls were singing words they didn't understand, along with Frankie Laine, Belafonte, and Pat Boone. Mothers, clacking over cobblestones on their wooden *zoccoli,* watched zealously that decorum was maintained.

In appearance Elbans are a catalogue of history's invasions.

The true Elban is like his Corsican neighbor: dark, short, and powerfully built on short legs like a Mediterranean donkey. There are curly haired blond Elbans with Norman or Greek blood, and small, wiry, dark types with Neapolitan or Spanish ancestors. On me, a stranger, all of them flashed wide smiles, as if I were an old friend. Tourists, mostly continental Italians and Germans, crowded cafés and souvenir shops to buy chunks of iron ore, statues of Napoleon, glassware, and embroidery. Sports shops did a brisk trade in all the *sub-aqua* paraphernalia, water skis, and even underwater cameras. Through this bustle one evening passed a black-and-gold horse-drawn hearse followed by black-robed mourners carrying torches. The crowd opened a way for the eerie funeral procession while Johnnie Ray sang *Just A-Wearyin' for You*.

Elba is an outdoor place. After obeisances to Napoleon's houses, there are no more monuments to waste your time. It is wise to leave Portoferraio and settle in one of the villages, many of which offer the most modern and comfortable accommodations. If a view is important, there is the Fonte Napoleone in Poggio, more than a thousand feet above the sea. This nineteenth-century villa has a high-ceilinged Victorian elegance, Flemish tapestries and hi-fi Beethoven symphonies in the garden. Its posh guestbook includes the signatures of the Duke and Duchess of Windsor, Rudi and Consuelo Crespi, and the late Dimitri Mitropoulos.

Preferring the sea, I stayed at the Désirée on the Gulf of Spartaia. This spanking new hotel owned by Tancredi Pasero, the famous opera basso, stands in wondrous isloation at the water's edge, against a background of empty green hills. For seven dollars a day I had a room and bath with excellent meals. The Désirée's high quality is equaled by other new hotels such as the Golfo in nearby Procchio and La Primula in the fishing town of Marciana Marina, neither of which, however, has the Désirée's splendid isolation.

Day and nights, the never-ceasing surf rolled toward my

windows, mostly softly, sometimes violently. Each morning I was roused from its lull by a donkey's nerve-shattering bray, followed by a series of unearthly staccato sneezes like a rusty pump. It was a week before I finally encountered the beast tethered to a fig tree a half-mile away. Under my balcony closed beach umbrellas stood rooted in the sand like spears; as the sun mounted they opened, one by one, like gaudy morning glories. Sails winged past like swans. Elba's deep and protected harbors make excellent yachting ports, and one midsummer weekend I counted more than thirty yachts flying the flags of fifteen countries. In and out of the little bay, the snorkel tubes of underwater swimmers floated by like submarine periscopes.

In the afternoons I swam out of the bay, exploring coastal cliffs and grottoes carved by the sea, as wondrous as Capri's. Deep dark caves in which the surf roared like thunder were too perilous to explore, but others were quietly lapping caverns with white sand floors lit by shimmering silvery lights. In one of these dreamlike Homeric chambers one lazy afternoon I found a northland siren asleep with her legs in the water. From this pagan encounter I swam in a burst of energy out to the Madonna dei Marinai, a bleached madonna patroness of sailors set on a rock in the sea, where prayers can be delivered only by stouthearted swimmers and oarsmen.

For seeing the island an automobile is necessary. Though Elba is small (nineteen by six and a half miles at its widest points) the primitive trails need time to cover. In Portoferraio I rented a little Fiat and found a chauffeur-guide named Speranto, which means "Hope." Hope, who had driven for Americans before, was wildly addicted to American "peanuts jam," and he begged me to secure some for our picnics. On most of our excursions we were accompanied by Hope's friend, Attilio, a high-spirited young Elban who had lived for a year in England and who was a repository of American popular music learned from phonograph records. Our first excursion for the purposes of orientation, was to the summit

of Mount Perone, one of Elba's highest peaks. Elba is part of
the Tuscan archipelago, and we stood as if on Mount Ararat
after the flood, looking down on mountains rising from the
water, named Pianosa, Capraia, Monte Cristo, Giglio, and
far to the west, the great shadow of Corsica. Elba and her
villages were spread around us like a small-scale relief map:
the high wild coast to the west, the central agricultural valleys,
and far in the east, the dark mining zone. Villages are also
of three types: coastal fishing, mining and inland agricultural
and wine towns.

With Hope at the wheel, guiding our doll-sized *macchina*
with nerve-shattering aplomb, and Attilio singing in the back
seat, we made day-long expeditions which included all three.
My favorite town was the old fishing center of Marciana
Marina, less than five miles up the coast from the Désirée.
It is built about a sweeping arc in the sea, guarded by Medi-
cian watch towers and nearly always crowded with a fleet
of brightly painted schooners. On its quay is an avenue of
Tamarici, a mimosa-like Mediterranean tree with thick foli-
age clusters that absorbs night moisture and drips it like rain
through the heat of the day. The trees are draped with red
fish nets and the fishermen repairing them look like huge
spiders spinning webs. The old houses in a variety of pastel
shades are covered in summer with red oleanders and purple
bougainvillaea. Here during the siesta hours you may hear
the explosion of a scooter motor, the whimper of a child or
the scrape of a pair of wooden soles on stone; otherwise
the early afternoon is one long hush.

In Marciana we rented a small fishing boat with an out-
board motor and put-put-putted along the cliffs and sea caves.
High above us, looking like rows of swallow nests, were
other caves, hollowed by Germans during the war for gun
installations and lookout stations, and now used by natives
for storing fish nets and as latrines. Our destination was the
Cape of San Andrea, Elba's northwest corner, where a young
Florentine had set a record in *sub-aqua* fishing by spearing

fifty-six kilos (123 pounds) in three hours. Hope introduced me to the sport. Wearing fins, masks, snorkels, and wielding five-tined spears, we resembled nothing so much as torturing devils in the *quatrocento* Last Judgments of Tuscan churches. Kicking up his black fins, Hope dived like a penguin, circled under water smoothly and silently as a shark, preying on fish named *obrina, dentice, occhiata,* and a blue-finned red-striped beauty called *pappagallo,* or parrot. My own fishing was not so fruitful, for I was too busy exploring a fantastic and iridescent world. Among rocks thirty feet down I saw schools of silver fish in a brilliant turquoise light, tiny pink clams clustered like hyacinth blossoms, and silver sea grass swaying like fields of windswept wheat. I also saw the menacing terrors of Elban waters, great *meduse,* or stinging jellyfish, with their foot-long tendrils floating like pink hair, and, growing on the rocks like puffballs, the nasty black *ricci,* or sea urchins whose stings are so unpleasant to swimmers.

From Marciana Marina we drove up through the great chartreuse fans of Elba's rich vineyards to the hilltop towns of Poggio and Marciana Alta. Elba's double villages, usually named Marina and Alta, date back to the Middle Ages when pirates made a habit of dropping in on coastal villages for beach parties and it was necessary to hide the womenfolk in the upper levels. Driving through a chestnut forest, we came upon the *Fonte Napoleone,* a spring at which, according to a bronze tablet, "Napoleon, his wings broken from hundreds of glorious flights, came for new strength and after drinking left in good health to begin again his fatal path."

Marciana Alta is a half-moon of red-tiled roofs curving about a mountainside. Behind its façade is a fascinating labyrinth of stairs and an enchanting little square hardly larger than a stage setting for *Cavalleria Rusticana.* On house stoops, behind bright pots of begonias, amaryllis, and geraniums, black-robed women gossiped softly and under the magnolia trees four old men played *passatella* on the face of a white

marble sun dial set in the square as a card table. At a table
outside a tiny bar we sampled island vintages. Other than
iron ore, wine is Elba's only export product. The most noble
is cool white Cerboni, comparable to mainland Frascati and
Verdicchio. We also drank golden Gasparri, Elba's substantial
and solid *vino ordinaire*, as well as a heavy red dessert wine
called Aleatico and a syrupy white Moscato, both of which
proved too sweet for my taste. Attilio told stories of Elba's
mountain folk, including the tale of a doctor who became
too ardently solicitous of some lady patients. One day the
doctor found his donkey tied outside his door wearing a card
with the farewell greeting, *"Arrivederci!"*

Attilio said, "The cheekie chap whiffed the drift and blew
town on his ass." As we rolled back down toward the sea
he sang, "Why can't the English learn to speak?"

From Marciana Marina to Portoferraio an excellent black-
top highway—built on a roadbed laid by Napoleon—curls
serpent-like over cliffs, connecting the hotels and villas of
Elba's fashionable north shore. Around its curves during the
summer months, Mercedes-Benzes, Jaguars, and Alfa-Romeos
shriek like whistling birds, carrying the high-born and rich
from one English-speaking cocktail party to another. Dress
for these affairs is bright pastel décolleté for women, ascots,
rope soles, and gay linen trousers for men. Drinks are martinis, "Americanoes," and such exotic inventions as gin,
grappa, and honey served with spices. Conversations deal with
motorcars, boats and fishing, the catastrophe of the lower-
class invading Elba and, during my visit, the art shows at two
rival hotels, the Fonte Napoleone, which was exhibiting the
work of a Florentine professor and the Désirée, which was
showing the paintings of an American artist. At each party
I picked up invitations to several others, so that my Elban
holiday became a pyramid of cocktails. At one I met the
wife of an Englishman who is a year-round Elban resident.
When I asked what her husband did with his time she looked
at me and said with chilling hauteur, "He shoots." Since

there is nothing to shoot but pigeons and the small larks and thrushes which the natives hunt with enthusiasm, the Englishman's sporting life did not appear an exciting one.

More industrious than the English were American expatriates Paul West, an ex-*Time* magazine executive, and his wife Peggy. Elbans are neither expert nor hard-working farmers, but the Wests' restoration of a two-century old farmhouse which German soldiers shot to ruins, and their energetic coaxing of olives and grapes from thirty acres of marginal lands have won them the respect of everyone on the island. "We live in a land of good neighbors," Paul West said. "The people are loyal, and so honest they never lock their doors. But they leave the key in the door to tell you they are not at home. They are too reserved and proud to thank you for a courtesy, but a day or two after you've done them a favor they will leave a bottle of wine or some newly baked bread at your door."

The lively West household, named *Picchiaie*, clamored with parakeets, parrots, a flock of guinea hens, a dog, and *Napoleone Seconde*, an amiable three-foot high Sardinian donkey. The house has an olive-shaded terrace which looks down on Portoferraio's shimmering indigo bay and on the softly veiled mountains beyond. There, dining one day on breast of guinea hen with truffles and drinking the marvelous white wines, I was seized with an impulse to follow the Wests' escapist example.

But practical research revealed that Elba is no longer a bargain paradise. In the ten years since the Wests settled there, a building boom has increased the costs of building sites as much as 1000 per cent. Since most of the irregular coastline is rugged rock, activity is centered about the beach coves, all of which are small. Procchio is an example. A few years ago this village was a sleepy country crossroads blessed with one of Elba's most beautiful beaches; today it is a large and noisy town with two luxury hotels and vast German tent colonies.

The foreign tourists are a result of the war. In Fascist times rich and noble Roman and Florentine families built summer villas on the tranquil "Capri without people" and maintained an exclusive social life. Well-heeled Milanese who followed were parvenus to be kept at a cool distance. In those days property was absurdly inexpensive and Elbans made docile and cheap servants. But in 1943 German troops occupied the island to work the iron mines and build fortifications everywhere. The sunny sea-washed island made a strong impression on a race addicted to romantic landscapes. After the war they returned as tourists, each year in increasing numbers. Commenting indirectly on the German economy, Paul West said, "At first Germans carried rucksacks, then they came in Volkswagens, and now they all drive Mercedes-Benzes." Swiss, French, and British followed until now tourism surpasses iron and wine as Elba's leading industry.

In spite of the invasion, Elba has remained, except for its beaches, a place of haunting solitude and primitive landscapes. More than one-third of its 30,000 citizens live in Portoferraio and the others are scattered in some twenty villages. Most of the inland areas are as empty and arid as ever. The wild and rugged mining zone in the east is an example. Hope, Attilio, and I spiraled over a new road through a landscape in which figs, olives, and chestnuts grew in untamed abundance. We arrived at Rio Elba, the oldest town of the island and from a distance one of the most handsome. Its tightly fitted concentric curves of houses, only a few shades lighter than the mountain to which they cling, appear as indigenous as lichen on stone. To enter the town is to suffer disillusionment. Rio Elba has a water problem and is the untidiest and smelliest of Elban towns. Garbage, lying in the pinched streets, was nuzzled by dogs and hens, and every alcove was a public latrine. Attilio pointed out a small house which belonged to him, a legacy from his maternal grandmother. "The house is for sale—very cheap," he said. "There is no real estate inflation here. I think it was very thoughtless of my grandmother to live up here instead of down in Procchio."

Directly below on the sea is the sister town of Rio Marina. "The ugliest town on the island," wrote Caitlin Thomas who chose to spend her tortured winter among its miners. It is also the richest, for it is the only Elban town where every able-bodied man is employed. From her loading piers Elba's ore is shipped to the furnaces of Piombino and Genoa. The town itself is a bleeding wound. Naked red earth rises steeply behind its red houses, and red dust covers everything. Piles of scrap iron stand in the public garden. Yet it has an elemental and violent beauty, like a town in Hades washed by a Stygian sea. It was Saturday, both pay-day and half-holiday, and the *birrerie* and *bottiglierie* were booming like Yukon saloons.

We returned to the Désirée by way of Volterraio, a Pisan watchtower on a sharp granite wall rising between the two Rios and Portoferraio, arriving at the peak in time for sunset. Sunset-watching is one of the diversions of Elba. Each evening cars gather at vantage points and people perch on slopes as on theatre tiers. For twenty minutes we blinked into an explosive spectacle. Not until the red sun had sunk into the silver sea was it possible to look toward the blinding west with comfort. Our incidental music was a saccharine violin version of Schumann's *Träumerei* wafted from a car radio. "Like a lousy movie," said Attilio disgustedly. A country boy sold us pine cones as large as pineapples, a dozen for 300 lire. With screeching tires and singing brakes, we flew down the mountain, past German pillboxes in which peasants were storing hay.

At the Désirée I resumed my daily battle with the bartender to *stir* and not shake martinis. I lost, as usual, and drank the milky substance the fellow produced so vigorously. That evening I went with Attilio and Hope to dance calypsos and tangos with some German girls in a brightly spangled tent on the Procchio beach. Later, on the sands where battle-fatigued Roman soldiers convalesced two thousand years ago, we roasted the pine cones until they burst, releasing the nuts inside. Attilio said dreamily, "I wish I had been born in Texas instead of on Elba. I would like to meet a Texas heiress with five thousand cows and much oil." He began to sing softly to himself, "I'm an old cow hand . . ."

The three of us made our last trip together over the sparsely settled south and west coasts. As Elba's north side is fashionable, so the south shore is Bohemian, overrun in summer by French and German campers. A perfect climate makes Elba a campers' paradise. In summer, rain falls perhaps once or twice a month, yet the island is kept fresh by winds so moisture-laden it is difficult to dry a towel in the afternoon. Nights are blanket-cool and the hottest hours are those of early morning before the wind stirs. After nine o'clock the day turns fresh and limpid all at once.

Sociable French campers crowd into their own Club Mediterraneo, a dismal nature colony of tents and straw huts set knee-deep in sand. The club resembles nothing so much as a penal colony. Some of the camp's Gallic diversions proved too merry for the puritanical Elbans, and the police made several raids. It was all settled in amicable Latin fashion, however, when the police chief was made an honorary member of the club.

Our road, the most perilous and undeveloped on the island, clung to a ledge high over the sea. The fiercely beautiful landscape was popular with German campers who, unlike the gregarious French, favor romantic isolation. For a week Hope had promised us Teutonic golden-haired Eves basking nude. From that standpoint the trip was mildly frustrating; the Eves we flushed were all wearing bikinis, but the settings in which they basked were unforgettable. We passed three tiny villages named Cavoli, Seccheto, and Fetovaia. With their curved white beaches, turquoise lagoons and cane bathing huts, they looked like colonies on a Pacific atoll. As on all our journeys, we picnicked on the fruits of the road. Stand-

[15] Germany: With the great-grandson of Richard Wagner and the great-great-grandson of Franz Liszt.

[16] Pilgrims at Loreto.

[17] The Republic of San Marino. Heads in the clouds and a revolution now and then.

[18] Nuraghi of Sardinia. Chimneys of hell left by a race of kings.

[19] St. Efisio crossing Sardinia. He pampered his belly.

[20] Orgosolo. Those in the cemetery died *tragicamente*.

[21] Oliena. Waiting for the priest to unlock the church.

[22] Oliena wedding. After the ceremony a corpse in the olive grove.

[23] Sardinian courting. "In Oliena only the women believe in God."

[24] Sardinia. I was haunted by the presence of Spain and sometimes Mexico.

[25] Lunch in Sardinia. "Hospitality was a one-way street."

[26] Sardinian strollers. The girls were like flirtatious nuns.

[27] Sardinia: a battle of wills.

[28] Portoferraio. Golden staircases for heaven climbers.

[29] Attilio of Elba. "Buick is on his way, won't it be bloody gay?"

ing on Hope's shoulders, swinging a bamboo stalk, Attilio knocked ripe prickly pears from giant cacti, and when we had eaten the pulpy fruit we rubbed road dust on our hands to remove the tiny thorns. We stopped at a vineyard and were busy pickings grapes when Hope shouted, *"Guarda!* Look out!"* A tall farmer we had not seen was climbing down a fig tree, gesticulating toward us. We leaped into the car and Hope started the motor. But the lean Zaccharia of the figs stood in the road blocking our way. "Those aren't my best grapes," he said. "Come with me." His voice was deep and friendly. We got out of the car and followed him to a terrace of vines sagging with gold and russet Biancone grapes. The man picked a dozen heavy pendants and gave them to us. "These," he said, "are grapes!" They were sweet as honey with a warm spicy flavor. The farmer refused to accept anything more than a handshake, and before we drove away he picked some of his ripest figs for us.

Our hazardous motoring came to a halt behind some workmen dynamiting a road-bed through rock. Below was the land's-end village of Pomonte which until one year before had communicated with the rest of the island only by foot, donkey, or boat. Now volunteer workmen were carving out of rock a road to connect with the highways on the north and south shores.

Down in the town barefoot old people warmed themselves silently in the sun, awaiting the arrival of civilization. Women sewing under fig trees heavy with black fruit watched us with eyes sharp as a forest animal's. Even the pigeons were black and seemed to be in mourning. Forming a beautiful design at the water's edge were several tall bleached poles, with booms, ropes and pulleys. These masts without ships were cranes for unloading granite, unchanged from the loading devices used by Caesar's soldiers. Only a donkey's bray broke the ancient stillness.

Yet there were signs that Pomonte was not as remote as it seemed, that at least some aspects of contemporary life had arrived before the road. On its little piazza stood three imposing buildings. There was a white church, a yellow *Posta-Telegrafo-Vendita di Vino* with a large gas Electrolux refrigerator, and a pink headquarters of the *Partito Comunista Italiano-Sezione Pomonte.*

Two rocky foot kilometers farther along the coast is the even more remote town of Chiessi. Here, up to the time of our visit, no automobiles had been seen. From the footpath above we looked down on an enchanting Arcadia. Spread in a thick grove of vineyards and fig orchards were blue, red, and yellow cottages covered with flowering vines. Doorways were draped with onion braids, and red-tiled roofs were spread with drying figs which scented the town with sweetness.

Chiessi has no beach, but a table-smooth granite slab which slopes gently into the water to become a sea floor. Here we splashed and swam with some local boys. Looking back up to the pretty village, it seemed as if we had severed our tie with time and had traveled in some dream spaceship, back to the pastoral and rustic peace of Daphnis and Chloe.

There were, however, familiar sounds to dispel the enchantment: the bone-chilling grind of a pneumatic drill, the ring of a mallet on steel, and an explosion of dynamite. The road was approaching. A bridge was being built over the top of the village and under it new houses for the strangers which the road would bring.

One of the boys announced that the road would be finished in two months. "My brother will buy a Vespa," he said. "Then I will go to the cinema in Marciana."

"My father ordered a Fiat," said another. "Of course, we will go to Portoferraio."

"My father is building three houses," said a third. "When the tourists come we will be rich."

In a shaded lane above I could see two dark-eyed maids, wearing trays of figs like hats, step aside for three mules carrying granite slabs to a building site, and a melancholia settled on my heart. Chiessi was preparing to leap into the twentieth century. I was happy I had arrived before the cars, the tooting buses and the tourists. Beside me Attilio dived into the sea and then climbed from the water on to a jut of rock. In his loudest voice he sang:

La Donna è Mobile
Buick is on his way,
Cinema every day,
Won't it be bloody gay?

nine

FROM BAYREUTH TO SALZBURG

Like the Minnesingers of medieval Europe my companion, an amiable English barrister named Ransom, and I had been hitting the musical trail—hitting it hard and handsomely in his Humber Hawk, named Wolfgang to honor the composer we both like best. Our pursuit had taken us over 9000 miles, fourteen borders, eleven mountain passes, and some forty musical performances. We had heard Strauss operas in Zürich, Mozart operas in Aix-en-Provence, where DDT was sprayed from planes to eliminate competing crickets, and *Carmen* with time off for a bullfight, at Arles. We had listened to Schubert and Brahms chamber music in Prades and, on a hot July night, to Bach's Christmas Oratorio sung by the Vienna Choir Boys at Ansbach. At Bregenz we had endured Johann Strauss's *One Night in Venice* floated on a pavilion in Lake Constance; and in the Swiss town of Fribourg, three thousand male and female yodelers.

Let me say at once in defense of what may seem a maniacal pursuit by a pair of music-crazy fools that what we were doing was not extraordinary. We were meeting familiar faces at every stop, and by midsummer strangers were greeting us like old friends. The most heavily traveled section of the Orpheus trail is a 250-mile stretch of Hitler's *Autobahn* known as "the music run." At opposite ends of this easy drive through green and rolling Bavaria lie Bayreuth and Salzburg, the Giants and the Dodgers of the music league. There is no reason at all for rivalry between the two, since their products are not competitive and neither can begin to meet its demand for tickets. But both are proud and jealous for glory, and the musical war between them is as intense as any fought out at Chavez Ravine.

No medieval lute-picking wanderers-on-foot were so weary and sore as we, rolling over the *Autobahn* toward Bayreuth on an August afternoon. Fortunately, we didn't have to search for a room; one was already reserved in the small apartment of a pair of honeymooners who slept on cots in their kitchen during the festival. Within an hour we were in dinner jackets driving to the Festspielhaus over sweeping chestnut-shaded Siegfried Wagner Allee. This was the boulevard over which in old days the queenly Cosima Wagner, daughter of Franz Liszt, led the procession to the opera in her four-horse carriage, and over which Kaiser Wilhelm rode to the theatre while Tchaikovsky watched from the window of a neighboring house.

Now, riding in the car with us was our friend Friedelind Wagner, granddaughter of the mighty Cosima and daughter of Siegfried, the man after whom the boulevard was named. Her presence made us *Familie Wagner*. The police bowed and trooped alongside, escorting us through the droves of *Zaungäste*, the "fence guests" who were there to watch the parade and not to hear music.

For Wagners are held in awe if not quite in reverence by their fellow citizens. Streets are named after members of the family and after operas. The people know Bayreuth would have no distinction at all if Richard Wagner hadn't settled there in 1870 because his patron, King Ludwig, wanted him in Bavaria.

Many of the ticket holders were studying librettos and carrying inflated rubber cushions. No lady can do these things and be chic; but she can be elegant, and the fence guests had a good show. The lavish finery was not necessarily of the most recent fashion. Old women blinking through *cloisonné* lorgnettes, their vintage lace covered with sequins, had a Victorian grandeur. In contrast a thick-necked industrialist was wearing a white tuxedo with white satin lapels, and his wife had a purple hair rinse and wore a gold brocaded gown. Celebrities included film and music stars and former Nazi big-wheels still alive and out of jail. Royalty was meager— there were reports of visits by the young Duke of Kent and former Queen Marie José of Italy, but the real royalty at Bayreuth was named Wagner.

The afternoon sun still high in the heavens made the evening-clad crowd seem more than ever like a curious tribal gathering. As outside a church, there was no laughter and few raised voices. Germans were terribly conscious that they were about to embark on the four-day sacrament of *Der Ring*.

Wotan's theme rang out over the plaza. The fanfare, played on a balcony of the theatre by a brass octet, was the signal for the congregation to enter the temple. We entered through Wagner's door into a funereal white marble foyer, where a bust of the composer peered out of a potted laurel jungle. The box upstairs was large, with more than twenty chairs. A Junoesque dowager in black satin was seating guests like an imperious dinner hostess. I recognized her from photographs. This was Winifred, the English-born daughter-in-law of Richard Wagner, one of the most enigmatic women of the twentieth century.

In the handsome photograph-filled brochure published by the Wagners we read: "The festivals were called into being by Richard Wagner in 1876; after his death (in 1883) Cosima Wagner, the daughter of Franz Liszt, assumed control. In 1908 Siegfried Wagner succeeded his mother. In 1930 after her husband's death it passed into the hands of Winifred

Wagner and she in turn entrusted it to her two sons, Wieland and Wolfgang, in 1951."

This does not quite tell the whole story.

Way back in 1921, at the home of a Munich piano manufacturer, Winifred Wagner met and was dazzled by the then unknown politician, Adolf Hitler. Through the twenties their friendship grew along with the politician's influence. After the death of both her husband and her mother-in-law in 1930, Winifred Wagner opened the doors of Bayreuth to her friend. Conductor Arturo Toscanini left the festival and never returned.

Bayreuth became a cultural activity of the Nazi hierarchy, and Winifred was the reigning queen of Nazi society. Hitler was a guest at Wagner's château, Wahnfried, and Winifred's four children called him "Uncle Wolf." In July 1934, while Austria's Chancellor Dollfuss was being assassinated in Vienna, Hitler was in Bayreuth listening to *Das Rheingold* from the Wagner family box.

One of Winifred's children matured to disenchantment. Her older daughter, Friedelind, the only Wagner political nonconformist, left Europe before the war and under the sponsorship of Toscanini became an American citizen. In Germany "Uncle Wolf" ordered Winifred's older son, Wieland, deferred from military service so that the Wagner blood would not be lost to Germany. Wieland's first child, a girl born in 1942, was Hitler's godchild; his second, a boy, was called Wolf.

After the war the Bonn government and the American Occupation Forces refused to return Bayreuth to Winifred. Instead they offered it in 1951 to her four children. Wieland and his brother Wolfgang had no money to build lavish naturalistic productions; so Wieland, a part-time painter who had studied the Greek drama, the theories of Freud and Jung, and the lighting principles of Gordon Craig, staged Grandfather's operas with lighting effects on a bare stage. The immediate result was a whooping controversy with traditionalists.

The press was on Wieland's side. When the sound and fury had subsided he was definitely Grandpa's boy. The New York *Times* said of Bayreuth: "Timelessness and spacelessness . . . a stunning achievement." The London *Daily Express* went all out: "Bayreuth has become the matchless untouchable opera house of the world."

Though officially banished from the Bayreuth realm, Winifred Wagner retains her hold over the festival's social protocol. She also keeps her family in turmoil. She does not like her son's productions and she cannot forget that her daughter fled Germany and adopted the enemy during the war.

We waited in silence more reverential than in any cathedral in Europe. I was apprehensive of what lay ahead. Perhaps I should say at once that I am not unreservedly Wagnerian in my musical tastes. My enthusiasm covers only the wondrously human *Die Meistersinger*, the lyrical *Tannhäuser*, and parts of the passionate *Tristan*. I had never been able to sit comfortably through even one evening of the *Ring*.

Now Conductor Joseph Keilbreth raised his stick, the double basses struck their E-flat pedal note. The curtains parted and we were plunged into Wagner's thirteen-hour apocalypse.

The stage was dark and beams of light came up to spot singers. By the use of ramps and platforms Wieland Wagner had turned the proscenium arch into a sort of monumental Cinemascope screen. Lighting tricks turned water into clouds and clouds into a steaming earth. We toured river beds, mountaintops, and subterranean channels.

Grandfather Wagner's elaborate paraphernalia—the winged helmets and breastplates, the stuffed animals and birds—were nowhere to be seen. Giants in Boris Karloff make-up loped across the stage like close relations of Peking Man. Rhine

Maidens were not tightly corseted dames in evening gowns and loops of pearls, but sleek sirens in strapless flesh-colored bathing suits.

What was obvious at once was that the music we were hearing was the most perfectly performed on the entire summer festival circuit. Also that the audience was the most deeply absorbed.

In Bayreuth there is only one opera a day, and performances have two one-hour intermissions. In 1900, Romain Rolland observed that during intermissions "French flirt, Germans drink beer, English read librettos." Today nearly everyone eats in one of the three Wagner-owned restaurants. In the grand Festspielgaste a meal and wine with celebrities may cost well over five dollars; in the more modest cafeteria one can lunch for a dollar, but the crush is murder. We usually went to the Canteen, an outdoor establishment for students and festival artists, where we had superb Franconian *Bratwurst* and beer for under fifty cents. All restaurants sell glucose pellets to energize anyone bogging down midway in the evening.

In the outdoor promenade the babel of tongues included Italian, Dutch, Scandinavian, as much English as German, and surprisingly a great deal of French. Europe's prettiest music critic, Nicole Hirsch of *France Soir*, explained why French pilgrims came to a shrine of German nationalism. "We are a very romantic people and we love romantic legends," she said. "Do not forget—*Tristan and Isolde* was originally our story."

When the electrified globes light up at ten or eleven o'clock—depending on the length of the opera—and the ovation has clapped itself out, it is time to go to the *Eule* or Owl. This dark grotto of several rooms is the only restaurant or night club that remains open in an otherwise curfewed town. Like everything else in Bayreuth it is a Wagner shrine. Its walls are papered with Wagner pictures and mementos. Conversation is about music and in the presence of so many

Wagners, corporeal and spiritual, it is heresy to say anything
not wildly flattering.

Anyone lucky enough to get in is happy to endure the
Owl's rather unpredictable service. The popular drink is a
sweetish Moselle wine; a popular dish is raw chopped beef
lubricated with raw eggs and garnished with raw onion. No
doubt Sieglinde and Brunnhilde dined like this in their caves,
but just watch a German blonde gulp this cannibal delicacy,
and you will be permanently disenchanted.

The week moved ponderously on like an exhausting novena.
As we progressed through *Die Walküre* and *Siegfried* into
Götterdämmerung, I forgot which day it was or what opera
I was in. Physically exhausted, emotionally drained, we would
swear we could bear no more, and still we could not stay
away. The tensions were mounting and we were trapped,
like all other members of the congregation, to await the
climax.

At *Götterdämmerung* it came, more violently than anyone
expected. During the last intermission a storm rolled swiftly
over the Czechoslovakian mountains on the eastern horizon.
Lightning flashed in the night; nature was competing with
the Wagner show inside. A curious nervous tension held the
people outdoors to watch the tempest rolling over the broad
Bavarian plains. Not until the third trumpet fanfare were
they drawn in.

As the act of demolition progressed inside, thunder shook
the world outdoors. The funeral pyre lit up and a crash of
hail blitzed the roof, so the music could hardly be heard. It
continued through the immolation; then, at the moment of
the closing of the cycle, the storm stopped and the theme
of tranquil nature purged of evil rose sweetly and gently
from the orchestra as the curtain fell.

In my hauntings of the theatres of the world I have
seldom had an experience to match it. Around me people
were weeping. For an hour they stomped and shouted. There
were twenty-one curtain calls.

After that I could not go with my companions to the Owl. Instead I walked the wild night, exhausting myself on the wet pavements of Niebelungen Strasse, Parsifal Strasse, Meistersinger Strasse, asking myself why they had wept, trying to understand the tears. Was it for the immolation in a bunker under the chancellery that they mourned? Was it their own death as gods? Was this the mystery of the rites of Bayreuth?

When Jan Sibelius visited Bayreuth he did not like the music, but he was enraptured by the landscape. Unfortunately, if one goes to operas there is time only for small excursions in and around the town. We went to Wahnfried, where we played Wagner's piano, saw Franz von Lenbach's lovely portrait of the young Cosima, and in the back yard visited Wagner's grave, a plain marble slab raised under weeping willows like the *Götterdämmerung* pyre. Nearby are the graves of Wagner's two Newfoundland dogs, Russ and Maussi, and of his parrot, Kochel.

On another day we saw the jewel-like rococo family theatre of the Bayreuth margraves and lunched at their hermitage in a garden as enchanting as Klingsor's in *Parsifal*. One day when there was no opera we took Nicole Hirsch and Friedelind Wagner on a roundabout of the Franconian countryside, past gabbling geese, oxen pulling hay, and tourist buses named Lohengrin and Tannhäuser, to Bamberg, one of the most captivating old towns in Germany, then through a series of pretty German Tudor villages to the gloomy gray castle of Coburg from which came Victoria's Albert.

At the Festspielhaus more music followed the *Ring*. There was a turgid *Flying Dutchman* and a pious *Parsifal* for which the program notes included Wieland Wagner's psychoanalysis of the characters (Parsifal had a mother complex, Klingsor a castration complex). Most memorable of all, both musically and visually, was Wieland Wagner's *Tann-*

häuser. This time the lights were bright, the costumes dazzling. The pictures on the stage were a stunning review of Italian art. The pilgrim's chorus was a Fra Angelico, the Wartburg castle a Giotto, Elizabeth's prayer an Annunciation by Botticelli. If there had been nothing but *Tannhäuser* at Bayreuth, it would still have been the most dazzling reward of the summer's pilgrimage. But it was enough, perhaps too much. With relief we steered Wolfgang over the music run to Salzburg. The *Autobahn,* an important occupation throughfare, was marked in English signs with German below. We rolled through dark sun-dappled conifer forests in which the young Siegfried must have hunted. The rich farmlands and soft hills reminded me of Ohio. Fields of wheat and rye were golden ripe, and crops of hops on stakes, faced westward by the prevailing winds, looked like fields of Jack's beanstalks.

We stopped at the Munich festival to hear, above all things, a performance of *Die Meistersinger.* Compared with Bayreuth's perfection it left much to be desired, but it was Wagner's own antidote to Wagner, richly human and gaudy, and bawdy as a Breughel fair.

Then on through the Alps of Bavaria and Austria to Salzburg. As we approached the most beautiful little town in central Europe our spirits soared. It is easy to understand why. Salzburg is a euphoric town! If you've ever been there its ingratiating personality has taken root in your soul and every return is a homecoming.

Laughter! A *Ländler* played in a restaurant called *Till Eulenspiegel!* Music that is a part of geography, along with the scenery and the architecture, the eating and drinking, the gorgeous girls smiling everywhere, the baroque air of playful venery and lechery that Mozart put into *The Marriage of Figaro* and *Così fan Tutte.*

For Salzburg is Mozart's town even more than Bayreuth is Wagner's. Wagner adopted Bayreuth in the last years of his life. Mozart was born in Salzburg and grew out of it. But where Wagner is a cult in Bayreuth, Mozart is business in Salzburg. In the Mozart industry everything is identified with the composer; even the famous marzipan balls are called *Mozart Kügeln*. In their prosperous devotion to their composer, most Salzburgers are not even aware that Mozart, aged twenty-four, repudiated his home town in protest against the meanness of its Archbishop Hieronymus, and never returned.

Our first opera was *The Magic Flute*, staged in the outdoor Felsenreitschule, or "rocky riding school," an arena carved out of a cliff in which horses were taught to dance for the amusement of seventeenth-century Archbishop Johann Ernst. Salzburg's most elaborate productions are put on in the horse academy, and the *Flute* was as magical as any in the fantasy's brilliant history. Its star was the designer, the famous Austrian painter Oskar Kokoschka, who exploded the whole production in a burst of turquoise, pink, violet, cobalt, orange, yellow, and brick red. The excitement of the décor stirred the Vienna Philharmonic Orchestra and the singers to a shimmering brilliance, and the show soared like a rocket to glory.

There are few days in Salzburg without three or four festival events. We had tickets for eleven performances in seven days, and established our record on Sunday with an orchestral concert conducted by George Szell in the morning, the traditional Max Reinhardt production of *Jedermann* in the afternoon, and in the evening a disarmingly racy *Seraglio*. The laughter during this gay lark was so loud and continuous that we could hardly hear the singers.

Performances in Salzburg begin at seven-thirty. Spectators snack lightly either before they go or on *Wurstli* in the foyer during intervals. After the music you wine and dine yourself properly in one of the town's several fine restaurants. Our favorite was the White Cross with its exotic Yugoslav menu, but others more popular are St. Peter's Keller, Stieglkeller, and the Powandra. For spectacular dining and dancing to a famous band, Salzburg has the Café Wintler, the most expensive night club in Austria. It overlooks the town from the Mönschsberg, and customers ride to it in a funicular. On sunny days the most rewarding lunching place is on the ramparts of the Hohensalzburg fortress, where the dark beer and the view of the Salzkammergut mountains are remarkable even if the food is not.

The fortress is also the place to go to watch natives dance Tyrolean style. Here one evening I negotiated a deal with a husky farmer named Rudi, wherein he would teach me the men's vigorous *Schuhplattler* if I would teach his wife a tango, the mastering of which was her heart's desire. After being pummeled about by Rudi and his lederhosened pals, I did what I could with the dirndled Mrs. Rudi. Apparently she was pleased; as we swooped over the floor she shouted happily to her husband, *"Guck mal, Rudi! Ich tanze modern!"*

On days when we were not bound by our packet of tickets to music, we swam in the cold waters of the glittering little Salzkammergut lakes at Bad Ischl, St. Gilgen (Mozart's mother's home town), and St. Wolfgang, where we lunched at the famous White Horse Inn on *Bauernschmaus*, an assortment of farmer sausages and smoked meats, and *Sachertorte*, a chocolate cake with butter cream filling and the inevitable *Schlag* or whipped cream.

The difference between Bayreuth and Salzburg is the difference between Germans and Austrians; the difference between church and carnival; the difference, indeed, between the music of Wagner, who wrote of gods, and the music of Mozart, who wrote of men. In Bayreuth, Wagner, worrying about his fame, built his own memorial. The Salzburg festival, disorderly and sparkling as a spring, bubbled into existence by itself. Mozart, lost in an unmarked grave, left only his memorial of music.

ten

THE TOWN OF MANY FACES

Not since the late Bunk Johnson's vespers in Manhattan's Stuyvesant Casino had I heard such Dixieland. The overcrowded, overheated hall was jumping. Six young musicians, wearing Levis and coonskin caps, rocked and swayed ecstatically to their own riffs and rides. Girls with blond hair tumbling over sticky faces flared through epileptic Charlestons; their partners' shirts were lacquered to wet backs and sweat spattered on kibitzers along the walls.

An old woman, so heavy she could not walk, raised herself up with two canes in a moment of jubilation and, tottering on swollen legs, boomed out with the music, *"Halt' den Tiger! Halt' den Tiger!"*

Basin Street? Harlem?

Not at all. God-fearing Zürich was on a spree. The occasion was the artists' annual Sylvester Ball on the night before New Year's Eve in a loft in Neumarktplatz. Outside, in the shadows of the twin spires of Grossmünster Cathedral, sweat-soaked youths tore off their clothes, poised naked on the brink of a medieval fountain and plunged in for a wash.

Watching these young Zürichers kicking over the traces, I did not wonder that Zürich is replacing Vienna as the psychiatric center of the world. The home town of Dr.

C. G. Jung is a schizophrenic city with more personalities than the Hindu deity Siva has arms. Consider some of its more striking masks.

Zürich wears a white collar. Her typical citizen is a physically fit, often athletic businessman who dresses conservatively and is polite with strangers, but not overfriendly. He is recognizable by two things: a briefcase and an anxious expression on his face. The briefcase was given to him the moment he was tall enough to lift it from the floor, and he will carry it—or subsequent ones—to his grave. The worried expression comes from the cares of his daily life. Zürichers are unsentimental and practical materialists who run their town as efficiently as a colony of ants. But entomologists tell us that even ant colonies have nervous breakdowns.

Zürich is virtuous. The town's self-righteous position as the moral bastion of Europe was firmly established more than four centuries ago by Reformer Huldreich Zwingli when he helped found the Protestantism which strongly influenced the development of England's national religion and which became the spiritual backbone of the United States. All you need to do is stand outside the Wasser-Kirche and look up into the glum face of the Zwingli statue, sword and Bible in hand, to understand his views on sin.

Zürich is Puritan. You actually breathe, see, and hear purity. Many travelers have called Zürich the most beautiful city in the world, and in summer they have an argument. The sharp fresh air blowing down from the mountains is sweetened by the scent of lavender which old ladies sell on the street and by the blossoms of thousands of linden trees. The town is a flower bed of red geraniums, roses, and begonias. Its streets are immaculately scrubbed; any sort of an eyesore is a personal agony to every Züricher who sees it. Sails hover over the blue lake like white butterflies. Soaring church spires form a heavenly lattice in the skies, and any strong-nerved visitor who has survived a Saturday night curfew, when all the bells are rung at once, will be convinced that the wrath of Zwingli is still in the town.

So far, so good. Virtue and purity belong together and go well with a white collar. But Zürich also has her exotic facets.

She is venal. Bluntly put, her people worship the Golden Calf. When they renounced the pleasures of the flesh, Reformation Zürichers substituted a lust for money and took up banking. During all the monetary crises that have shaken Europe during the first half of the twentieth century, the banks of Switzerland stood solid. When the last war ended, Zürich's Bahnhofstrasse was the banking center of Continental Europe and a world-wide deposit vault. The Swiss love other people's money almost as much as their own and they have never had any scruples about whose money they husband. Fascist fortunes were secure behind the red-geranium window boxes and Latin American dictators stashed away their piles there. Guatemala's Jacobo Arbenz, whose Swiss name came from his grandfather, was reunited with his personal fortune in Switzerland, and it is no secret that Argentina's Juan Perón hoarded some of his money there.

Most surprising of all, Zürich is lecherous. Without giving up their substitute deity of the Golden Calf, modern Zürichers have returned to a worship of Aphrodite. Women and money have always been a natural twosome, and tired businessmen, especially if they are rich, need relaxation.

All Puritans like to kick over the traces now and then and Zürichers do it with startling alacrity. When GI's in Germany discovered that a lot more than chocolate and Emmenthal cheese was for sale across the border, the gray town on the Limmat became known as one of the gayer fleshpots. Zwingli, stalking through his fortress of virtue today, would probably see it as Babylon pepped up with considerable spice from the cities of the plains.

No one knows quite how many professional prostitutes there are in Zürich. Estimates range from 1000 to 15,000;

a social agency's director conservatively put the figure at 2500. There is no accurate check. Every adult in Zürich must register a profession for tax purposes and the favorite *Berufe* of the girls are hairdresser, beautician, and masseuse. A few register as language teachers, and the toast of the police department is one girl who listed her profession as "import-export."

The girls are chic, with flashy good taste in make-up and dress. Almost all are Swiss; a chauvinistic policeman said, "We feel the work should go to our own people." Many are country girls who come to town to earn the dowry which they hope will enable them to marry. Since at least part of their business comes from young country bachelors on a fling in the big town, it is reasonable to suppose that some of the hard-earned francs complete their cycle in a chalet in the Alps: that the young farmer marrying a hometown girl with a city dowry is getting back some of his investment. However, it is a moot question how many of the girls make it back to the farm.

The Zürich philosophy is that everyone minds his own business and, since almost everyone has so much business to mind, the girls prosper with police and civic blessing. Virtue is admirable enough so long as it doesn't interfere with business. Furthermore, many solid God-fearing burghers, like the respectable entrepreneurs in Shaw's *Mrs. Warren's Profession*, make monthly collections of high rents from the girls' apartments which take up several square blocks in one of the pleasanter residential districts.

Theatres of operation are centered about the opera house in the Old Town's Bellevue Platz, a hub of traffic and night life across the Limmat from the banks. On dark Dufourstrasse (named after a heroic general of Switzerland's 1847 Sonderbund Civil War), where I once lived, or on shaded Limmat Quai nearby, I could watch girls negotiating any night of the week. On weekends the activity in these posts was not unlike that of cattle markets in the squares of Alpine villages. Buyers never hurried. They strolled about, silently appraising what was on the hoof, comparing prices, ages, and qualities conspicuously bovine. Chauffeured black limousines rolled by and unloaded dark-suited, diamond-ringed tycoons, who stepped out to shop around like everyone else, temporarily inflating the market. Younger and more modest shoppers swooped on bicycles from one market to another like silent bats.

There was always a policeman or two watching discreetly in the shadows. The police knew, of course, about the Swiss penal code's *Gesetz 206* making liable to punishment any girl who "solicits in public for the purpose of misconduct." But negotiations were soft-voiced and well mannered and occasions to enforce the law seldom arose.

In 1954, this efficient operation of a profitable business was momentarily interrupted. As the Rabelaisian tale is told in Zürich, it began on a night when one lady told another outside the opera house, to get the hell off her beat. Unfortunately, the second lady was the wife of a public official and she was waiting for her husband to drive up in his car. The result was a stern reminder to the police of *Gesetz 206*.

The police did not, as police might have in an American city, launch a sweeping "clean-up." Instead, with typical Swiss caution, they arrested one girl, who became known as "Frau M." and charged her with "soliciting by public loitering with intent to get money in a period of six months at least three hundred men for non-matrimonial intercourse."

Immediately Frau M. was famous. Swiss, with their strong sense of fair play, organized into two camps of public opinion. What shook the little country was not the guilt or innocence of Frau M., but the question of when is a whore a whore and when is she a lady?

In Zürich's district court Frau M. was acquitted on the grounds that walking in a street and stating one's address is not persuasive solicitation. The case was taken to Zürich's higher court, which found that a woman is not guilty for her alluring appearance and that if, as a result of her allure, she agrees to intercourse, that is her own business.

Finally, the case went to the Federal Court in Lausanne. This judicial body, equivalent to the Supreme Court of the United States, ruled that in the matter of soliciting, "The penal code is on the same ground as the commerce code which recognizes that the display of merchandise in a shop window is an offer even if it does not address itself toward a particular customer." The court found Frau M.'s dress and behavior comparable to a store window and judged her guilty.

Back in Zürich the girls did not stew over the decision for long. They went out and bought dogs. Dogs have to be walked and no one can arrest a lady for walking one. The smartly barbered and (in winter) corseted poodles and terriers tugging on taut leashes are high bred and mostly black, since black fits best with the girls' business wardrobes. Some girls, discovering they loved dogs, now have two or three. As a result one respectable secretary of my acquaintance found it was no longer safe to walk her little Musette; Papa has to do it for her.

The outcome of Frau M.'s tangle with the law surprised no one and pleased almost everyone. Officialdom won a moral victory over the girls—whose business, if anything, improved. The dogs turned out to be especially useful for striking up acquaintanceships. No policeman would question the motives of a gentleman who, moved by a love for animals, bends to pat a furry head. Nor has anyone bothered to question the erratic hygiene of the dogs.

In the two thousand years of its history Zürich has never been known as a warrior city. But ever since Zwingli's time another kind of war, the war of sex, has been smoldering in the town. Hostility between men and women comes naturally in a city where even the churches have genders, where Fraumünster and Grossmünster face each other across the Limmat. Zürichers boast of their family life, but they have one of the highest divorce records in Europe. A local psychiatrist said, "Swiss men talk to their women as they talk to their cows and goats." He was speaking somewhat metaphorically of a sexual relationship that is at best inarticulate and unsentimental.

It is a startling fact that Switzerland, which blows its loudest alphorns to advertise its social advances, has never permitted women to vote. The women, who have fought for the ballot without success for sixty years, know they will not get it until the men vote it in—and the men are sitting in the catbird seat. The inference is clear enough; the men will not accept women as their physical and mental equals. They mean to bind them forever to the female trinity of *Kinder, Küche,* and *Kirche,* with lots of *putzen* thrown in.

If you talk to a man about the subject, he will do his best to convince you of the logic of his attitude. Across the Limmat from the Zwingli statue there is another statue which offers a clue. It stands on the Lindenhof, a lofty square rising over the river like a pulpit. This statue of an armored woman commemorates an episode in the Middle Ages, when the women of Zürich gathered up spears and swords to scare the tar out of an approaching Austrian army and save their town. Looking at this statue, one does not doubt who the real warriors of Zürich are, and that the women aren't letting the men forget it. Men don't like to think what would happen if women ever got to the polls. They have more than a hint in the *Frauenvereine,* a formidable "ladies' society" with which, without casting a vote, the ladies virtually run the town. Adhering to the Puritan ideology that the male is base and sinful and the female is a guiding angel, they attack their men where it hurts most—through their drinks. A Swiss likes his beer and *Kirschwasser;* next to the Frenchman he is the heaviest drinker in Europe.

So the *Frauenvereine* went after the public houses. The ladies managed a midnight curfew which brings Zürich night life to an abrupt and frustrating end when it seems to only

have begun (and incidentally, has increased the function of
the prostitute in the town). Having accomplished this, they
set up their own *alkoholfrei* establishments. Almost half of
Zürich's thousand restaurants fall into the dismal "alcohol-
free" category. Those which the *Frauenvereine* operate are
graceless places where one can get a substantial meal for two
and a half francs—about sixty cents—with no tipping allowed. Inexpensive food is popular and a large clientele re-
sults in many converts to such *Frauenvereine* beverages as
apple and grape juice.

Another depressing feature of Zürich's dietary landscape is
her vegetarian restaurants. Zürichers are food faddists and
many of the ladies have been converted to the theories of
Dr. Bircher-Benner, a raw-vegetable prophet who died in
1939 at the age of seventy and whose greatest apostle has
been Dr. Gayelord Hauser. It is no wonder that a hungry
male served a supper of *Birchermüesli*, a health pudding of
oatmeal, fruits and nuts, sneaks off to his favorite *Bierstuben*
to bootleg a *Bratwurst* or some *Schinken*. As a Philistine
carnivore, I am happy to add that, aside from such gastro-
nomical aberrations, the Zürich cuisine is excellent, com-
bining the best of German with a counterpoint of French
and Italian.

A by-product of the ladies' temperance drive is the coffee-
house. There are now about 350 in the city. Coffeehouses are
a tradition in Germanic cities and Zürich's most famous is
the fifty-year-old Odeon, an Edwardian parlor on Bellevue
Platz which has marble tables, crystal chandeliers, potted
rubber plants and a highbrow literati clientele. Here the price
of a cup of coffee entitles you to stay all morning, read a
large library of newspapers and magazines, and chin with
whatever celebrities are on hand. The late Thomas Mann
used to be one of them. The second floor is a night club
at which tables of peroxided doxies watch for signals from
tables of unattached males. Once, when a department store
tried to take over the Odeon property, a public clamor saved

the café. It is no secret, however, that the booming second floor pays the rent.

Coffeehouses with exotic names like Java, Bali, Turco, and Hawaii appeal to the university crowd. Young Zürichers drink far less alcohol than their fathers, but they keep themselves hopped up with unlimited quantities of coffee. Police dealing with crime trace more youthful delinquencies to coffeehouses than to bars.

Zürich's crimes are of a special sort. Murders are almost unheard of and, surprising as it might seem in this Midas town, big-time hold-ups and burglaries are virtually nonexistent. There are occasional small robberies and forgeries. But the kind of crimes for which Zürichers—and Swiss generally—seem to have a special disposition are sexual, a fact which will surprise no students of Puritan psychology.

The amount of sexual crime became a public scandal when newspapers accused public officials of minimizing the horrid truth. One journal even ventured that two-thirds of the sex crimes were suppressed by prudish victims and never reached the attention of the police. The police argue that by minimizing such statistics they reduce the hysteria which only increases the crimes. Care is taken not to expose offenders who are given psychiatric therapy. A large part of the offenses are rape, with the offenders ranging from eighteen to seventy-seven years of age. A social agency director blamed erotic films and cheap literature for provoking sensuality and violence in the curiously inverted Swiss temperament. He scored sentimental German films rather than Hollywood pictures and praised the good influence of American Western films based on action rather than sensuality. Other factors in the sex problem are insufficient and bad education, and too much prosperity, providing economic and social independence for young people under twenty years of age.

An obvious product of any sexual spree is babies. Although there are no slums in Zürich and very little poverty, there are many unmarried mothers. As in the rest of the world, more females are born in Switzerland than males. Add to this natural surplus of women almost 100,000 women workers, largely domestics who come from Italy, Austria, and Germany with the hope of finding a Swiss husband, and the result is a sexual market which, either sacred or profane, is decidedly in the male's favor. It is a circumstance which makes the men somewhat irresponsible and not at all disposed toward marriage. ("Why?" Zürich's bachelors ask one another in their bumblebee language, "buy the horse when you can ride it free?") But in cases where paternity can be legally proved, the government forces wayward fathers to support their offspring.

A Puritan after a binge has a guilt complex bigger than his hangover and that is why the psychiatrists are needed. Swiss are naturally depressive types; they lead Europe in both suicides and mental disturbances. A psychiatrist credited this *"malaise Suisse"* to "an internal emptiness": "We have no national crisis upon which to externalize our emotions. Business is good. We don't fight wars. There is nothing to unite us to each other in a common effort. We're unhappy and we don't know why."

Part of the trouble is the inferiority complex which mountains give to people living intimately with them. Alpine people are high-tempered and taut-nerved and they crack more quickly under strain than do plains dwellers. Zürich has the *Föhn*, a hot high-pressure air pocket which rolls down from the mountains and settles over the city. During its fomenting days, blood courses wildly through the veins, death notices increase in newspapers and clinics report an exaggerated unrest in patients. Other factors in the Swiss' spiritual disquietude are his materialism, represented by those banks full of other people's money, and, most important of all, old Zwingli's smothering blanket of Puritanism.

By far the most attractive quality of Zürich's many-sided personality is her tradition of humanism. Zürichers like to refer to their town as "Athens on the Limmat." The claim is modest and entirely justifiable. As cities go, it is small (415,000 citizens; one-tenth of the population of Switzerland), but it has an intensity of culture superior to most larger cities. Its university is famous for medicine, its Institute of Technology for the colony of Nobel Prize winners on its staff, the Jung Institute for bringing the fountainhead of psychiatry from Vienna.

The Zürich playhouse is the best German-language theatre in Europe, and the state-supported opera performs more modern and experimental works by Hindemith, Honegger, Kodaly, Menotti, and Britten than any other major opera house on the Continent. Its Richard Strauss festival each June is a high spot in Europe's summer music. Zürichers have twenty-seven concert halls, fifty-seven male choruses, and five hundred professors of music. The characteristic attitude toward music is expressed in a probably apocryphal story of a visiting gentleman who accosted a beautiful young woman near the opera house and was told, "Not tonight. They're performing the *Missa Solemnis* of Beethoven."

For the visitor who understands German, the most unusual feature of Zürich's night life is her cabaret theatres. These startling manifestations of free speech were begun by Erika Mann in the early thirties with "The Pepper Mill," the only German-speaking public house in Europe that dared to laugh openly at Hitler. Today the best cabaret is the "Federal," in a pub called *Hirschen*. Here you see well-wined and dined burghers guffawing at malicious parodies of themselves. Swiss humor, often sadistic and cruel, is redeemed by a broad gift for self-ridicule.

The most diverting street in town is the winding Münstergasse, which begins at Grossmünster Cathedral, changes midway into Niederhofstrasse, and continues to the Central Hotel across the river from the station. An alley so narrow that the slumming bankers and tycoons can't drive their black Cadillacs and Mercedes through it, the Münstergasse is a gaudy casbah of clubs, bars, theatres, and cafés which ring nightly

with the cacophony of American blues, cowboy songs, sentimental German ballads and Swiss yodeling. There is also a
cluster of existentialist cafés and cinemas, for Zürichers are
cultists. The art movement known as Dadaism was born in
Zürich in 1916, and in our time the existentialism which has
sputtered to a low fizzle in Paris is still burning bright on the
Limmat.

Jazz balls and jam sessions are weekly affairs and in the
winter Dixieland combos accompany ski trains to the Engel-
berg or Graubünden. There are usually two or three such
groups waiting for trains, transforming the station into something like a New Orleans ward heeler's funeral.

Because of its humanistic spirit and lively interest in the
arts, Zürich has always attracted creative people. Richard
Wagner lived there for ten years, composing *Das Rheingold*,
Die Walküre, and parts of *Tristan* and *Parsifal*. James Joyce
worked on *Ulysses* and *Finnegans Wake* there, and died in
Zürich in 1941. Thomas Mann wrote for long periods in
Zürich before he died there in 1955.

The Reformation which made Zürich Puritan also made
her an asylum for political refugees. The first to come were
English Protestants fleeing Bloody Mary Tudor. During the
First World War a mild little refugee lived with his wife
in a poor room in Spiegelgasse, where, the landlord noted,
"He never quarreled with his wife. They lived on almost
nothing—tea and bread and butter for supper." Things liv-
ened up considerably in the humble room during the Rus-
sian Revolution, for the mild little tenant was named Ulianov,
otherwise Lenin.

During the last war some of Germany's luckier Jews escaped to Zürich and are still living there. What warms the
émigré is a prevailing spirit of optimism. Like Americans,
Swiss believe stanchly in the future. "In Zürich we can do
anything," is a popular saying, and a psychiatrist said, "We
are essentially a peasant people and it is our peasant instinct
to face tensions and anxieties with a calm imperturbability."

The imperturbability was strong in the character of Zürich's three legendary patrons: Saints Felix, Regula, and Exuperantius. Beheaded for their Christian faith, the sturdy trio, according to the myth, picked up their own heads, carried them to the hill where Grossmünster now stands, dug their own graves, lay in them and covered themselves with earth.

Today in Zürich no heads are chopped. Heads are occasionally somewhat fuddled, but Zürichers still aren't letting go of them. Zürich's curious human comedy has its shade of dark northern gloom, but then a buoyant merriment will waft in from the south which invariably lays the ghost of Zwingli to rest.

The lively counterpoint never ends. Church bells are pealing, but someone in a café is singing *On the Sunny Side of the Street*. The money of the world is being counted while grandmothers are knitting furiously on Lindenhof benches, as if they had to cover the nakedness of the world before nightfall. *Frauenvereine* ladies brood over the sins of the flesh while their menfolk negotiate quietly under dark trees with the mistresses of dogs.

A gray northern city with swooping gulls, and coots and divers quarreling over fish in the winter, Zürich changes in the summer into a bright southern town with swans, splashing fountains and the scent of lime trees. Benvenuto Cellini, seeing it in summer, cried out, "City of wonder, sparkling like a jewel!" and Thornton Wilder said, "The only city in Europe in which I would like to live." It is difficult not to agree with both of them.

eleven

THE VALLEY OF THE MASKS

My pursuit of demons began in a Zürich museum one wintry day when I was confronted by some terrifyingly evil faces, leering at me as if I were a sinner trapped in a purgatory designed by Bosch.

The faces were masks of wood carved and painted by peasants in the Swiss cantons of Graubünden and Valais to wear at carnival. The most fearful ones, distorted monkey-like faces with chancred noses and hollow eyes and finished with horses' hair and boars' teeth, came from the Lötschental, one of the highest and most archaic valleys in Switzerland.

During the long winter and spring I returned to the museum several times to see those demi-human faces which haunted me like half-forgotten nightmares from my childhood. In February the Lötschental was sealed with snow so I could not go to the carnival, but I talked with a Zürich professor of medicine and he gave me a confusing prognosis of the men who carved the masks. In spite of centuries of in-breeding and an unvaried diet of bread and cheese, the Lötschentalers, said the doctor, were the healthiest people in Switzerland. Unattended by doctors from birth to death, they were noted for their longevity, usually dying in their eighties of "water" or dropsy, a circulatory failing of old hearts worn out by hard labor. The dropsy death rate was probably abetted by alcohol, for in heavy-drinking Switzerland, Lötschentalers were the undisputed champions. Cancer, one of the major killers in Switzerland, was almost unknown in the valley. And though Switzerland leads the world in mental illnesses, the piously Catholic Lötschentalers seem never to have heard of nervous breakdowns. Were they happy? The word, said the doctor, does not exist in the valley. Because the Lötschentalers do not pursue happiness they were, in discontented Switzerland, an island of contented people. Nevertheless, I was sure this enigmatic picture must, like those fearful masks, hide some astonishing secrets.

In May, by a curious coincidence, I rented a house on the shores of Lago Maggiore which was owned by the German Baron Eduard von der Heydt who had collected the Zürich masks. When I told the old baron I was planning a journey up into the Lötschental, he said, "Find yourself some laughing masks. They are rare and most valued."

It was storming in the north so I had to wait out June on Maggiore's steaming shores. Finally, early in July, word came that the rains had ceased beyond the Alps and that the sun was shining in the valley of the masks. On a Sunday morning I set out with my guide, a nineteen-year-old student from Zug named Willy Hofstetter, a merry and jaunty boy with a round puckish face. He had come to me by way of his aunt who now packed two rucksacks with emergency food rations—chocolate, powdered milk, and cheeses together with first aid equipment—and harnessed us to the sacks like donkeys. Lötschental bread, she warned us, would be hard as stone.

We started from Locarno on the Centovalli train, a hairsbreadth Toonerville Trolley which wound perilously along precipices and squeezed through canyons so narrow that we plucked a bouquet of bluebells from the mountain walls as we passed. It required three railroad transfers and two border crossings in and out of Italy to get us to the foot of the

Lötschental. Our debarkation was at a jolly station in Goppenstein. The waiting room was a public house crowded with family groups singing and laughing at tables loaded with salamis and cheeses, with beakers of beer and bottles of *Fendant*, a golden wine shot through with sunlight from the Rhône Valley below.

I wanted to stay but my guide was eager to move on. We had climbed three hours by train and now we began climbing by foot. A chilling gust blew out of the short tunnel in the mountain which was the gateway to the valley. In a niche inside the tunnel, in a bower of fresh flowers, was a Madonna; above her, carved in stone, we read, "*Wanderer grüss Uns, Ich segne Dich*" ("Wanderer greet me, I bless you").

On the other side of the tunnel we were blinded by the glitter of glaciers above us and deafened by the thunder of the Lonza River below. We met bare-legged youths and pink-skinned flaxen-braided girls, carrying their Sunday trophies of Alpine roses. "*Grüss Gott*," they said to us. A hilariously drunken little man had sense enough to cling with his hands to the right side of the road; if he had wandered to the left he would have been plunged into the foaming white torrent below. "The wine must be good," said Willy. "Let's hurry."

Since it was the end of the day we were alone going up. We passed through the first town, Ferden, a tight cluster of brown huts built of larch logs, the only trees growing at that altitude. The town had a ripe gamy odor which came from piles of fermenting manure crowded between the houses. Manure is wealth which a Lötschentaler hoards like gold. Status is measured by the height of the heap outside one's door, and in winter the steaming piles help warm the houses. Finely chopped wood, piled against the walls up to the tiny windows also gives protection. Continuing up the valley, we passed a series of stone crypts dug into the side of the road like the tornado cellars of my native Midwest. Willy explained that these were travelers' refuges from *Fer-*

denlaui, the dangerous avalanches which thunder down the mountains in winter and in spring. On the slopes above were V-shaped stone avalanche walls, and still higher were avalanche guards of aluminum, a metal light enough for lugging up the mountains. In the evening sun these great rectangular mirrors shone too brightly to look upon.

There were summer hazards too. I saw a smallish snake in the road and, to my regret, called it to Willy's attention. He identified it as a poisonous viper and put it into one of Aunt Lisi's plastic cheese containers and into his rucksack to take home to Zug.

Another mile and we were in Kippel, the main town of the valley. Its low profile of steeply sloped dark buildings was broken by a gracefully spired church and a large barn-like hotel, the Lötschenberg. On a high ledge over the town stood a forty-foot cross of wood dedicated to St. Nicholas, beloved in the valley because he was a farmer. On the upper side of the single street the buildings were windowless stables, and hay huts built on stilts. Each pylon had a mushroom-like disc of flat stone at the top to keep out rats. Below the road were the dwellings and shops, the church and the cemetery. This curious design of the town made me think at once of hygiene and typhoid. Though there were no mosquitoes at this altitude, flies swarmed over the manure heaps. The houses, in *Oberland* chalet style, were crowded together for protection from cold and avalanches. Their soft-wood stairways were concave, the steps gnawed away by the heavy Lötschental boots. The more affluent homes had balconies with boxes of red geraniums, bright splashes of color in the otherwise unrelieved brown of wood and dung. Many houses had pious mottoes burned or carved into the walls, like brand marks. *"Wer Gott vertraut hat wohl gebaut"* ("Who trusts in God builds well"), I read, and *"Alles welkt und wird zu Staube, Nur nicht Hoffnung, Liebe, Glaube"* ("Everything crumbles and returns to dust, except hope, love, and faith"). The house mottoes were the ceaselessly burdened Lötschentalers' pie-in-the-sky, their promise to themselves for a happy eternity.

Women and children were carrying wooden buckets into the stables for the evening milking, and in addition to the pungency of manure there was the sweetish smell of milk and cheese. The people were lean, angular, and small with strong brown faces. There were few young women. Willy explained that the maidens were up in the Alpine pastures where they cared for the cattle from June 30 to September 15. All the people we saw in the streets walked with long swift steps, as if each were carrying some great imaginary load on his shoulders. Even the children loped in this way, gripping the earth with their thick soles, their faces turned downward. These silent, solemn, miniature adults going about their work—which at this hour was carrying wooden buckets of fresh milk on their shoulders—awed me. They never seemed to laugh, and if they spoke it was to greet us politely, to murmur a soft *"Grüss Gott."* Beasts of burden from their first steps, Willy said they attended school only in the deep months of winter when there is no work on the land. Clearly no such thing as childhood existed in the Lötschental.

I saw a tiny aproned girl carrying a long loaf of bread, holding it lovingly, kissing it like a doll, and I asked her if she could take us to the house of the prior to whom I had a letter. She led us through several tight alleys toward the church, pointed to a door and ran off, caressing her loaf. The bell was answered by the prior himself. His name was John Siegen; he was a tall old man with flowing white hair and a lean sculptured face that was itself a mask, benign and beautiful. Gentle in manner and soft of voice, he radiated a holy sparkle. In his furled black frock he appeared to be levitating from the floor, like a saint in an El Greco assumption.

He invited us into his study, a low-ceilinged brown cave of unpainted vertical boards with a porcelain stove in a corner and walls filled with paintings and books on painting, mountain climbing and Swiss history. On a shelf stood a bronzed bust of the prior, a gift to him from the Swiss government on his seventieth birthday two years before. The statue had a craggy sort of distinction, and yet it rested heavily; metal was not a proper medium in which to capture the prior's spirituality. But my impression of his frailty was a delusion. He was not only the valley's religious leader; he was also cultural arbiter, historian, photographer, and one-man chamber of commerce. The author of a book about the valley, he had traveled all over Europe giving illustrated lectures, and he was a dedicated mountaineer who had climbed the Matterhorn to read the first mass on its summit. The prior told us he had risen that morning for a five-thirty Mass, then climbed to an altitude of 6500 feet to read a Mass for the pastured maidens, descended again to Kippel for a third mass at twelve-thirty, after which he had taken his first nourishment of the day, and then conducted vespers in the afternoon.

He made us tea, serving with it bread, butter, thick honey, a plate of apples, and a bottle of white wine. The tea was excellent and the bread, indeed, was toothbreaking, so we followed the prior's example of pouring wine into the tea and dunking the honeyed bread. I guessed that this would be our host's supper, for he seemed an abstemious man. Weaving his thin bony hands in and out like flying shuttles, he talked of his people, how they had to sell their dairy cattle because there was not enough forage in the valley to keep them for milk, how they ate vegetables in summer and lived in the winter on cheese, milk, bread (from imported wheat), and *Bündnerfleisch*, which is air-dried beef. Lowering his voice almost to a whisper he said, "My greatest parish problem is . . ." He finished the sentence by pointing to the wine bottle.

I said I did not wonder that alcoholism might be a problem in a valley where snow falls from September to May, where in winter avalanches destroy even the telephone wires and a single-file tunnel is the only avenue to the outside world, where people had not even the diversions of movies and television. Speaking with fierce intensity the prior said, "Movies and television would spoil and corrupt our people and teach them discontent. We permit them to dance, but only on the fourteen days of carnival." I asked him to tell me about the explosive mid-winter fête when the people hid their faces behind the haunting masks. "They dance and they sing," he said, "and they move in caravans from house to house, with only their masked heads visible above the tunnels like a caravan of huge bugs crawling over the snow." In his battle against modernism the prior was resolute. He disapproved of the lotteries and gambling games which the people of Ferden were conducting that summer to raise money for their church, and he took a dour view of the new modern-design church, not yet dedicated, in the village of Wiler farther up the valley, and of its progressive young rector, Father Bloetsor. "He is not yet ordained," said the prior sternly. "But it gives him pleasure to call himself a *Pfarrer*. He does not understand that when modern civilization enters our valley we will lose our identity and become like everyone else."

The prior told us he had performed more than five hundred marriages in the valley and more than a thousand christenings. Autumn was a popular season for marrying and early summer the season for births. I supposed the vital statistics had much to do with the summer sequestering of the maidens. The prior was worried about a young parishioner, an innocent lad just past twenty who, having no sisters, had been sent up into the meadows to care for cows with the summer vestals. My companion, Willy, rolled his eyes heavenward and said, "That poor unlucky fellow. Just think of it, he doesn't have any sisters!"

The prior walked with us to the church to show us some columns from the first church built in 1250. In the cemetery there was no grass, just anonymous mounds of dry earth squeezed tightly together, each with an unnamed cupolaed crucifix. Still, the identities of the graves were known, for each was lovingly tended with flowering plants, and in a special corner for children the small graves were covered with edelweiss.

The cavernous Hotel Lötschenberg was deserted. Wandering in empty halls, we heard a silvery spiral of song from the basement. In a moment a pretty red-haired girl came running up the stairs, yodeling merrily. When she saw us she stopped and blushed. A room? Yes, she had one for five francs a night. She produced a great ring of iron keys and, clanking like a jailer, took us to a large and pleasant room.

After a wash—with water from a jug—we went down to an excellent supper of veal, potatoes, and salad, and a bottle of the marvelously delicate *Fendant*. The same girl was our waitress; she was a *Wirtstochter*, a daughter of the inn, and her name was Katie. When a fly landed in Willy's soup she was sympathetic. "There are flies occasionally," she said. "Where do they come from?" I could have told her. We asked if it was true that there was no dancing except at carnival. She arched her brows impishly and said, "There are many things the prior does not know." For instance, that very evening in Ferden there would be a *Kirchenbau*, literally a "church-building," but actually a fête to raise money to pay for the building. She herself was going after her evening chores.

A moment later Katie ran to our table, trembling and pale. Did we know, she asked, that there was a viper in our room? We did. Well, the chambermaid had run screaming into the kitchen and after a restorative cognac had refused absolutely to have anything more to do with the room. Either the viper went or . . . I was inclined to sympathize with the chambermaid, but Willy's inexplicable affection for the snake was deep. The viper, he told Katie, would eat some of the flies. A crisis was circumvented when we agreed to care for the room ourselves.

After supper Willy and I read in the prior's book that the Lötschental's Alpine pastures are not privately owned but are community property and that their use is prudently pro-portioned according to the number of sheep and cattle they can support. Each family owns some wooden keys known as *Tesseln* which are good for a summer's grazing of one cow or ten sheep. These keys, sometimes centuries old and marked with strange symbols like cattle brands in the Ameri-can West, are inherited from father to youngest son and as a medium of exchange are bought, sold or rented. The curious custom of property inheritance by the youngest in-stead of the oldest son is based on the longevity of the people. It is the custom of the unfortunate elder sons to leave the valley and seek their fortunes elsewhere. When there are no sons, keys and property are inherited by a son-in-law. When a family dies out or leaves the valley there is high bidding for its *Tesseln*. Keys in use are fitted into a large slotted board controlled by the *Alpvogt*—alp master—who in this way knows exactly how many livestock are grazing in the meadows and to whom they belong. In the autumn all *Tesseln* holders gather to drink wine and arrange for the descent of their women and cows into the valley.

A tradition for which the valley is famous is called *Holz-tragen* or "wood-carrying." Whenever someone builds a house or hay hut in the Alps, larch logs are prepared in the forests below. The transporting of the wood up the steep slopes is a community effort usually beginning at 3 A.M. Like a well-organized insect colony, the carriers—women as well as men—trot in pairs, carrying a log on their cush-ioned shoulders for ten steps, when they put it down to be picked up by another pair of human trotters who carry it ten steps farther. The trotting is done in rhythm, like a dance, with the carriers singing their own music. By 11 A.M. the animated human chain has delivered enough wood for the house and the building begins. Children arrive carrying sacks of food from the village and mules bring up sixty-liter bar-rels of wine. At 3 P.M., when the construction is finished, the prior arrives to bless the new house; then there is a feast followed by dancing which continues on the new floor until dusk when everyone descends to the village.

During Holy Week the youths of Lötschental play a game called "Whipping Christ," in which they flail each other with wooden clubs, pantomiming the flagellation of Jesus. For two weeks preceding Easter there is a relay of uninterrupted praying in the church with a lottery assigning each person's hours of prayer. On the Sunday after Easter, called *Spendensontag*, tithings of cheese are brought to the cathedral. This custom goes back to the fifteenth century when the cows of the valley were stricken with a disease and then suddenly were cured, presumably by a miracle. On *Segnessontag*—blessing Sunday—which is just before the women go up into the Alps in June, 100 *Herrgottsgrenadiere*—knights of God—wearing bright pre-Napoleon white trousers, red jackets and black fur hats, accompanied by a brass band, lead the people in a noisy "welcome to summer" procession up and down meadows of flowers.

Popular names in the valley are of classical origin: women are called Opportuna, Aloysia, Klotilde, and Appolonia; men are named Elgius and Longinus. Other names are contractions of saints: Josefmaria, Johantonius, and Peternaz. The last, a contraction of Peter-Ignazius, pronounced *Paternuts*, appealed to Willy who promptly so christened his snake.

Later, walking down to Ferden through a pink twilight we could hear the sounds of the roistering ahead. Willy warned me to be cautious; the men of Lötschental, he said, were known to be taciturn, humorless and sometimes violent. We found the crowd around Town Hall, a square two-story house which doubled also as the school. Women in black skirts, white aprons and embroidered vests and shawls, offered us chances on a lottery. The men, not the women, were the preeners. They wore large rakish yellow hats with black bands and elaborately cross-stitched girdles, inherited father to son and dated like heirlooms: 1907, 1913, etc. A good many of the men were drunk and there were some

efforts at yodeling which never really took flight. The older
men were banging at a game of bowls with wooden balls
so chipped and battered that they were no longer round.
The younger ones were rat-a-tat-tatting in a *Blumenschies-
sen*, rifle sharp-shooting in which the targets were flowers.
They wore their blossom trophies in their hats and the best
marksmen among them were as exotically adorned as bride-
grooms.

Inside, the scene was like a Breughel wedding, with long
tables of men and women drinking *Fendant* and beer and
eating *Wurst* and cheese. Waitresses were young girls wearing long dark skirts and printed cotton aprons and their hair
in long flaxen braids. Many children stood about, gravely
quiet in their too-large hand-me-down clothes. The music
was a disappointment; instead of the lively local *Ländler* for
which I'd hoped, it was American two-steps from a phonograph. A few young couples thumped awkwardly in a
dance. The young bucks, wearing their flower-shooting
chaplets, whirled with a spark of spirit, but the graceless
girls didn't seem to enjoy it at all. No doubt their knitted
woolen stockings and the heavy mountain boots they wore
took all the joy out of it.

The mayor, a swarthy small man with a snappish voice, was
standing on a chair, reading out the names of the lottery
winners. A basket of potatoes went to the man who most
closely guessed the number of potatoes, a ham to the woman
who named its weight, an electric grill to a woman holding
a lucky number which was drawn from a milk bucket. After
the lottery there was an auction. Crucifixes, gesso bleeding
hearts, electric appliances, toy poodles, rubber ducks, cheeses,
shirts and aprons were sold, all for extraordinarily high prices.
A man drinking beside me said, "For the church we will
give anything." The sum to be raised during the summer, he
said, was 300,000 francs.

Looking up and down the tables, I became aware of a
phantasm of faces, gaunt, unhappy, used-up faces, distorted

by scarred cheeks, toothless gums, and broken noses, and resigned despairing faces in which the maiming was not of the flesh but of the spirit. Willy, an art student, whispered that they were faces to delight Rembrandt. I was thinking of the grotesques drawn by Leonardo. I had the feeling that the faces which surrounded me were familiar, that I'd seen them before.

Then I remembered the masks of Zürich. It was like the museum—I was in a room full of masks. Women's masks with black kerchiefs hiding hair, the jowls, nostrils, and boggle eyes gleaming as if from a tube. Men's masks, torn-eared, paralysis-twisted, time-limned like tree bark. Those grotesque wooden bogies in the museum were brutally ironic parodies of all the afflictions of the flesh with which I was now surrounded. I recalled the baron's tip that mirth in masks was almost nonexistent and Willy's warning that the men of Lötschental were humorless. Both were wrong; by carving their masks in their own images, these stern smileless people showed they had humor after all. Like African tribesmen, they engraved their sufferings and their fears into wood to exorcise them from their lives.

I had drunk too much *Fendant* and the room was steaming with human heat and odors. We went outdoors. The moonlight shone coldly off the snowfields above. St. Nicholas' cross, illuminated by electricity, seemed to hang in the skies, and under it the houses of Kippel lurked dark and ominous. Walking back, we could hardly speak for the roaring of the waters, but the night smelled sweet away from the villages.

Halfway we met a young Swiss guest of the hotel, Ursula, walking with a tall, muscular youth wearing an embroidered girdle and on his hat a wreath of flower-shooting glory. Ursula greeted us warmly, inviting us to return to Ferden to dance with her. The suggestion did not please her young man; remembering the hot violence of Lötschentaler men I declined the invitation. Ursula told us that the hotel would be locked and she gave us a key which she said would open the front door. We said good night; icy breezes were descending from the snowfields and I was eager to get into bed.

It was not to be, not yet. The key Ursula gave us did not fit the front door, did not fit any door as we found out by circling the dark hotel, trying them all. I rang the bell, but there was no reply. I rang it again holding my thumb to it for a quarter-hour. Nothing happened. The owner's large family and several guests were all in bed. Willy offered to return to Ferden to find Ursula and I waited, huddled, shivering, on the stoop of the hotel.

Willy returned very soon with Ursula. She had quarreled with her flower-shooter and was walking home alone when Willy met her. The key she had given us was not for the front door at all, but for the door to her room! She was sorry to have made such a silly mistake. However could it have happened?

Ursula let us in and when we got to our room we discovered in our confusion that we still had the key to her room. Willy and I had begun a deliberation about what we should do with it—and which of us should do it—when we heard a loud crash of glass and an angry drunken voice. The flower-shooter had returned, and when Ursula refused to come out, he had thrown a rock through the window of her room. We listened to their loud Rabelaisian quarrel filling the night and decided we would return the key in the morning. Though the hotel did not have many guests it seemed to have a great many ghosts. Whenever I rolled over in bed I roused an echo several corridors away, and a footstep on the uncarpeted floors set off a syndrome of pulse-quickening creaks and groans all through the hollow building

At breakfast we missed our cheerful *Wirtstochter*, Katie. Our waitress, a less larkish version of Katie, was her younger sister, Teresa. It was the first fair haying day after a fortnight of rain, Teresa explained, and Katie was working in the hayfields. Teresa was going herself as soon as she was finished with our breakfasts. She told us that she and Katie operated the hotel, their mother cooked in the kitchen and the father took care of the office. A brother managed the family fields where everyone was haying.

Carrying the lunches Teresa packed, we started up the valley, following the churning white gorge of the Lonza. All around us men were swinging scythes and raking. Women were pushing or pulling loaded carts of hay, or carrying great bundles of it on their backs. As we approached the village of Wiler we saw a young man in the flapping robes of a priest loading huge mounds of hay on the backs of some very young girls. We guessed that this must be the unordained *Pfarrer* Bloetsor and introduced ourselves. He was boyishly handsome with thick curly black hair and heavy black-shelled spectacles, and he told us that the girls, now staggering and swaying up the slopes like female Atlases, were his sisters. The young *Pfarrer* raced ahead on his bicycle, from the handlebars of which there unfurled two black velvet pennants, one with a crucifix and one with an image of the Madonna. "I embroidered them myself," the priest shouted over his shoulder to us. There was also a medallion of St. Christopher in which he obviously had faith, as he peddled dangerously over the precipitous trails.

Wiler is a new town with an open sunny atmosphere. The old town had burned down (fire is a constant hazard in the tightly huddled wooden villages) and the modern chalets were widely spaced with green lawns and red geranium beds. There were no manure piles and the air was clean and sweet. As in Kippel, the street was deserted; only the silent faces of the old and infirm peered at us from behind latticed windows.

We passed through Ried where we found some masks, but they seemed dull and casually turned out for tourists. The next town was Blatten where winter sleighs hung on the outside of the houses as in Lapland. Here in a hayfield we saw the old prior swinging a scythe, appearing with the wind billowing his black skirts and white hair like an avenging dark angel of death. As we ascended toward the glaciers the light grew brighter, the air chillier. There were many wayside prayer stations, all of them crucifixions. To the toil-burdened Lötschentalers the anguished cross spoke in a voice that no placid Virgin ever could. When a Madonna appeared at all it was in a pieta with the dead Christ. One of the pietas was in a tiny grotto filled with fresh flowers, a. memorial to the members of one family who had died in the mountains. We read the carved words:

Peter Joseph Kalbermatten, aged 12, lost in a storm in 1885.
Johann Kalbermatten, aged 23, killed by an avalanche 1896.
Magdalena Tannast Kalbermatten, aged 43, died in an accident 1936.
Johann Kalbermatten, aged 73, was surprised by death in this place 1939.
Peter Kalbermatten, aged 6, was killed by a tree falling on him 1945.

The last town was Eisten, and here Willy crossed a bridge to visit a cluster of tents just visible beyond the foaming gorge. "They belong to Boy Scouts from Zürich," he said. "In one of the tents I have a friend who is sharing it with a Finnish girl."

Pondering Switzerland's liberated views on scouting, I climbed alone through fields of wild pansies and roses, bluebells, sweet peas, mustard, carnations, daisies, lupins, a lavender puff called Rapunzel, and finally, on the high slopes just under the glacier, edelweiss. Over the flowers whirred the myriadly jeweled world of insects, and I imagined myself walking through a flower-carpeted meadow in one of Fra

Angelico's golden paradises. On every green patch of the goat-challenging precipices someone, often a girl, was swinging a scythe. Each mower carried a whetstone in an ox horn fastened to a belt over the buttocks.

At the top of the valley was *Kuhmatt* (cow meadow), a huddle of twenty *Stahlen*, or hay huts, built around a small chapel. It was like a deserted toy village, and the old huts, rooted in the landscape like trees, seemed to have grown up among the manure piles. Empty now, they would soon be filled with hay. Since it is almost impossible to move hay on the steep slopes, the farmers build such huts in the vicinity of each hayfield. In the winter they move their cattle, like nomads on Mongolian steppes, from one set of huts to another, letting the cattle eat up the hay and at the same time distribute their precious manure over the fields.

The chapel, built in the seventeenth century, was wildly baroque. A great iron screen before the altar protected the massive gold ornamentation like a grill in a bank. On the walls were voto paintings of miraculous healings, of rescues from avalanches, and of donkeys hurtling from footbridges into the Lonza torrent. From the pulpit railing a disembodied wooden hand clutching a crucifix reached out eerily into the sanctuary. On a sudden impulse I pulled the bell ropes and the tolling echoed up and down the valley. Then, having broken the oppressive solitude of the place, I returned to the sun to wait for Willy.

He returned presently to report he had not found his friend. "The mountains are large," he reported laconically. "My friend is small and the Finnish girl is smaller." We ate our lunch. There were cheese and ham sandwiches, Sunkist oranges from America, eggs stamped in Denmark, and Swiss chocolate. While we were eating, a small boy arrived with an adult-sized pack which bent him almost to the ground. He unloaded it, greeted us with a softly sibilant *"Grüss Gott,"* went into the chapel for a quick prayer, and then, taking up his burden again, continued on his way. Willy said he was carrying food to haymakers above the glacier. Soon a man arrived, leading a mule loaded with beer, and then some young women carrying bundles fashioned by knotting the corners of blankets, from which loaves of bread protruded. The light was blinding and mists rose like steam from the white cascade of *Gletschermilch* thundering below us. "I could listen all day to this *Bach* symphony," punned Willy. He took out his sketch pad and began drawing huts and mountains and I stretched in the sun and napped.

In the afternoon, walking back to Kippel, we fell in with a procession of home-bound haymakers. We followed a bent old couple holding hands like lovers, he bearing a scythe on his shoulder and she a rake. The perfume of drying hay filled the air and covered the smell of manure like a deodorant.

Willy had heard rumors of a mask carver down in Ferden, so after supper he went to investigate. I wandered in the twilight through the back lanes of Kippel, following the sound of a hammer to a carpenter's shop. Outside, in the dusk, I found the carpenter's wife sewing. She was a handsome brown-haired woman in her thirties, dressed in blue with a blue kerchief covering her head, like a Madonna by Filippo Lippi. At her feet a golden-haired boy of four was busy with his child-sized tools, playing at building a house. He was the happiest child I'd seen in the valley, the only one who played, the only one who laughed.

The woman's name was Frau Rieder; her child's was Markus. She told me she was one of fifteen children born in the valley, that she had a brother, a Swissair official who lived in New York. "He wants to be a rich and big man and he will," she said. In her young womanhood she had lived in Zürich where life was "carefree and easy." But she had come back to the Lötschental to marry, to have her family. "Life is a struggle," she said, sighing, complaining softly. "Everyone works too hard. The summers are short and the winters are terrible. No one has any time and people get old

too soon. Especially the women. You would not believe how
young they are, these women who look so old. Sometimes I
think we are all old, even the children, that we are a valley of
old people."

Her husband, the carpenter, heard our voices and came out
of the shop. He was a strong, noble-faced man with a warm
smile and a great mane of wild blond hair. "It's not a bad
life," he said, wanting to soften his wife's judgment. "The
valley offers hard work and good health. When I was young
we climbed the Alps in the evening with jugs of wine to
visit the girls up there with the cows. Then, in the mornings
we came down to make the hay. Now the young men don't
go up any more at night. They have lost some of the joy."

From an upstairs window came the music of an accordion,
the first live music I had heard in the valley. The one who
was playing was the carpenter's older son, Cyrill, aged fifteen, who was home for the summer from his collegium in
St. Moritz. Little Markus stopped his hammering and saw-
ing, laid down his tools and buried his face in the blue skirts
of his mother. The carpenter's glowing eyes embraced them
both. Sitting there, watching and listening, I felt a strange
and warm exultation.

Women were walking home from church, their hands
crossed over prayer books. The *Gemeinde Weibel*—the town
crier—blew on his brass bugle and read the names of the
persons·drafted to make hay in the communal meadows in
the morning. Around the public fountain youths were gathered in soft conclave, feigning indifference to the girls strolling by with arms interlocked, as if in barricade against the
world of men. Boys on bicycles swooped in silent circles,
their jackets flapping like bats' wings in the night. Then the
church clock began to toll, and the murmuring youths said
good night to one another and leaped off like rabbits into
the dark. It was the curfew hour at eight. The only light
left in the street came from the upstairs room where the
carpenter's son was playing. In the darkened windows of

the houses I could see the silhouettes of children and old people listening to the accordion playing, not mountain music, but *Arrivederci, Roma*.

Willy returned, excited because he had located some masks in the house of a farmer who carved them as a hobby. Together we went to see them. A solemn little girl answered the door. Her parents, she said, were still raking hay, but she knew the prices of the masks. One had a grimacing apoplectic leer, the closest I had seen to a smile. For 160 francs I bought it and three others: a shawled witch, a demon with feverish cheeks sticking out its tongue, and an angry old man with white horsehairs emerging from his nostrils and ears. We carried them to the hotel where the two *lustige Wirtstöchter*, their hair caught up in ribbons like young Roman matrons, asked us to dance an "English waltz" with them in the taproom. The sisters were the only women we had seen smile and the only ones wearing nylon stockings.

That night it stormed. Black clouds rolled over the snowfields and the thunder rumbled louder than the Lonza. Lightning blinked out the electricity. Willy was singing like a snake charmer to Paternuts; it appeared to be a great love between them. In the flares of lightning the masks propped like devils on a chest came to vivid and terrifying life, and I got up to turn them face down. As I passed a window I saw in a flash the figure of a man carrying two logs up the mountain. His rain cloak was as long as a robe and he was bent almost to the ground by the weight of the logs meeting at right angles on his shoulders, forming a perfect crucifix. Too startled to move, I watched with each flare from the heavens the form of that man struggling upward, dragging his burden to the heights. Walking behind him, following, was a woman holding the hand of a child.

twelve

SIEGFRIED'S WINE JOURNEY

The last time I made the Swiss Rhine journey I took with me a young Swiss cousin who, just incidentally, is named Siegfried. I was in Zürich alone and since, if the season is right, I never visit this part of Switzerland without making an excursion on my favorite river, I invited Siegfried to come along.

Siegfried is a relaxed lad who on my last visit had just hit the bull's-eye in the annual *Knabenschiessen* or Boy's Shooting Match, but there had been some question about giving him the prize because the bull's-eye was in the target next to the one at which he aimed.

Now he was sixteen and had sprouted to a man's height if not breadth. His leanness I credited to his diet. The Swiss are food faddists and during the years since my last visit Siegfried's doctor father had zealously launched his family on a raw-vegetable diet. The doctor was also vehemently *alkoholfrei*, a reaction, I gather, to tradition in a family which has never been notably abstinent. "Meat and alcohol poison the body," Siegfried warned me solemnly.

In spite of such notions Siegfried turned out to be an amiable traveling companion. I was surprised to discover that, while he had traveled over considerable areas of Europe and

Africa, he had never made a journey on the Rhine, which is only thirty miles from his home.

The Rhine journey was a classic summer holiday in the pre-automotive nineteenth and early twentieth centuries, not only with Swiss but with English and Americans on the grand tour. No doubt Richard Wagner had much to do with it. It is always a blow to the German national pride to have it pointed out that Wagner lived in Zürich during the writing of much of the *Ring* and *Tristan,* and the stretch of river that inspired his famous *Siegfried's Rhine Journey* might as well have been Swiss as German. Though it changes nationalities at Basel, the north-flowing Rhine is very much a Swiss river. Its gray headwaters spring from the melting Zapport glacier in the wild canton of Uri, plunge into a gorge named Hell from which it churns around Switzerland until it widens into the great reservoir known as the Bodensee or Lake Constance, flows on to Basel and finally empties into the North Sea in Holland.

It is the part from Lake Constance to Basel which I know best. Since navigation is abruptly terminated at Schaffhausen by the Rhine Falls, the traditional one-day outing was a morning train ride from Zürich to Kreuzlingen on Lake Constance, a boat trip down to Schaffhausen, and an evening train ride back to Zürich with a fleeting glimpse of the falls from the coach window. One could also reverse the trip, taking the boat upstream from Schaffhausen to Kreuzlingen. Automobiles both simplify and complicate the trip. For one thing, travelers can stop off to see the largest and most spectacular waterfall in Europe. But Rhine steamers are too small to transport cars, and drivers must make a round trip on the boat to return to their cars.

For this reason Siegfried and I made only half the Rhine journey. We drove to Schaffhausen and took the boat upstream to Stein-am-Rhein, a medieval fishing village which is the prettiest town on the whole length of the Rhine.

We drove through fields of shocked wheat and bursting

tomatoes and through villages glowing with red geraniums. By my side Siegfried, who had a Swiss passion for facts and statistics, checked that everything was in its place from an old guide book which had once belonged to his grandfather, many years dead. The book said nothing of course about Zürich's glistening new airport, or about the zigzagging concrete walls which resembled a medieval city bastion and which Switzerland built during the war for fear of German tanks.

Near the town of Eglisau we had our first view of the Rhine from a 200-foot-high bridge. We crossed into a tiny triangle of Germany which extends down into Switzerland and after less than five miles were back in Switzerland and at the spectacular Rhine Falls. It was still early enough in the day to see the morning rainbows. Raising his voice against the roar Siegfried read from Grandfather's guide that the falls were 370 feet wide, 100 feet high, and that they delivered 88,000 cubic feet of water per second. Comparison of Europe's greatest falls with Niagara is inevitable. The Rhine Falls are smaller, but the landscape surrounding the chute is more romantically picturesque than the urban setting of Niagara.

Ten minutes and we were in Schaffhausen, capital of the only Swiss canton north of the Rhine. This is the town which American planes bombed in April 1944, killing some thirty persons and destroying many monuments. Modern structures, which cost the American government some $10,000,000 in reparations, stood out conspicuously in the medieval streets. Its picture gallery, one of the best in Europe, is in the eleventh-century Benedictine Monastery of All-Saints around which the town grew. Many Rhine towns grew up about monasteries. One reason is that the terraces along the river grow a moderately meritorious vintage of grape. Benedictines, as Siegfried was startled to learn, were never an abstemious order.

A boat was leaving almost at once. It was a smooth Diesel,

quieter and cleaner than some of the picturesque smoky steamers I have taken in the past. The Rhine fleet, which operates from April to September, includes three Diesels carrying 250 passengers and two steamers carrying four hundred. The price of a round trip ticket from Schaffhausen to Stein was seventy-five cents.

We took seats on the sunny top deck and Siegfried joined the rest of the Swiss in waving. The Swiss are the wavingest people I know. Inarticulate in verbal communications, the moment they are separated by a bit of landscape they flail at one another like windmills. There were plenty at whom to wave. Both the German and Swiss sides were thick with swimmers, fishers, campers, and sunbathers, and the water was a regatta of the canvas kayaks which Germans fold into a rucksack, and long orange shells with clubs of eight rowers, their paddles going like centipedes' legs.

It was a glorious day. The blue sky was flecked with white clouds which, passing over the sun, mottled the green landscape like camouflage cloth. The Rhine has a mystic romanticism which inspired not only Wagner but the poets, Schiller and Ruskin, and the painter Böcklin. It is never blue like the brown Danube, but green, taking its color from the rich vegetation on its shores. When storm clouds roll over the Rhineland, it will turn solidly black. It is frequently covered with mists which, in the winter at least, can make navigation perilous. Because it is a shallow river, varying from under two meters in low seasons when navigation often ceases, to eight meters in high season, the Rhine flows swiftly and is covered with the whorls of angry rapids. River swans lurch fitfully against the tide like chugging toy steamers.

Siegfried, who had been on the bridge gathering facts from the skipper, came back to report that the trip from Schaffhausen to Kreuzlingen takes four hours, the return three hours. During the high season there are four round trips daily beginning at eight in the morning. Sunday or holiday passengers may total 6000; the record for a season was 280,-000. He also reported somewhat smugly that heavy rains had caused a blight to attack the terraced vineyards on the river bank and that the wine season would be a bad one.

We left the vineyards behind and passed through brooding fir forests in which the river turned dark and rows of poplars were reflected in the water like pylons. Toy-like villages passed swiftly one after another, each a covey of brown-beamed, high-gabled houses huddling about a church and perhaps a convent or monastery. We saw Paradies, St. Katherinental, Diessenhofen, Hemishofen, and Wagenhausen, and finally, at the spot where the river widens into the Untersee or lower Lake Constance, we came on the jewel of them all, Stein-am-Rhein.

On first sight it is almost too perfect, like one of those glistening postcards with the river reflection so pure one is never sure which is right side up. On top of a hill stands a great fortress, the Burg Hohenklingen, seat of the barons of Klingen who were the medieval overlords of Stein. Below, in a grove of willows whose graceful fronds lay on the water and tugged downstream like the skirts of maids caught in the wind, stood the town of white houses bright with red geraniums, clustered about a soaring church steeple. It looked like a fairy-tale village rising from the river.

No fairies, good or evil, guarded it and a three-minute walk took us to St. George's Monastery, a handsome old building with its front side in the river. Cousin Siegfried read from his book: "With this monastery Stein was founded in the year 1007. It took five hundred years to build and is a combination of Romanesque, Gothic, and Renaissance. Secularized during the Reformation, it is now controlled by the Swiss government. The order was a small one and there are cells for only twelve monks. . . ."

A merry dozen they must have been. The first thing one sees on entering is their great wine cellar. There is something comically Rabelaisian about it. The mammoth press has a lever four feet square and twenty-five feet long. My mind conjured up a jolly Benedictine riding like a circus aerialist on the end of it, yodeling his happy *Te Deums* as he zoomed up and down. Four barrels lay on platforms along the wall. There were pedestals for at least ten more, so that a barrel a monk was a reasonably conservative estimate.

Siegfried was troubled. "Who drank the wine?" he asked.

"The monks, naturally," I answered him.

"All of it?"

"Well, they must have made some for their patrons up in the castle. And I'm sure boats were always arriving on the river with guests to whom they served wine."

"What kind of guests?"

"Knights and traders and no doubt other monks."

"I suppose they had to drink with their guests."

"Naturally they were gracious hosts."

"All that wine must have made them sick," Siegfried said.

"On the contrary, it probably kept them healthy," I said. "It must have warmed them on cold nights."

Estimating that each of the barrels measured one and a half meters across and two meters deep, Siegfried began a series of computations to determine their contents. He continued his mathematics as we walked through the monastery.

That the good brothers did not spend much time brooding in their cells was obvious from the large number of handsomely paneled and heated parlors, chapter rooms, and dormitories. Walls were covered with lively frescoes of medieval fairs and horsemarkets, of bloody Roman battle scenes and a touching St. Christopher portaging the Christ child across a river alive with ducks, pickerel, and Nordic mermaids. With their front door opening on the waters, I had the feeling that the monks may have been on fairly intimate terms with the buxom Loreleis, a species which according to legend are indigenous to the Rhine.

The frescoes are credited to a Schaffhausen artist named Thomas Schmid, but a young apprentice who did much

of the work cleverly managed to hide his own name in the
design of the paintings. It is there, on one wall, woven into
the necklace of a woman: Ambrose Holbein. Holbein died
at twenty-four and his go-getting younger brother, Hans,
kept things in the family by taking over both his studio and
his wife.

A tiny chapel was the only room in the monastery that
seemed neglected. "They couldn't all have prayed at the
same time," said Siegfried, counting places, and added, "I
guess they had too many other things to do."

The bells chiming twelve in the tower reminded Siegfried
he was hungry. In three minutes we were on the Town
Hall Square, in an inn called The Sun, famous for its fish
dishes. Since the Rhine is the best fishing river in Western
Europe, the eating of fish is one of the joys of a Rhine
journey. The river's supply of salmon, trout, pickerel, bass,
and perch never seems to diminish, and as the glacial waters
are continually cold the quality is always of the best.

Freed from parental discipline and, I feared, already somewhat under Benedictine influence, Siegfried ordered a baked
pike which, when it came, extended well over the ends of a
silver platter about twenty inches long. The pike was as far
as I was willing to go in corrupting youth, so I was relieved
when Siegfried refused wine. Looking at my half-liter of
native white *Twanner*, he said sternly, "That will be very
bad for your head and for your liver."

I was eating pickerel baked in egg batter which is the
famous speciality of The Sun. "How much wine do you
drink a day?" Siegfried asked.

"The question is a difficult one to answer," I said. "There
are many days when I don't drink any."

"Then you are not yet an alcoholic," Siegfried said. "Alcoholics drink every day. No doubt the monks were alcoholics."
Then he returned his attentions to his pike and his mathematics.

Stein is the second Swiss town that was mistakenly bombed

by Americans. Nine people were killed and twenty houses were destroyed or damaged. Fortunately, none of the damage was in the square, an open sunny place with fountains surrounded by geraniums and statues of armored warriors bearing pikes. It is not a square at all, but a triangle, an enchanting storybook place of high-gabled houses with names like Stag, Pelican, Crown, Red Ox, Black Horn, and Titmouse, each covered with lively frescoes. On first sight it is hard to conceive that grown-ups might live in such a magic place, but on closer examination one sees that the pictures of venuses and satyrs are somewhat robust for children.

No one can tell quite why the citizens of Stein have so gaily painted their houses on the outside. A lady in the hotel said the frescoes were painted by itinerant Italians nine hundred years ago and that they retained their freshness because they were painted with unperishable vegetable dyes and because they were scrubbed once a year in Rhine water. It is a story that a non-critical tourist might accept if he weren't aware that the late Gothic houses could not be more than five hundred years old and that much of the subject matter of the frescoes did not exist nine centuries ago. The truth is that sometime in the sixteenth century, Thomas Schmid, the same Schaffhausen artist who worked on the monastery frescoes, was commissioned to paint the façade of a house called the White Eagle. He made such a roaring success of it that the idea caught on. The people of Stein have been painting pictures on their houses ever since. Some buildings, including the Town Hall, were painted as recently as 1920.

Subjects include anything that entered the fancy of either owner or artist. You can see boar and stag hunts, spirited vintage scenes that might have been painted by Breughel, legendary heroes such as St. George, patron of Stein, and Wilhelm Tell, patriotic hero of Switzerland. There are stories from Roman history and Italian folk tales, medieval processions, cattle and birds, family histories and coats of arms. Under a picture of a red ox one owner had printed, FOR MY RED HAIR I AM KNOWN AND NAMED THE RED OX. The house was covered with such bloody episodes as Lucretia stabbing herself, Judith severing the head of Holophernes and David dealing with Goliath. The house of The Sun in which we were eating fish showed the philosopher Diogenes in his wine barrel house, darkened by the shadow of Alexander falling across it. "What would you like most in the world?" Alexander asks the philosopher, and Diogenes replies, "That you step out of my sunlight."

Imaginative as they were, none of the artists has been able to touch the ribaldry of Thomas Schmid's White Eagle. Like any medieval moralist, Master Schmid illustrated far more interestingly the vices of which he disapproved than the virtues of which he approved. On a wall surface cut by six windows, he crowded Roman legends, a tale from Virgil about a king who doubts his wife's chastity, two stories of illicit love from Boccaccio, and an assortment of remarkably ugly naked women, including one with a goat's hind-quarters and a suckling infant, called "profane love."

Siegfried was especially fascinated by a pot-bellied, pinheaded lady named *Prudence*, looking at herself in a mirror. Finally, he said, "I don't think undressed women are very pretty."

Without overdoing it I tried to explain that the artist's conceptions were neither standard nor flattering.

"I suppose he didn't like women very much," Siegfried said. I agreed it was probably the answer. Schmid was a misogynist.

A boat returning to Schaffhausen called at Stein at five o'clock. A half-hour before Siegfried excused himself to return to the monastery. At the dock he reported he had measured the wine barrels both in the center and on the ends to determine their slope. He worked over his calculations during the boat ride back.

As we slid quietly downstream the sky turned darkly ominous and swans harbored up for the night. At Schaffhausen Siegfried confessed he was hungry again and we went to the riverside *Fischerstube*. Most Rhine towns have their feet in the water and Schaffhausen's "feet" include several good fish restaurants. The one we selected had a board walk over the water and only a box of red geraniums separated us from the black waters. I ordered a steamed trout. "If the fish does not please you," Siegfried said, "you can throw him back in the river." Sadly he added, "Of course he will not be able to swim away."

Succumbing recklessly to his innate carnivorousness, my young cousin ordered not a fish but a pair of sizzling bratwurst. I had not fully recovered from the surprise of that when he said, "I think I should like a glass of wine."

In the interests of family relations I rationalized that it was the Benedictines and not myself that were leading a young Calvinist astray. I thought of an old Currier & Ives print called "The Drunkard's Progress," beginning with one innocent glass and climaxing in an alcoholic's grave. The wine I had ordered for my trout was not the local sharp red vintage but some light *St. Saphorin* from the sunny shores of Geneva in the south. I poured Siegfried half a glass. He tasted it carefully like a *cognoscenti*. "It is rather good," he said, and drank it up.

"Could I have some more please?" he asked.

"I'd rather you didn't."

"Why not?" He produced his computations. "Each of the barrels held 3500 liters of wine. That is ten liters of wine for each monk each day. If a monk could drink ten liters of wine . . ."

"It is quite impossible," I said. "You are forgetting the Klingens in the castle."

"Even if a monk drank only *five* liters, I do not think it would be dangerous if I had one full glass."

I let him have it. He drank it rather solemnly and said, "Now I shall see how it is to be drunk."

A Wagnerian storm was brooding as we started toward Zürich. Passing the Rhine Falls we got a quick and stirring glimpse of the steaming chute by lightning. As we drove along, rain beating against the car, I tried to minimize as best I could the wine consumption of the Benedictines.

"No doubt the Klingens had many warrior knights with a wine ration," I reasoned. "That would use up a lot."

"*Doch,*" said Siegfried, "*Es ist a meineid hufa wii.*"

I had to agree. It was still a hell of a lot of wine.

thirteen

THE MARQUISE'S HOLY MOUNTAIN

The summer, like Bottom's dream, had no bottom.
Was I alone in the New Hampshire woods? I was not
always sure. I was there because a marquise had asked me
one winter's afternoon in New York if I believed in fairies.
My reply was that I hadn't thought on the matter since I
was a child. "Since you are Anglo-Saxon I am not surprised,"
said the Marquise. "Celts are more conversant with little
folk. Come live on my Holy Mountain. You will begin
to think of them again."

My benevolent sorceress was the Marquise Dedons de
Pierrefeu who despite her French title is one of the last of
New England's great individualists. Though she is the Dowager Marquise of the Provence town of Pierrefeu, she lives
most of each year in a pink house in a rose garden in the
New Hampshire village of Hancock. Five miles away is her
"Holy Mountain"—900 acres and a lake as primeval as the
fifth day of creation, inhabited by all God's creatures but
man. The Marquise calls cities "hells which man creates for
himself"; her sanctuary is "a place of peace to restore the
spirit."

Many men boast of a desire for wooded solitude but few,
even if they have the opportunity in our increasingly

crowded earth, have the courage for it. My own courage was limited. As an insurance against too much solitude I invited a few well-spaced guests before I left the city. "You will regret them," the Marquise said. "The unseen life is strong and you will not be lonely."

To live on the Holy Mountain I had to make a pact to destroy no life. Nailed to a tree at the entrance was a board painted with a line from the book of Isaiah: "They shall not hurt nor destroy in all my holy mountain." Actually, it was not one mountain, but a series of mountains and hills joined by a stream which flowed through the lake. Here and there little patches of meadow where once men had farmed were a précis of New Hampshire history. "We've returned to the forest," the Marquise said, "back to the bears and the beavers. When the sheep stopped grazing—about the time of the Civil War—the deer came back."

At first my Teutonic eyes saw the deep forest and its hidden lake as a German opera setting, as devastatingly romantic as the Königsee above Berchtesgaden. German music kept surging through my head: Siegfried's *Forest Murmurs* and arias from *Der Freischutz*. Swimming through the blue mists on the lake, watching wisps of it crawling up through the pines on the mountains, I sang *Durch Die Walder* so vigorously that a game warden, thinking I was calling for help, rowed out to rescue me.

The cave-like house where I lived I called Hunding's Hut. Its unpainted boards had taken on nature's protecting colors; like an animal it had withdrawn back into the forest. But the house was primordial only in its façade; it had four bedrooms, a country kitchen with electric stove and refrigerator, a city bath, a marvelous library of old books and a fireplace large enough to roast a boar.

It was at night when the trees dripped with limpid lights that I began to realize the forest was really Shakespeare's and not Wagner's. Floating—or so it seemed—through silvery cobwebs, hearing the sighing of water and the nocturnal rustlings of beasts, I remembered that Oberon is identified in mythology with Alberich, king of the elves and guardian of the Nibelung treasure.

Around the house was a copse of flowers: Shakespeare's nodding violet and thyme, cowslips, columbines, and Canterbury bells. There were also azaleas and lilacs, ladyslippers, sweet william, orange day lilies, blue plantain lilies and mock orange bushes like wintry snowdrifts. After each rain the fragile waxen Indian pipes appeared miraculously.

In my first restless week in this wilderness the daytime quiet was unnerving and the night's eerie noises terrifying. Animals crashed through the forest and a rabbit sounded like a bear. In the daytime I would see them or their tracks— deer, woodchucks, squirrels, raccoons, fox, and the fishing animals, otter, mink, and weasel, slithering over the shore rocks. In the house some mice gnawed on the bindings of an early edition of the *Spectator*, and across the road a city of beavers cut "popples" to build their private pond. At night the mists rising from the beaver pond made it look like a volcanic crater on the moon. One night the green eyes of a lynx faced me from the porch and I had to wait in the car until the cat decided to slink away.

In the lagoon there were snapping turtles two feet wide. Blue herons, perfectly camouflaged by the blue-flowered pickerel weed, would rise from the swamps with a great fuss of flapping and coast across the lake looking for fish. A pair of snakes kept house under the front stoop and thousands of bats lived in the walls. One could hear them rustling and whimpering under the boards during the day. At night a dark cloud of them emerged from the crevices and swooped about the house until dawn, like the birds whirring over the Church of the Swallows on the Italian shore of Lugano.

Quickly I discovered what good friends the bats were, for there were no mosquitoes around Hunding's Hut and I could sit on the terrace listening to the evening epiphanies of the Wilson thrushes. By playing a record of violins

or a soprano on my phonograph I could bring them out
an hour early. Kirsten Flagstad's recording of *Elizabeth's
Prayer* drove them ecstatic. Later there would be a *Boris
Godunof* choir of bullfrogs—stripling tenors, virile baritones,
and grandfather bassos—booming in the swamp, and sometimes the chilling hootings of two loons. In vain I held my
ears tuned for the song of the Hermit Thrush. This shy
bird sang after midnight, the Marquise said, and kept his
distance from the habitat of man.

There were leeches in the lake. The day I discovered some
luminous orange newts in a patch of moss, I looked up the
witches' recipe:

> *Fillet of fenny snake . . .*
> *Eye of newt and toe of frog*
> *Wool of bat and tongue of dog,*
> *Adder's fork and blind-worm's sting,*
> *Lizard's leg and howlet's wing . . .*

Howlets are owls; I lacked only a dog's tongue.

One day, without realizing quite how it had come about,
I was aware I had made my peace with the wood, that my
life had become part of the forest's life. I resented the trips
to town for groceries and mail. I hated the phone to ring
and I played my records less.

My guests came, and each brought problems. A painter
was unable to paint. "Too many stars, too much horizon,
too many birch," he said. "I shall go mad." A Radcliffe
senior paddled out like Minnehaha and filled the bottom of
the canoe with golden lotus—which I had to hide since their
picking was prohibited both by law and by the Marquise.
A pair of Norwegian nudists had their *derrières* blistered by
poison ivy. A writer with a vivid imagination found the
"unseen life" promised by the Marquise very nearly un-
hinging. At night he heard ghosts, and when I explained
that they were bats and not spooks rustling in the walls, he
recalled frightening tales of rabid bats biting humans in Texas.

Twilight, when the bats began swooping, he called "Dracula time." He insisted that a daddy longlegs on his bed was a black widow, and one night when I was swimming he swore he heard shrieks of laughter in the woods. When I returned, the doors were locked and the shades pulled and my friend, trembling in a cold panic, was remembering all the lonely murders of which he had ever heard. One shattering day, returning from the lake with blood flecks on his body, he reported he had been attacked by a school of piranhas. The fish were actually little sun bass, called "kibbies," which sometimes followed a swimmer, nipping at him. Once when I bathed in the lake they ate my cake of soap.

Sometimes the Marquise would drive out in her little sports car to swim or walk in the forest. She was, she boasted, in her eighty-second summer (her birthday was not until November). Thinking of her age I worried about her scrambling over the rough terrain. I needn't have; dressed in green corduroy slacks, a green khaki shirt (with U.S.N. stenciled on the pocket), a chartreuse velvet hair ribbon, and Indian moccasins, she led me down canyons and over streams, more sure-footed and agile than myself. She would pick up an old beer bottle or potato chip bag left by picnickers, tending each foot of her 900 acres like a garden. "Don't step on the Solomon's-seal," she admonished. "They're a kindly healing plant." One day we sat on a granite boulder watching trout flashing in the stream below and the green gossamered dragonflies mating in mid-air above. "Did you ever see the dance of the atoms?" the Marquise asked. She directed me to focus against the sun and I saw movement, the shimmering flashes of dancing light.

"We are on this planet to learn perfection," she said. "But we are not given enough time. Like Plato's prisoners, we have our backs turned to the light and we perceive only the shadows of objects and think them the realities."

The silence was shattered by a passing military jet. The Marquise flushed with anger. "I have written to congressmen asking that they stop those planes from tearing apart the walls of houses and destroying men's souls," she said. "Sometimes, alas, I think I have lived too long."

Not surprisingly in Puritan New England, the Marquise was a legend. At the post office I heard stories of the ceremony of her second marriage in a forest with the Marquise and her groom mounted on steeds. The barber, recalling how the Marquise once reviled him for shooting a deer, said, "She was so sincere there were tears in her eyes. I felt sorry for her. She's a good lady. But she doesn't know how a deer or two a winter can take a chunk out of the meat bill." A twenty-year-old Cherokee guide told a fantastic tale about the Marquise entertaining a flying-saucer-load of nude Venutians on the Holy Mountain. "Their bodies were dark brown from flying so close to the sun," he said.

The truth was almost as fanciful, as I found one evening while reading some family chronicles in the library of Hunding's Hut. The Marquise was born in Boston a Tudor, descended from the Welsh Tewdwr (*sic*) family which produced England's kings, and, through her grandmother, from the kings of Scotland. The first American Tudor, Dean John, kept a Revolutionary War diary in which, in April 1775, he modestly wrote: "Fine weather but terable News from Lexington, just after 6 this morning we had a rumer that the 1,000, some said 1,200 Regular soldiers that marched oute of Boston privately last night had kil'd 30 men of Lexington who were exercising. . . . I forebare at present a farther Acct & leave it to som faithfull Historian to tell the dismal story to posterity."

The Marquise's cousin Delia was the mother of Ireland's Charles Stewart Parnell, and her Aunt Sophie was a Polish countess. Named Elizabeth after the Tudor queen, the Marquise changed her name to Elsa, her favorite Wagnerian heroine, when she went to Paris to become a singer. "My voice was too light for the great roles," she said. "I became a dancer, and my mother wouldn't permit me to dance in the

Folies Bergère. Then I became a pianist, but I fell in love and was married."

The handsome Count Dedons de Pierrefeu died in World War I, leaving his New England countess (she became Dowager Marquise by succession only five years ago) with four small children whom she brought to America. Through sorrow she had arrived at her convictions about peace, and the Holy Mountain with its surcease from killing was a memorial to her love.

One ominously brooding day when hurricane warnings were coming over the radio I drove to the Marquise's pink fairy-tale candy house. The high pressure had given her a headache and she was reclining. In a violet dress on an aquamarine chaise, she was a creation by Colette. Her delft eyes glistened, her heart-shaped face was youthful and soft, her blond-gray hair was tied with the usual ribbon. Around her were five vases of roses and a bouquet of lilies. I was surprised how small she was. Standing, her regal womanly elegance made her seem tall. She had been thinking, she said, about love, "that still white flame that burns forever in the secret heart."

"Ah," she said, and it was like Colette sighing, "to have known passionate love and be separated from it by death is heartbreaking. But real love cannot be broken, nor can death cancel it. After you have become one with eternal love, life need no longer be lonely. My friend, you are still young. Love vehemently, with all your heart and soul. Love is all that life really is." She chided me for what she called my "egocentric interest in pretty women." She said, "Don't you demand anything but physical good looks? Don't you know that sometimes plain women are more passionate?"

We drank white Bordeaux wine and ate oatmeal cookies while waiting out the storm. It was no hurricane, but an electrical cannonade with rain. Sitting there, I saw a minute red ant climb into the cookie plate. I made a move to crush it, but the Marquise stopped me, rose from her lounge, picked

up the tiny ant and carried it to the door to release it outdoors. The storm had thinned the air and cooled the earth
and the Marquise was feeling better.

Two evenings later on the Holy Mountain I had a summer's night fête. About forty friends came: artists from
MacDowell Colony, students from Cambridge, neighbors
from Hancock. We drank martinis at Hunding's Hut and
then carried supper and wine to the birch meadow on the
lake, where a pair of new aluminum gates glistened like silver
in the light of a full moon. We danced on the grass and a
student, gifted both musically and linguistically, sang songs
of Norway, Denmark, Israel, France, and Germany while
accompanying himself on the guitar. The forest glowed with
mysterious lights. The birches were mints of flashing coins
and the silhouettes of firs took the shapes of castles. Clearly
it was the time of night when "everyone lets forth his sprite."

Suddenly, with a soft cry, a girl slid into the water and
swam into the mists. A strange madness swept over my
guests; like lemmings following a secret urge, making strange
cries, they fell pell-mell into the water or pursued one another into the forest.

I was left alone. Softly I heard a new sound, a long flute-
like trill in descending scale. I rose, enchanted, to follow the
call into the silvery forest. I fought through tangles of briars
and stumbled on branches and stones, beckoned by the liquid-
toned melody. From the darkness came another music, that
of running water. I came to a cliff and climbed its steep sides,
coming at the top upon two trees, a birch and a pine, em-
bracing, their roots tangled together in the same crevice, their
trunks entwined. High above me, their branches interlocked.
Before me was a misty canyon; I took a step forward, then
lost my foothold and fell, down through branches and briars
on and on until I came to rest on a soft bed of moss. I lay
under a sea of silvery cobwebs, listening to the Hermit
Thrush singing more beautifully than the nightingales I had
heard in the marshes of the Po.

Someone called my name, plaintively, over and over, but I had not the will to answer. White nymphs dripping light from their flowing hair were plunging through the forest, pursued by gigantic green frogs. Brown tritons flashed in and out of the mists and a plain little lady stumbling in too-big shoes was overtaken by a Japanese wrestler covered with fish scales. Pink clouds soared like flamingoes over the moon and a beautiful undine rose from the water clutching to her breast, like Cleopatra's asp, a black leech.

Hours later, in glittering dawn, I brushed the cobwebs from my face and looked around. I was surrounded by crumbling green-lichened stone walls that might have been the ruins of some ancient troglodyte's villa. Below me was the cascading stream, filled with clusters of red flowers which, reflected in the water, made the dark pine-canopied pools seem like pools of blood. Around me were clumps of shoulder-high golden rod, blue gentians, white asters, and orange jewel flowers and ferns. I was in a secret enchanted garden, the most beautiful I had ever seen. Suspended in the air above me on green fairy wings the dragonflies were making their suspended love. I looked into the sun and saw atoms move.

I climbed out of the canyon. On the lake the water was as bright and clear as glass. I heard the chilling hoots of the loons; they were alone on the waters, their heads swerving like periscopes, diving and emerging like submarines from another side of the lake.

As I unlocked the gleaming gates I heard a scream and then laughter. Outside in the back seat of a car a little girl cowered in terror; in the front two adults pointed to me and rocked with mirth.

"She kept asking, where are we going, where are we going?" the mother cried. "We were passing the Holy Mountain sign and her father said we're going where God lives. . . ."

The child looked at me, screamed louder, and the car drove away with the parents laughing harder than ever.

I raised my hands to my head to see if ass's ears might have grown there during the night, and remembered something the Marquise had said during the storm: "If there had been psychiatrists when I was young, whatever would have become of me. I'd have been ruined!"